W9-CAD-693

**FROM GALLUP**

BASED ON OUR LARGEST GLOBAL STUDY
OF THE FUTURE OF WORK

# IT'S THE MANAGER

**GALLUP FINDS THAT THE QUALITY OF MANAGERS AND TEAM LEADERS IS THE SINGLE BIGGEST FACTOR IN YOUR ORGANIZATION'S LONG-TERM SUCCESS**

JIM CLIFTON | JIM HARTER

GALLUP PRESS
1330 Avenue of the Americas
17th Floor
New York, NY 10019

Library of Congress Control Number: 2018967010
ISBN: 978-1-59562-224-2

First Printing: 2019
10 9 8 7 6 5 4 3 2



Printed in Canada

♻ This book was printed on chlorine-free paper made with 100% post-consumer waste.

**TO THOSE WHO BELIEVE MAXIMIZING HUMAN POTENTIAL IS NOW THE PRIMARY PURPOSE OF ALL ORGANIZATIONS**

# TABLE OF CONTENTS

# How to Read This Book

This is a reference book for CEOs, CHROs and managers. It is not meant to be read cover to cover on a plane ride from Chicago to Los Angeles. We wrote it to advise you on whichever burning issues your organization faces right now.

This book includes more than 50 breakthroughs grouped into five sections: Strategy, Culture, Employment Brand, Boss to Coach and The Future of Work.

All companies are at a different stage in their journey. Your organization may have addressed some of these topics but is still struggling with others. So find the chapters that have answers to your biggest problems.

As you read this book, keep in mind that the quality of your managers and team leaders is the single biggest factor in your organization's success.

# INTRODUCTION
## The New Will of the World

While the world's workplace has been going through extraordinary historic change, the practice of management has been stuck in time for more than 30 years.

The practice of management has fallen behind how people work, live and want to experience their lives. We need to adapt.

To better understand this situation, Gallup analysts reviewed everything we could find across almost all leading institutions and management literature — as well as our own data from more than 30 years of U.S. and global workplace tracking. Our work included tens of millions of in-depth interviews of employees and managers across 160 countries.

We conducted roundtable interviews with CHROs from 300 of the world's largest organizations.

We interviewed several of the world's pre-eminent economists.

Gallup concludes that the world's most serious short-term (five- to 10-year) problem is declining economic dynamism and declining productivity (GDP per capita). We also conclude that these problems can be fixed just as surely as lean management and Six Sigma once fixed U.S. and global production quality.

This time, the defects that need to be eliminated aren't failures in processes but failures in maximizing human potential.

Politics and policies won't fix declining economic dynamism and declining productivity. CEOs and CHROs will. The people who lead the world's 10,000 largest organizations — including government organizations and nongovernmental organizations (NGOs) — can fix the world's biggest problems.

American businesses should play a big role. According to the Census Bureau, there are roughly 6 million firms in the U.S. Of the 6 million, 4 million have four or fewer employees. These are mom-and-pop shops. So that leaves only 2 million small, medium and large businesses in the country. They are made up of 1 million firms with five to nine employees, 600,000 firms with 10 to 19 employees and 500,000 firms with 20 to 99 employees. There are only 90,000 businesses in America with 100 to 499 employees. And about 18,000 with 500 employees or more.

Those top 18,000 companies could significantly change U.S. outcomes of GDP growth and productivity by changing their cultures to high employee development cultures.

The solution lies in aligning the practice of management with the new *will* of the world's workers. The great American dream has changed. So has the great global dream. What the whole world wants is a good job. This is the new will of the world.

Everything will change when organizations respond to that will.

As with lean management and Six Sigma, when management practices are transformed, people are transformed, and organizations save enormous amounts of time and money. Everything gets better. People and teams grow and develop, and they're far more successful because their work aligns with their will to have a good — or even great — job.

Failing to maximize the potential of a team member is — to use a Six Sigma term — a *defect*.

One large global professional services company estimated that it was wasting $1 billion of leadership time per year on managers filling out ratings forms rather than developing employees and having ongoing coaching conversations with them. Like so many CEOs and CHROs are discovering, there's no evidence anywhere in the world, in any institution of management science, that existing massive employee evaluation and rating processes are effective.

CEOs and CHROs ask us: *How exactly do I know — or how can I audit — if I have a culture of high development?* The best item to measure this anywhere in the world is: "There is someone at work who encourages my development."

When 60% of your employees give a strong "yes" to this item, you have transformed your workplace and changed the world a little to a lot.

The data and analytics in this book present major discoveries that conclude global economic productivity has slowed in the past three decades because of a failure to make significant changes in how managers lead and develop people and teams.

While Gallup analytics faults the practice of management, Gallup also concludes that this problem is fixable. We define "fixable" as creating an upward trend in global employee engagement. Currently, just 15% of employees worldwide are engaged at work, meaning they have great jobs in which they are developing with rich mission and purpose. If that number were to rise to 50%, workplaces everywhere would change — and so would the world.

And research shows exactly how to dramatically increase the percentage of engaged employees. Volumes have been written on the subject; the knowledge is already there. The problem is, while the *science* of management has advanced significantly in the past three decades, the *practice* of management hasn't.

The longtime purpose of business has been to create shareholder return. We like that — but it isn't enough for the future of work.

Peter Drucker wrote, "There is only one valid definition of business purpose: to create a customer." We like that too. But it isn't enough for the new workplace.

The new purpose of business — and the future of work — has to include maximizing human potential.

## WHAT IS PRODUCTIVITY?

Maximizing human potential not only has a positive impact on your company, but on your nation's and the world's productivity too. The stakes are that high.

The core metric of economists and academics throughout most institutions around the world is GDP, which is basically the sum of everything all citizens make, buy and sell to one another.

If a country had "total sales," that would be its GDP — the sum total of all transactions of its citizens and organizations. And pretty much all national governments report this quarterly.

GDP defaults to being the primary metric for societal progress and the health of nations. For example, China's GDP per capita is doing well, and Russia's is not. So important academics and thought leaders conclude that China's human development is better than Russia's.

It isn't quite that simple, but at least GDP is one consistent metric across nations and societies that is generally very helpful.

GDP growth divided by total population or "per capita" is what economists refer to as "productivity."

As an example, think of the United States as a company, and you are the CEO or CHRO. You have about 125 million full-time employees and 27 million part-time employees and roughly $20 trillion in sales (GDP 2018) and almost $20 trillion of debt. The most serious problem facing your gigantic company, America Inc., is declining growth and skyrocketing expenses.

Your employees are grumbling, as 50% of them are making less than they were 35 years ago. In real terms — overall — your employees have not received a raise in more than 35 years. Their expenses of housing, healthcare and education are exploding while paycheck sizes are frozen or declining.

CEOs and CHROs are in a better place than their national governments to change their countries' and the world's economic dynamism. While good fiscal policy is better than bad fiscal policy, the biggest levers are in the hands of CEOs and CHROs, not national lawmakers.

## WHY WALL STREET IS RUNNING ON EMPTY

When employees at all levels aren't developing, neither are their organizations. No spirit, no ideas, no organic customer growth. Add this all together, and you have declining economic dynamism. With the exception of about 20 companies, this is the same story for big U.S. businesses too — so they grow through acquisitions.

When companies are failing to grow organically, CEOs give up, go back to their offices, acquire their competitors and cut prices.

Shockingly, the majority of publicly traded boards of directors encourage this.

This graph shows what a world of declining economic dynamism looks like.

## Global Economic Growth — World Bank

*GDP per capita growth (annual %)*

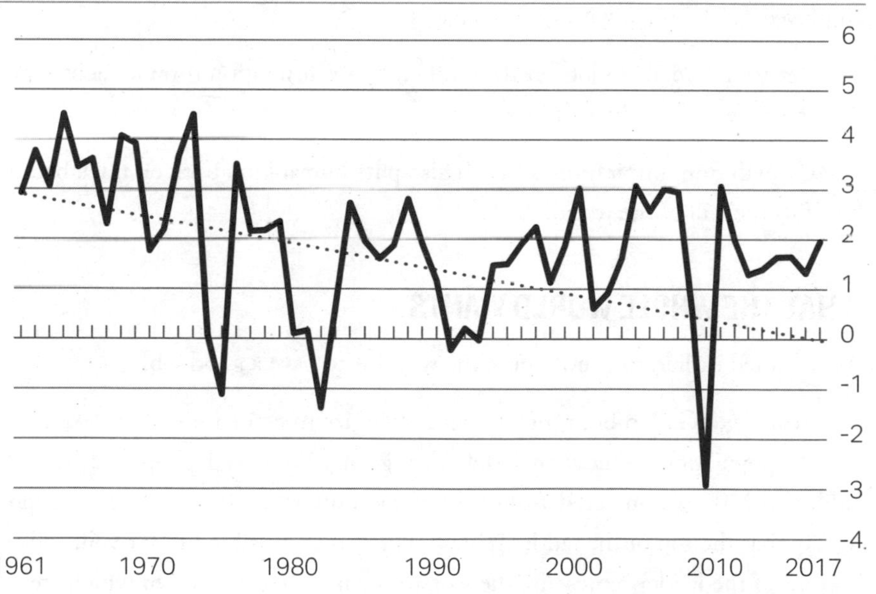


Acquiring competitors is the current growth strategy of nearly all Fortune 1000 companies. As a result, the number of publicly listed companies on U.S. exchanges has been nearly cut in half in the past 20 years — from about 7,300 to 3,700.

The herd is getting pretty small.

At some point, this acquisition strategy hits a wall. It makes you wonder how long we'll need the New York Stock Exchange and Nasdaq.

Gallup analytics finds that most companies can still double their revenue by simply selling more to their existing customer base. But for whatever reasons, they don't. They take the easier road of buying customers rather than building them through highly inspired teams.

**Note to boards of directors:** Rather than pay unrecoverably high prices for acquisitions, Gallup recommends immediately implementing an authentic organic growth strategy — one built on a fully transformed workplace culture of high employee development with great managers.

Bet your leadership job on this: When team inspiration grows, client build-outs, revenue and quality earnings grow.

Growth from inspiration is free. It also puts humankind back on track because it fulfills the will of the world.

## WHAT THE WHOLE WORLD WANTS

As we noted earlier, the new will of the world is to have a good job.

Years ago, Gallup built global methodologies to estimate — for 98% of the world's population — how their lives are going. We asked people, "Imagine a ladder with steps numbered from zero at the bottom to 10 at the top. Suppose we say that the top of the ladder represents the best possible life for you, and the bottom of the ladder represents the worst possible life for you. On which step of the ladder would you say you personally feel you stand at this time, assuming that the higher the step the better you feel about your life, and the lower the step the worse you feel about it? Which step comes closest to the way you feel?"

We went on to ask them what exactly makes a great life.

What we found surprised us. While law and order and food and shelter remain primary basic needs for people everywhere, we found that the great global dream is realized primarily when someone has a "good job."

Likewise, Gallup's tracking of the American dream for more than 80 years found that people wanted the basics of law and order (safety) followed by food and shelter — and then to have a family and to own a home and live in peace.

Now in America and around the world, the great global dream is to have a good job. This is one of Gallup's biggest and most surprising discoveries ever. Family, children, owning a home and peace are still important, but they are lower priority.

The "best life imaginable" — especially for young people and increasingly for women — doesn't happen unless you have a great job with a living wage and a manager or team leader who encourages your development.

What exactly is the difference between a lousy job, a good job and a great job?

A "lousy job" is one in which you are underemployed, receive a very low wage and work less than 30 hours when you want to work full time.

Gallup defines a "good job" as working full time for an organization, with 30+ hours a week and a living-wage paycheck.

A "great job" has all the qualities of a good job but with one big differentiator: Employees are engaged in meaningful and fulfilling work and feel they are experiencing real individual growth and development in the workplace.

People with great jobs have very different life outcomes. Besides booming your business, they inspire teams, solve problems instead of create them, volunteer in their community, have far better health and wellbeing, and have fewer workplace accidents and little to no mistakes and defects.

The problem is, just 15% of the world's workers are engaged at work — or appear to have great jobs. These global few drive the world's economy. They provide extraordinary value to organizations and societies.

The remaining 85% of working adults in the world tell Gallup they are either not engaged at work — just going through the motions — or worse, they hate their jobs, managers and companies. Among many other things, they report that their jobs have no meaning, which in the new millennium, translates to: Their lives have no meaning.

The global workplace is in much greater need than we knew.

For example, look at Japan, a great country trying hard to get it right — where an alarming 94% of Japanese are either not engaged or are actively disengaged at work. The problem is so serious that the government has intervened with new policies and laws to address the stress and clinical burnout in the workplace and tragically high suicide rates.

The current practice of management is not only destroying the future of work in Japan, it is destroying Japanese culture. Just 6% of the country's workers report being engaged at work.

World leaders, CEOs and CHROs have solved much harder problems than dramatically improving employee engagement. However, they may never have solved one with so much upside — for their own organizations' growth, but also for global growth of free enterprise and the next big leap in human development.

## IT'S THE MANAGER

Most CEOs and CHROs are probably thinking, "I agree with all of this, but what can I do right now to get better outcomes? What lever do I pull to make wholesale changes in my culture so it aligns with the new will and future of work?"

Of all the codes Gallup has been asked to crack dating back 80 years to our founder, George Gallup, the single most profound, distinct and clarifying finding — ever — is probably this one: 70% of the variance in team engagement is determined solely by the manager.

It's the manager.

If you have 50,000 employees, you have about 5,000 managers or team leaders — all the variance is right there. Clever benefit packages, new scoring systems, free lunches and on-site volleyball courts are great. But they don't change growth outcomes. Only improving your ratio of great to lousy managers does.

If, of your 5,000 managers, 30% are great, 20% are lousy and 50% are just there — which are about the U.S. national averages of employee engagement — double the 30% to 60%, and cut the 20% to single digits. Do this, and your stock price will boom. Literally nothing a CEO or CHRO does will authentically, structurally and sustainably change the value of your organization more.

So what is the lever? Usually, there isn't a single lever to create change. In this case, there is: It's the manager.

When you have great managers who can maximize the potential of every team member, you have delivered on the new global will: a great job and a great life.

That is the future of work.

# STRATEGY

**INSPIRATIONAL MESSAGES ARE IMPORTANT. BUT THEY'LL HAVE NO SIGNIFICANT IMPACT UNLESS LEADERS BUILD A STRATEGY TO BRING MULTIPLE TEAMS TOGETHER AND MAKE GREAT DECISIONS.**

# CHAPTER 1

## WHAT EXACTLY SHOULD CEOs AND CHROs CHANGE?

Most millennials (people born between 1980 and 1996) and Generation Z (those born in 1997 or later) are coming to work with great enthusiasm. But the old management practices — forms, gaps, low individualization and annual reviews — grind the life out of them. Current worldwide practices of management are producing very little development.

What does this mean for your organization's productivity? It means that if you have old management practices, you need to significantly change your workplace — transform your culture.

Changing your culture begins by changing what CEOs and CHROs believe. Then changing what their organization's managers believe. And then changing how those managers develop every single team member.

Gallup has found that millennials in particular have disrupted how the world works — how people communicate and how they read and write and relate. And there's no going back. Millennials and Generation Z are disrupting retail, hospitality, real estate and housing, transportation, entertainment, and travel — and they will soon radically change higher education.

Millennials and Generation Z are changing the very will of the world — and changing what it means to have a great job and a great life.

### THE SIX CHANGES

Gallup recommends that organizations immediately change their cultures from *old will* to *new will*. These are the six biggest changes that we discovered:

1. ***Millennials and Generation Z don't just work for a paycheck — they want a purpose.*** For people in these generations, their work must

have meaning. They want to work for organizations with a mission and purpose. In the past, baby boomers and other generations didn't necessarily need meaning in their jobs. They just wanted a paycheck. Their mission and purpose were their families and communities. For millennials and Generation Z, compensation is important and must be fair, but it's no longer their primary motivation. The emphasis for these generations has switched from paycheck to purpose — and so should your culture.

2. ***Millennials and Generation Z are no longer pursuing job satisfaction — they are pursuing development.*** Most members of these generations don't care about the bells and whistles in many workplaces today — the pingpong tables, fancy latte machines and free food that companies offer to try to create job satisfaction. Giving out toys and entitlements is a leadership mistake. And worse, it's condescending.

3. ***Millennials and Generation Z don't want bosses — they want coaches.*** The role of an old-style boss is command and control. But millennials and Generation Z care about having team leaders who can coach them, who value them as individuals and employees, and who help them understand and build their strengths.

4. ***Millennials and Generation Z don't want annual reviews — they want ongoing conversations.*** How these generations communicate — texting, tweeting, Skype, etc. — is immediate and continuous. Millennials and Generation Z are accustomed to constant communication and feedback, and this dramatically affects the workplace. Annual reviews on their own have never worked.

5. ***Millennials and Generation Z don't want a manager who fixates on their weaknesses.*** Gallup research shows that weaknesses never develop into strengths, while strengths develop infinitely. Your organization should not ignore weaknesses. Rather, you should understand

weaknesses but maximize strengths. A strengths-based culture also helps you attract and keep star team members.

6. ***It's not my job — it's my life.*** As we noted earlier, one of Gallup's discoveries is that what everyone in the world wants is a good job. This is especially true for millennials and Generation Z. More so than ever in the history of corporate culture, employees are asking, "Does this organization value my strengths and my contribution? Does this organization give me the chance to do what I do best every day?" Because for millennials and Generation Z, a job is no longer just a job — it's their life.

## Changing Demands of the Workforce

| **Past** ⟶ | **Future** |
|---|---|
| My Paycheck | My Purpose |
| My Satisfaction | My Development |
| My Boss | My Coach |
| My Annual Review | My Ongoing Conversations |
| My Weaknesses | My Strengths |
| My Job | My Life |

# CHAPTER 2

## WHY ORGANIZATIONAL CHANGE IS SO HARD

Only 22% of workers strongly agree that the leadership of their organization has a clear direction for the organization.

Changing cultures from old will to new will and adapting management to the six changes won't happen without C-level leadership. The problem is, only 22% of workers strongly agree that their organization's leadership has a clear direction.

Why is organizational change so hard?

One answer is that over the millennia, humans have existed mostly in small groups, or tribes. To provide value, each tribe member has a role and incentives to build bonds within the tribe. The survival of the group depends on everyone doing their part.

*Also, there are incentives to distrust outsiders who might try to take the tribe's resources.*

"Us versus them" had value in hunting and gathering. Tribalism is built into our brains.

What's more, sociologists have found that there are limits on the number of allies people can maintain in a group. So, for a large organization to function, your loyal friends need to have loyal friends, and so on.

It is only through second- and third-degree connections that your networks become influential. Your success as a leader depends on your reputation extending beyond your closest confidants.

Gallup workplace research supports these sociological discoveries. There is a ripple effect in successful organizations: The engagement of leaders extends to the engagement of managers, which then extends to the front line. But it doesn't happen if left to chance.

It is only in recent human evolution that large societies — and companies with leaders in charge of many teams, with thousands of people — have emerged. There are countless examples of large organizations' successes and failures. Failure often results from a breakdown in the ally network. Tribalism re-emerges, and teams work against other teams and therefore against the larger goals of the organization.

In fact, a major challenge for leaders of large organizations is that there is no common culture — often even in prominent companies. One of the counterintuitive discoveries in Gallup's bestselling book *First, Break All the Rules* was the wide variation in the engagement of teams in the same large organizations — some teams' engagement levels ranked at the top of our engagement database, some were at the bottom and the rest were spread in between.

On the other hand, large organizations and societies have developed for good reasons. They have built great efficiencies that have made life easier and longer, with less pain and hardship for everyone.

The old boss-to-employee, command-and-control leadership environment has "worked" when it comes to building process-efficiency systems, engineering large buildings and creating infrastructure. But the top-down leadership techniques of the past have not adapted to a workplace that now demands coaching and collaboration to thrive.

# CHAPTER 3

## TWO NON-NEGOTIABLE TRAITS FOR LEADERS

- Bring multiple teams together.
- Make great decisions.

There's a common misperception that leaders can be successful through the sheer force of inspiration. If only that were true.

Think about it. Why do motivational speakers often fail to have any evidence of lasting change? Because most well-intended motivational messages don't match *actual daily experiences*. It's similar in leadership.

At first, most employees want to believe the inspiring messages. But their day-to-day experiences make them question leaders' authenticity. They are asked to change their course to align with a new initiative, but don't know why. They get their annual review and have no idea why they didn't get the bonus or promotion they expected. Some slacker who plays office politics got it instead. A benefit just got cut. Their manager blames it on upper management. What do employees think about their inspiring leader now?

Gallup has studied leaders for five decades — from top leaders to middle managers to front-line supervisors. What have we discovered that separates great leaders from all the rest?

We can list more than 20 dimensions we've found in successful leaders: the ability to create a vision, thinking strategically, building influential internal and external networks, courage to make tough decisions, and so on. Successful leadership is multidimensional for sure. But most of the traits of successful leaders can be distilled down to two elements. They know how to:

1. bring multiple teams together
2. make great decisions

And these two elements have a lot to do with whether organizations are agile.

Inspirational messages are important — but there will be no significant impact until leaders have a strategy for how they bring teams together and make great decisions.

Neither of these two demands can exist without the other if a leader is going to be successful.

# CHAPTER 4

## BRING MULTIPLE TEAMS TOGETHER

When your managers are developing, they see the bigger picture of their work and are more likely to work effectively with other managers.

All organizations have problems they need to resolve. Whether people work through friction to fix problems or point fingers depends a lot on what they think of their leadership.

Like their employees, your front-line managers and supervisors need to have jobs where they feel they are continuously developing. Many managers try to shield their teams from corporate problems — sometimes taking the blame themselves. Other managers will choose to blame upper management for their problems — "It's not my fault. It's corporate."

Us-versus-them takes over. Silos develop.

Managers at all levels — whether they are team leaders, managers of other managers or executive leaders — need a well-defined and well-articulated mission and purpose that everyone can easily relate back to the work they do every day — their contribution. They need clear expectations that are continually redefined with the ongoing, often changing, corporate strategy. And they need continual coaching and accountability so that they can see their progress and potential.

Before your managers can deliver what they need to their employees, they must first get what *they* need as employees. The teams they are on are made up of other managers who are either on the same page or not. They see other managers as either allies or enemies. How connected your teams of managers are as a group will determine whether the teams they manage will support other teams or not.

Managers are much more likely to inspire big-picture, cross-team cooperation in their employees when they themselves are engaged and developing. In upcoming sections of the book, most notably "Boss to Coach," we provide a roadmap for how to develop your managers.

For any organization to change effectively, its managers must be able to work together.

# CHAPTER 5

## MAKE GREAT DECISIONS

Organizations are decision factories.

Daniel Kahneman, Gallup senior scientist emeritus, Nobel Prize-winning psychologist and generally considered the world's leading authority on decision-making, once told us, "Organizations are decision factories."

Organizations succeed or fail based on leaders' decisions — decisions regarding strategic direction, mergers or acquisitions, key hires, new technology, the company's mission, or serious ethical dilemmas.

If a decision is not "right," all the talent and energy aimed at the decision is wasted.

Making the right decisions is a science in itself. Beyond *luck*, which some right decisions are attributed to, there are three keys to being right more often than not:

1. **Know your limits.** Leaders need to have an honest understanding of their decision-making strengths and weaknesses. In what situations are you most vulnerable to making the wrong call? For example, a leader may have extremely strong self-confidence that makes them prone to decisions that aren't well-thought-out. Or they may be highly competitive, leading the team to put winning in the short term over stronger long-term objectives. Or they simply may not know a subject well enough without the support of experts. Great decision-makers are keenly aware of their limitations.

2. **Apply critical thinking.** Does the decision make sense? What's the logic? To make good decisions, leaders have to engage in deep critical thinking with colleagues to identify high-risk blind spots. Almost all leaders are subject to confirmation bias because they surround themselves with people who think like they do and who

are consciously or unconsciously motivated to agree with them. In many cases, as a leader, you will have to fight "groupthink" and make decisions that go against the grain.

Before making major decisions, assess whether your decision-making is biased by a strength or a weakness. And test for confirmation bias: Are you surrounded by "yes people"? Challenge every member of your team to present a dissenting idea. What are the most likely short- and long-term consequences of the decision?

3. **Use analytics-driven evidence.** What do the numbers say? Are there patterns in the data that support — or conflict with — your decision? (See Chapter 52.) One of Amazon CEO Jeff Bezos' famous statements is: "The great thing about fact-based decisions is that they overrule the hierarchy." Analytics, if done right, also have the potential to overrule politics and bias.

When great decision-making is combined with teams that work together, your organization has the best chance to build a *culture* that is truly agile in the workforce of the future.

# CULTURE

**YOUR ORGANIZATION'S CULTURE HAS A DIRECT, MEASURABLE IMPACT ON PERFORMANCE.**

# CHAPTER 6

## WHAT IS AN ORGANIZATIONAL CULTURE?

41% of employees strongly agree that they know what their organization stands for and what makes it different from competitors.

*Culture begins with your purpose — why you are in business. It lives or dies day to day through your managers.*

While most leaders can articulate their organization's purpose, most employees can't. Only 27% of employees strongly believe in their company's values. This disconnect has a negative impact on everything.

*Culture determines your brand — how employees and customers view your company.*

A world-class culture inspires your most talented employees to create superior customer experiences. When an organization makes a brand promise but fails to deliver, it loses credibility with customers — and especially employees.

Unfortunately, this situation is all too common: Only 26% of U.S. workers feel their organization always delivers on the promises it makes to customers.

An organization's performance improves when its employees understand what differentiates its brand. But Gallup analytics reveals that less than half of U.S. employees (41%) strongly agree that they know what their organization stands for and what makes it different from its competitors.

And 71% of millennials who strongly agree that they know what their organization stands for and what makes it different from its competitors say they plan to stay with their company for at least one year. That number falls to 30% for millennials who strongly disagree.

In short, if your best employees don't know your organization's purpose, they will leave.

# CHAPTER 7

## WHY CULTURE MATTERS

Culture has a direct impact on performance.

Ask yourself these questions about your culture:

- How well do your purpose, brand and culture align?
- How clear is your purpose to employees and customers?
- Are your employees committed to your culture?

The best applicants join an organization because of its reputation. And social media greatly heightens awareness of a company's culture — good or bad.

Gallup analytics finds that employees and teams who align with their organization's culture consistently perform better on internal key performance metrics than those who do not.

*Culture has a direct, measurable impact on performance.*

One in three employees worldwide strongly agree with the statement "The mission or purpose of my organization makes me feel my job is important." By doubling that ratio, business units have realized a 34% reduction in absenteeism, a 42% drop in safety incidents and a 19% improvement in quality.

### SYMPTOMS OF A BROKEN CULTURE

Sometimes organizations don't initially see problems with their culture as "culture problems" at all. Here are some warning signs that your culture might be broken:

- the inability to attract world-class talent
- difficulty maximizing organic growth based on customer-employee interactions
- leadership initiatives that don't go anywhere
- lack of agility in responding to customer needs
- loss of best performers to top brands

## WHY STANDARD SURVEYS DON'T WORK FOR CULTURE

Culture is unique to every organization. Your culture is personal.

Many culture survey tools attempt to fit organizations into certain cultural "types" based on predetermined views of "good" or "bad" culture. They compare their organizational culture to external benchmarks rather than to their leadership's aspirations. While these benchmarks might reveal how an organization compares to a generic standard, they fail to measure what is fundamentally unique to your enterprise.

Organizations need an approach to culture that is flexible enough to identify their uniqueness — and one that is grounded in rigorous science.

# CHAPTER 8

## HOW TO CHANGE A CULTURE

Merging cultures is hard because tribes, by nature, want to maintain their identities.

Most CEOs and CHROs list "culture" as a top priority. They know they need to change.

They want a culture that is agile and adaptable to changes happening around the world. They especially want a culture with high collaboration where they can make good decisions and execute them quickly. They want a culture that attracts and retains the biggest stars.

Following record levels of mergers and acquisitions, many organizations around the world are trying to blend cultures and brands. Merging cultures rarely works because tribes, by nature, want to maintain their identities.

What has to happen to change a culture?

1. **Identify your purpose and brand.** The CEO, CHRO and executive committee need to clearly identify your purpose — why you are in business — and how you want applicants, employees and customers to perceive your brand. Purpose and brand set the stage for everything else. The employee experience starts with applicants' first impression of your organization — how they perceive your culture and brand — and then how their employee journey, from onboarding to development and eventually departure, validates those impressions. Top executives need to be aligned, consistent and committed to the purpose and brand. That is the starting point for bringing teams together and effective decision-making.

2. **Audit all programs and communications** — including human capital practices, performance management, values and rituals, and team structures — for alignment and consistency with your organization's purpose and brand. Gallup has found that this can be a quick process and recommends performing this audit annually.

3. **Reposition your managers as coaches.** Only your best managers can implement the culture you want. A great culture is one of the few things an organization can't buy. Managers at all levels make or break your culture change. And traditional performance management systems have struggled to inspire and develop employees, which can result in billions of dollars in lost productivity. (See Chapter 20.) Today's employees want a coach, not a boss. Moving your managers from *boss* to *coach* not only increases employee engagement and improves performance, but it's also essential to changing your culture.

We will discuss specific types of cultural change — such as building a strengths-based culture and creating a culture of high development — for the new future of work in the chapters ahead. In those chapters — which include the topics of attraction to departure, diversity and inclusion, and artificial intelligence — we will present important realities in your organization that determine your culture and your brand. And, we will provide science-based insights into how you can change your culture and build your purpose and brand.

# EMPLOYMENT BRAND

WITH SOCIAL MEDIA AND INSTANT COMMUNICATION, YOUR ORGANIZATION'S REPUTATION TRAVELS MUCH MORE QUICKLY NOW THAN IN THE PAST.

# CHAPTER 9

## ATTRACTING THE NEW WORKFORCE

Companies spend time and money on marketing campaigns to build a loyal customer base. But they often neglect to develop an equally strong employment brand to attract the best applicants.

### Employee Experience

*The journey with your organization*

Thanks to the prevalence of technology and social media, employees can reveal — and share — how they experience a company's brand. Now everyone knows what actually happens inside organizations. This includes the entire employee experience, from hiring and onboarding to career development opportunities and departure.

Millennials are highly networked. When searching for jobs, they seek out referrals from current employees of potential organizations and suggestions from family members and friends. This is different from going on Facebook or other social network platforms to find a job. *They go to trusted relationships.*

The new workforce is less interested in career fairs, professional recruiting services and other types of recruiting events. Other avenues are easier and quicker to access — and, to them, more authentic.

Millennials prefer to go straight to the source of companies they're interested in. But they also cast a wide net in their job searches, leaning toward online sources in their career field, professional network sites, other online job sites, employee ranking sites and general search engines that allow them to explore many options. They're less likely to use social network sites and college career centers or websites.

Specifically related to workplace culture, millennials are seeking jobs that fit their lifestyle. While overall compensation is still extremely important to nearly half of younger employees, it is *less important* than opportunities to learn and advance, the quality of their manager, and having interesting work.

What does all this mean for recruiting? It means your workplace reality is now more transparent than ever. Your actual culture — how management works, how people advance, what kind of flexibility employees really get, the office space and place — determines your employment brand.

The most important thing you can do is maintain a strong employment brand and a workplace culture that lives up to that brand. Reputation travels much more quickly now than in the past.

And organizational transparency will become even more magnified with Generation Z entering the workforce. All they have known from birth is digital communication.

If there's a discrepancy between how your organization presents itself to the world and how it *really is*, prospective employees will find out about it online and from their friends. And the word will spread.

# CHAPTER 10

## HIRING STAR EMPLOYEES

Predisposed biases can cause managers to choose the wrong candidates.

The wrong hire — or just plain bad hire — can be immensely costly. Not only did you miss the chance to hire a star, but you have to spend more money to train a replacement.

Hiring star employees who are engaged costs organizations less because they boost customer engagement, revenues and profitability.

The right selection decisions establish a culture of high performance. They also establish how easily people will integrate into your culture, how quickly they'll develop, how long they'll stay, how they'll represent your organization and whether they'll persist when times are tough.

To give you some perspective, reducing predisposed biases with a valid assessment system can triple the success rate of your hires.

### TYPES OF BIAS:

- **Glare factors.** Hiring managers give disproportionate weight to characteristics that appear on the surface during an interview, such as how candidates look, dress and present themselves.
- **Experience fallacy.** Hiring managers had an applicant from a previous employer turn out to be highly successful, so they assume everyone from that company will be successful.
- **Confirmation bias.** Hiring managers form a distinct impression of a candidate based on the school they attended or a club they belonged to and only hear comments that confirm their beliefs about the person.

- **Overconfidence bias.** Hiring managers believe that they have a special ability to judge applicants based on their gut and don't consider other information.
- **Similarity bias.** Hiring managers select and hire people who are like them.
- **Stereotype bias.** Hiring managers have unconscious stereotypes associated with gender, race, sexual orientation, ethnicity and age.
- **Availability bias.** Hiring managers rely on their memory of an interview and make a decision based on a few high or low points rather than taking a comprehensive view.
- **Escalation of commitment.** Hiring managers feel pressured to move forward with a candidate because they have already invested so much time or energy in the process.

In a meta-analysis published in the journal *Psychological Bulletin*, researchers Nalini Ambady and Robert Rosenthal coined the term "thin slices" of behavior, later popularized by Malcolm Gladwell in his book *Blink: The Power of Thinking Without Thinking*. The science was rooted in the fact that people often form judgments based on very small samples of interaction with someone else — for example, first impressions.

In some cases, these thin slices provide valid insights. For example, when a medical doctor or nurse takes your blood pressure, pulse or blood sample, this is a science-based thin slice to draw inferences about your health. And in other cases, thin slices can reveal unconscious biases, such as those listed above, that can lead to snap judgments, bad decisions and failed outcomes.

Because of these biases, it's not unusual for managers to make hiring decisions they later regret after actually spending time with the person on the job.

In some fields, massive amounts of data are readily available. When college athletes are recruited, for instance, professionals spend hours studying stats and watching game film prior to making a decision. Recruiting bureaus use a five-star system to rate each potential player. The system, while imperfect, does remarkably well in predicting which colleges will have teams that are in the running for a championship each year.

Most organizations don't have the luxury of gathering "game film" on job candidates. But fortunately, as with the rigor of medicine, organizational psychologists have spent a century developing *psychometrics* — the science of measuring psychological characteristics. And now there are efficient measures and methods that can substantially reduce hiring bias by providing science-based thin slices and that have been shown to predict performance after the hiring decision.

# CHAPTER II

## HIRING ANALYTICS — THE SOLUTION

### Four criteria for successful hiring:

1. Prior experiences and achievements
2. Innate tendencies
3. Multiple interviews
4. On-the-job observation

Gallup researchers have spent five decades asking questions, studying responses and tracking individuals' performance in hundreds of jobs across more than 2,000 clients. Our scientists have discovered five general innate traits, or tendencies, that predict performance across job types:

1. Motivation — drive for achievement
2. Workstyle — organizing work for efficient completion
3. Initiation — taking action and inspiring others to succeed
4. Collaboration — building quality partnerships
5. Thought process — solving problems through assimilation of new information

Within these five traits, unique subtraits can be used to improve prediction of performance for individual contributor roles, managers and executive leaders.

Gallup Senior Scientist Frank L. Schmidt, a pioneer in meta-analytic methods, along with colleagues In-Sue Oh and Jonathan A. Shaffer, reviewed 100 years of assessment research in organizational psychology. They examined the selection methods that organizations have most commonly used.

Their review included 31 different measures and methods. Some of the methods, such as tests of intelligence, personality and structured interviews, take 30 minutes to an hour to complete. Other methods, such as in assessment centers and job tryouts, are more time-consuming and involve more substantial observations. Schmidt and his colleagues found that the less time-consuming measures performed just as well, or better, than the more time-consuming observations as a result of many years of refinement of these more efficient methods.

Taking into account the Gallup research, the 100-year findings and what we've seen work most practically and effectively in organizations, we recommend using the following criteria for successful hiring:

1. **Prior experiences and achievements.** Collect substantial background information on candidates, including key experiences that align with job demands, educational achievement and evidence of job knowledge.
2. **Innate tendencies.** Evaluate candidates on the five traits above — motivation, workstyle, initiation, collaboration and thought process. Screening for these five innate tendencies will encompass most of what you need to know about a candidate in this category. You can do this efficiently and cost-effectively using Gallup's structured interviews and web-based assessments.
3. **Multiple interviews.** At later stages in the hiring process, have the hiring manager and team members conduct multiple interviews with candidates. These interviews allow you to contextualize candidates' fit to their role, manager, team and organization. Gallup has developed listening guides to improve the quality of these conversations. Combining evaluations from several interviews will substantially reduce the potential bias of a single-interview approach.
4. **On-the-job observation.** Use internships and other project-based experiences to gather "game film" on each candidate's individual achievements, collaboration and customer value. Collect ratings from their supervisors and peers.

Using these four criteria, you can design a hiring process that is an engaging, positive experience for candidates *and* scientifically tied to high performance. Advances in artificial intelligence will make the hiring process more efficient in the years ahead.

# CHAPTER 12

## WHERE TO FIND "GAME FILM" ON FUTURE STARS

Less than one-third of college graduates strongly agree that they worked on a project that took a semester or more to complete or had an internship or job that allowed them to apply what they were learning in the classroom.

Attracting star employees and building your employment brand should start while your future stars are still in college — or even high school. One of the best ways to prepare students is through meaningful internships and apprenticeships.

And those students would greatly appreciate the opportunities. Gallup has found that only one-third of college students strongly agree that they will graduate with the skills and knowledge they need to be successful in the job market (34%) and workplace (36%). And just over half (53%) believe that their major will lead to a good job.

These are among the key findings from the *Strada-Gallup 2017 College Student Survey* — a nationally representative survey of students that examines their perceptions on preparedness for the workforce and the career-related support they receive from their institutions.

In further research, the Gallup Alumni Survey (formerly the Gallup-Purdue Index) — designed to measure the quality of the college experience from the perspective of college graduates — has identified six positive college experiences with a strong link to post-collegiate success:

1. having at least one professor who made them excited about learning
2. professors who cared about them as a person
3. having a mentor who encouraged them to pursue their goals and dreams

4. working on a project that took a semester or more to complete
5. having an internship or job that allowed them to apply what they learned in the classroom
6. being extremely active in extracurricular activities and organizations while in college

These six experiences link to postgraduate wellbeing and employee engagement, among other key outcomes. But just 3% of graduates have had all six of these experiences in college.

Within this Gallup Alumni Survey finding lies a massive opportunity for organizations.

Specifically, companies can play an active role with three of these six college experiences: *having a mentor, working on projects that allow them to apply what they learned* and *having an internship.* To prepare your next wave of recruits, consider partnering with colleges and universities to create intensive work-integrated experiences for students.

Who is in a better position to mentor the future workforce than the professionals who are currently doing the work? Internships, mentorships and practical work projects can close the gap on one of the most difficult prehiring criterion to obtain — how well individuals actually perform on the job.

If your organization depends on high-quality graduates, be proactive about creating high school and college experiences for your future workforce. Offering internships is an obvious way to take the lead. You might also look at how to integrate your business into college curricula — for example, offer to design semester-long creative projects for students.

Only half of college graduates strongly agree that their education was worth the cost. This perception is related to how leaders design the college experience. It is also based on how intentional businesses are about working with colleges to prepare their next wave of recruits.

Of course, not everyone attends a traditional four-year college. Many students go straight to work from high school, and the model of school-to-work will dramatically change in the coming years.

Take employee branding to a whole new level, and give students a realistic idea of what working for you would be like. Not only will this greatly benefit your organization in selecting future stars, these experiences will provide infinite value to students.

# CHAPTER 13

## FIVE QUESTIONS FOR ONBOARDING

1. "What do we believe in around here?"
2. "What are my strengths?"
3. "What is my role?"
4. "Who are my partners?"
5. "What does my future here look like?"

Once recruited and hired, how does an employee who just walked through your company's doors become "one of us"?

You can take a variety of approaches to onboarding new workers based on your organization's culture. Some companies focus on building social bonds, while others leave people to figure things out on their own. Some follow a set process for orientation, while others have a "sink or swim" approach.

The goal of onboarding should be to introduce foundational elements that employees can build on throughout their career — those that influence their performance over *decades* not quarters.

First impressions matter. They set the tone for the employee's career, and it's never easier to influence employee behavior than when they are a blank slate and eager to learn and change.

Yet while organizations have paid great attention to improving onboarding processes, only about one in 10 employees, managers and leaders strongly agree that their organization does a good job of onboarding. And roughly four in 10 employees are engaged in their first six months of employment — when engagement is typically at its peak.

Why does early attention fail to result in lasting impact as people progress through their tenure? Do you and your new employees have a clear view of your organization's purpose, desired brand and desired culture?

Here are five questions you must answer for every new employee to have a successful onboarding program:

## 1. "WHAT DO WE BELIEVE IN AROUND HERE?"

The first thing new employees need to know is your organization's stated purpose — your shared beliefs. Then, you can frame everything else as an expression of what the organization stands for and is trying to achieve.

Naturally, you must communicate a lot of "nuts and bolts" information during onboarding — the basic benefits, rules and policies that govern all employees in your organization. These seemingly pragmatic matters are actually expressions of your organizational culture.

How leaders practice and reinforce details like safety, family leave and reporting ethics violations says a lot about your culture as a whole. For example, if you have a stated policy of flextime and send messages that you value employee wellbeing, can employees *really* leave their desk to go to the gym or leave the office early to attend a child's event? Do your benefits, rules, ethical boundaries and culture align with your organization's stated *purpose* and *brand*?

## 2. "WHAT ARE MY STRENGTHS?"

To become "one of us" and to be productive, employees must know themselves. But organizations almost always overlook this crucial early step.

Your organization has a vested interest in making sure that all your new employees approach their roles using their strengths. When employees know their strengths, they can take conversations with their managers to a deeper level. And when team members know one another's strengths, new members can quickly assimilate into a team, and everyone can better collaborate to get work done.

Effective orientation needs to provide opportunities for employees to explore how they use their individual strengths to achieve outcomes. New employees also need to be aware of what they *don't do well* so they know when they need to rely on others and ask for help.

But strengths training isn't only about performance. It's an upfront investment of time and money in employees as individuals. Offering strengths training shows that you care about developing your employees and demonstrates that you're interested in their long-term growth. We'll discuss the science of strengths in the next chapter.

## 3. "WHAT IS MY ROLE?"

According to Gallup's global study of workplaces, only about 50% of employees know what's expected of them at work. Most employees get a sense of the demands of their future job during the recruitment process. But too often, reality doesn't match what was advertised. Being clear and accurate about the responsibilities of the job and how you evaluate performance seems basic, but this step is often overlooked.

The next step is to figure out how new employees can use their strengths to achieve great things for themselves and your organization — and how their work connects to your mission or purpose. Strong fit-to-role is predictive of performance and longevity.

It's critical for new employees to quickly gain the confidence that they can master their role. New employees should be able to look back at their first six months on the job and name their successes.

## 4. "WHO ARE MY PARTNERS?"

New employees need to feel like they belong. They need to know that their superiors and peers accept them. They also need to know who they can depend on to support them as they experiment and learn their role.

Each new hire should develop a strategy for building partnerships in the organization — a "relationship map." Social network analysis in the academic literature illustrates how someone's influence in an organization is determined based on their first-, second- and third-degree connections.

First-degree connections are the people you know personally and trust — your friends. Second-degree connections are the friends of your friends, and so on. Second- and third-degree connections can have a big influence on an employee's reputation and influence, because the second- and third-degree connections multiply their influence through others.

In short, your relationships at work determine how much work you get done and reinforce that you belong in the organization.

## 5. "WHAT DOES MY FUTURE HERE LOOK LIKE?"

All people need to learn and grow. Younger employees in particular see new jobs as learning and growth opportunities. Regardless of their age, however, *all* employees need to be able to see a plausible path forward in their career at your organization.

Nearly nine out of 10 people say that the last time they switched jobs, they switched organizations. That means that nearly all organizations made an investment to hire and train their workforce — and then could not provide a plausible career path for it. In contrast, employees who have an opportunity to learn and grow at work are twice as likely as those on the other end of the scale to say they will spend their career with their company.

**A note of caution:** Your onboarding employee experience must align with your *real culture*. After six months in a role, the honeymoon starts to fade, and your new idealistic employee has probably met a few veterans who are quick to share "how things *really* work around here." If the values you preach on Day One do not match the true values that your structure, benefits and recognition, and leadership exhibit, your new employees will suffer long-term shock as they realize that what they thought they signed up for is something quite different.

# CHAPTER 14

## SHORTCUT TO DEVELOPMENT — STRENGTHS-BASED CONVERSATIONS

If you're a manager, ask yourself, "Am I an expert on my team members' weaknesses or on their strengths?"

Our brains are hardwired to critique others. When a coworker asks us to review their presentation, our first instinct is to look for mistakes and "opportunities for improvement." When we're assigned to train a new employee, we focus on the steps they miss or the information they get wrong.

Traditional performance management reflects these instincts. It's set up to rank and rate employees and to "correct" their weaknesses. But this approach often fails to actually improve performance. Just 21% of employees strongly agree that their performance is managed in a way that motivates them to do outstanding work.

We may be naturally wired to give criticism, but we sure aren't wired to receive it. We crave praise any time we can get it.

So how can managers know the right balance between praise and criticism for employees?

Serious review of an individual's strengths *and* weaknesses is essential to exceptional career development. Critical feedback is necessary at times, and everyone needs to be aware of and accountable for their weaknesses. But to inspire exceptional performance, managers have to lead with — and continually revisit — meaningful feedback based on what each person naturally does best. This is the starting point to building trust, which increases the likelihood that the critical feedback will result in growth and development.

As organizations ask managers to interact with employees more frequently, managers must be careful not to turn ongoing conversations into ongoing criticism.

Constant criticism makes it nearly impossible for a manager and employee to build a relationship of trust, which makes it difficult for the employee to accept any critique with an open mind. It also makes it difficult for employees to be engaged at work.

A typical day for an engaged employee looks much different than a typical day for an actively disengaged employee. One of the underlying reasons for that is engaged employees' abundance of positive experiences.

Engaged employees aren't immune to negativity or job stress. Gallup research shows that, whether they are engaged or not, employees experience more stress during the workweek than on the weekend. That's not surprising. Most employees deal with unexpected requests and workplace drama in the office. But the structure of an engaged employee's day and their interactions with managers and peers allow them to spend more time doing what they do best.

How then should managers structure the "ideal" day for employees to encourage higher engagement and performance?

In a study of 8,115 employees, Gallup asked respondents to think about their most recent workday (if it was the previous day) and to report the number of hours they spent doing various activities. What best differentiated engaged from actively disengaged employees was the time they spent focusing on their strengths — feeling so absorbed in their work that time passed quickly — and less time spent focusing on what they don't do well. Engaged employees spent four times as much of their day focusing on their strengths compared with what they don't do well. *Actively disengaged employees spent about equal time focusing on their strengths and on what they don't do well.*

A strengths approach to performance is not about glossing over weaknesses or ensuring that employees *only* get to do tasks and projects they like. Everyone's role will include responsibilities that aren't much fun.

Likewise, there will be times when managers need to give constructive feedback to help employees improve in their roles. But managers shouldn't treat feedback like it's a balancing act. They shouldn't equally match criticism with praise. The scales should be heavily tilted toward what employees do best.

Gallup data suggest that employees in today's workforce expect their managers to coach them — primarily based on their strengths. And a high-performing workforce should set this expectation for its team leaders, because it produces much better results.

# CHAPTER 15

## CLIFTONSTRENGTHS 34: A TAXONOMY OF HUMAN POTENTIAL

### THE 34 CLIFTONSTRENGTHS THEMES

| | | |
|---|---|---|
| Achiever | Deliberative | Learner |
| Activator | Developer | Maximizer |
| Adaptability | Discipline | Positivity |
| Analytical | Empathy | Relator |
| Arranger | Focus | Responsibility |
| Belief | Futuristic | Restorative |
| Command | Harmony | Self-Assurance |
| Communication | Ideation | Significance |
| Competition | Includer | Strategic |
| Connectedness | Individualization | Woo |
| Consistency | Input | |
| Context | Intellection | |

*"What would happen if we studied what was* ***right*** *with people versus what's wrong with people?"*

This deceptively simple question posed decades ago by Don Clifton is what launched the global strengths movement that we know today.

The question was a particularly personal one for Don. As a child, he was bedridden for months due to a severe leg injury. Instead of obsessing over this painful obstacle, he read voraciously and focused on honing his intellect and talent for mathematics. This experience taught him something about emphasizing strengths over weaknesses.

During World War II, Don put his mathematics skills to the test as an Army Air Force navigator and bombardier flying B-24s, for which he received a Distinguished Flying Cross for his heroism among his 25 successful bombing sorties. While flying over the Azores in severe weather, his flight went off course. He had a hunch about how to correct it. But when he did the math, he realized his intuition was wrong. He learned to trust science over personal intuition.

When Don returned home from WWII, he had seen enough of war and destruction. He wanted to spend the rest of his life doing good for humankind. This led to his intense interest in studying human development.

In the late 1940s and 1950s, the field of psychology was focused primarily on diagnosing and treating psychological problems. To Don, this seemed to be entirely backward.

"In my graduate study in psychology, it became evident to me that psychologists had historically studied what was wrong with people rather than what worked," Don said. "I realized then that too often, people were being characterized by their problems and weaknesses rather than their talents. That realization led me to the necessity for studying successful people. The only way to learn to identify the differences in any professions is to study the successful performers."

In 1949, Don and his colleagues started the Nebraska Human Resources Research Foundation at the University of Nebraska. The foundation served as a community service for students and as a laboratory for graduate students to practice strengths-based psychology.

Don and his students and colleagues discovered that successful students — those who would persist to graduation — had notably different character traits than less successful ones. They also learned that successful students had the same counselors.

These early discoveries about successful people stirred other hypotheses. Don and his colleagues began to study the most successful school counselors, teachers, salespeople and managers. Don discovered that there were certain traits that successful people in a role shared. He defined these human tendencies as "naturally recurring patterns of thought, feeling or behavior that can be productively applied."

Notably, Don was not interested in creating a personality test, though he became world-famous for having created the CliftonStrengths assessment (formerly Clifton StrengthsFinder), which identifies users' talent themes. And — as of this writing — more than 20 million people worldwide have taken the assessment. Rather, Don wanted to identify those universal but practical traits that were predictive of real high-performance outcomes. And he wanted to identify tendencies in people that were unique to each individual but that could be developed into true strengths with practice. *The purpose of Don's work was to bring focus to conversations so that people could better understand not just who they are — but what they are capable of achieving.*

Over his 50-year career — near the end of which he was honored by the American Psychological Association with a presidential commendation as the father of strengths-based psychology — Don continued to gather data with his team in hundreds of studies of the most successful people across all cultures, industries, roles and walks of life. By the mid-1990s, a meta-analysis of all this research coalesced into 34 distinct talent "themes" that highly successful people develop into strengths. (See definitions for the 34 CliftonStrengths themes in Appendix 1.)

These themes outline the primary dimensions of human potential. Every person has a unique mixture of these themes, which begin as innate potential but that can be unleashed through practice and intentional development.

**To discover your own strengths, use the access code in the packet in the back of the book to take the CliftonStrengths assessment.**

# CHAPTER 16

## FIVE STEPS TO BUILDING A STRENGTHS-BASED CULTURE

1. Start with the CEO or it doesn't work.
2. Require every employee to discover their strengths.
3. Build an internal network of strengths coaches.
4. Integrate strengths into performance management.
5. Transform your learning programs.

Few organizations in the world can honestly say their culture is "strengths-based." This is a massive missed opportunity. Organizations and teams with strengths-based cultures consistently outperform their competitors.

Building a strengths-based culture is hard work. Simply knowing everyone's strengths is not enough to create change. It takes ongoing conversations, reflection and practice to successfully integrate strengths into your organization's daily routines. The most effective way to accomplish this is with strengths coaches certified by Gallup.

True strengths-based organizations have strong leadership and great managers they have cultivated over time through selection and development programs. These leaders have an impact on the organization's performance because they have a deep belief in the business value of human development.

Strengths-based organizations have strengths-based teams as their cultural default — the norm for how they get work done. And strengths-based teams have higher engagement, better retention of top performers, better customer service and higher profitability.

Given the real and measurable benefits of having a strengths-based culture, how can your organization instill a culture based on strengths that is a respected part of the organization's foundation?

1. **Start with the CEO or it doesn't work.** If you want a strengths-based culture, executive leadership needs to explain how capitalizing on the strengths of each person in the organization will empower the company to achieve its purpose and business objectives. Executive leaders should share their strengths and communicate how they use them. In the book *Strengths Based Leadership*, Gallup outlines how individual leaders with very different talents and strengths achieve exceptional performance in their own way.

2. **Require every employee to discover their strengths.** Strengths measurement gives teams a common language to talk about how they can collaborate and perform effectively. Awareness is just the beginning. A strengths-based measurement approach is designed primarily to improve constructive communication and development.

3. **Build an internal network of strengths coaches.** Internal strengths coaches give managers practical strengths insights and tools. They serve as internal consultants who can advise your managers and provide ongoing support.

4. **Integrate strengths into performance management.** Your managers need to become strengths-based performance coaches for their teams. This means they must first understand their own strengths and how they can use them. Then, they need to understand their employees' strengths so they can have effective ongoing conversations that lead to performance and competency development. When your individual contributors learn how to apply their strengths in their unique roles, strengths become a vital part of your ongoing business operations, rather than a temporary side program.

5. **Transform your learning programs.** Conduct a thorough audit of your existing programs and practices — recruiting, hiring, onboarding and the entire employee life cycle. Identify any programs, practices or policies that wear down your workforce by philosophically

contradicting a culture that leads with strengths. Then change them. Identifying weaknesses is important, and everyone in your organization will have tasks and responsibilities that don't perfectly align with their strengths. To effectively develop competencies, first understand who each person is and what their natural tendencies are. Then position them to maximize the time they spend using their strengths to improve competencies.

# CHAPTER 17

## THE RIGHT EXPECTATIONS — COMPETENCIES 2.0

**Seven expectations that are necessary for success in any role:**

- **Build relationships.** Create partnerships, build trust, share ideas and accomplish work.
- **Develop people.** Help others become more effective through strengths, expectations and coaching.
- **Lead change.** Embrace change and set goals that align with a stated vision.
- **Inspire others.** Encourage others through positivity, vision, confidence, challenges and recognition.
- **Think critically.** Gather and evaluate information that leads to smart decisions.
- **Communicate clearly.** Share information regularly and concisely.
- **Create accountability.** Hold yourself and your team responsible for performance.

For a strengths-based approach to be successful, each person needs to aim their strengths at something important to them and to your organization.

What behaviors do you expect from every employee?

If you can give a short answer to that question, you've already identified elements of the culture you want. If the list is too long to remember — or includes descriptions and labels that don't resonate with most people — then your culture doesn't match your aspirations.

Large organizations create competencies that they expect employees to master. Competency labels range from "provide constructive feedback" to "be decisive." Some are vague or confusing — "be purposeful" or "discourage regressive movement."

The practice of "competency modeling" has become increasingly popular despite not having a commonly accepted definition or methodology or clear linkages to organizational effectiveness.

Competency models usually include a wide variety of traits, skills, capabilities, knowledge, behaviors and responsibilities. This hodgepodge creates confusion about what competencies represent and how to use them.

Until recently, there had been no attempt to define a universal set of competencies that apply across jobs and organizations.

To do that, a Gallup team reviewed research spanning three decades and conducted a content analysis of 360 unique behavioral job demands in 559 job roles across 18 industries. Data came from job-analysis studies that Gallup experts originally conducted — which studied top performers in a wide variety of roles — and competency models created independently at other organizations. Hundreds of competency statements have been written. We tried to collect them all.

After pooling the unique demands and competencies we collected from all the roles we studied, Gallup scientists found considerable redundancies. Many different labels had been used to describe the same competencies. When our team conducted an exhaustive coding process, we discovered seven higher-order categories that described the expectations necessary for success in literally any role.

These seven categories — listed above — don't contain every competency that has ever been conceptualized. But chances are, most or all of the competencies that you've identified in your organization — if they are predictive of high performance — will fit into one of the seven universal categories.

This list is Gallup's simplest and most comprehensive explanation of the job demands required to achieve excellence for all employees in any organization.

## DO THESE COMPETENCIES REALLY APPLY TO EVERYONE?

You may be asking yourself how these seven competencies can be expectations for *every* role, from the front line to executive leadership. Should a manufacturing employee or bus driver be expected to develop people, lead change and inspire others? In an optimally run organization, yes. *Everyone* should play a role in developing their colleagues by providing meaningful feedback and coaching.

Leaders need to be the first to model these demands because their behavior dictates what employees interpret as a real expectation.

But how can someone who doesn't have natural tendencies in Developer or Individualization *develop people*? How can someone who doesn't lead with thinking themes like Analytical or Strategic *think critically*? Or how can someone who doesn't lead with Communication *communicate clearly*? (See definitions for the 34 CliftonStrengths themes in Appendix 1.)

Not everyone will meet these expectations the same way. Based on their strengths, people will find some competencies easier to achieve than others. But everyone can use their unique strengths profile to meet these demands.

For example, someone who is highly competitive can *develop people* by creating clear criteria for progress so that "winning" can be defined. Or a person who is highly harmonious can *think critically* by discovering and emphasizing what people have in common and bring resolution to conflict.

Each of these seven competencies aligns with effective performance management practices that increase engagement and produce high performance. How do you know how well you are doing at meeting these demands? Ask your constituencies — your peers, direct reports, managers and other partners. The seven competencies bring focus to a 360 developmental process.

In the future workforce, people will increasingly need to improve in each of these seven areas. Everyone is better off when they build relationships, contribute to developing others, lead change in their role, inspire others, think critically, communicate clearly and hold each other accountable.

And, everyone should think about how they can use their strengths to meet each of the seven expectations.

# CHAPTER 18

## GETTING SUCCESSION PLANNING RIGHT

- Start with objective performance measures.
- Analyze the key experiences that create success.
- Tap in to innate tendencies.
- Design highly individualized leadership development.

Effective succession planning is essential for retaining world-class talent at all levels of the organization, not just the C-suite.

The problem most companies have is that their succession planning is primarily a subjective process. It's prone to biases that result in poor decisions about who should advance in the organization. And poor succession decisions undermine the entire organization because people are promoted into roles that they lack the capacity to perform.

Many companies have no succession plan at all and make these crucial decisions as needed. The absence of an organized system leads to extraordinarily high costs in external hiring.

When done right, decisions to promote from within the organization result in higher success rates. This is because decision-makers can closely observe and use on-the-job performance to make better decisions.

But having a system in place is just one step. You also need a system that dramatically reduces bias.

To illustrate how bias can affect management decisions, Gallup asked 645 leaders where they would assign their best performer if they had two managerial jobs available: one in a loss-making territory and another in a territory that was already profitable. Two-thirds of leaders said they would put the top manager in the loss-making territory in an attempt to recoup the loss. This decision process reflects a loss-aversion bias — a tendency toward avoiding losses.

High-performing leaders were more likely to position the top performer in the profitable territory. They knew they could get a greater return on their investment immediately if they combined a somewhat successful territory with a highly skilled manager — and research supports their decision. The high-performing leaders chose a data-driven decision that corrects for the loss-aversion bias.

Confirmation bias also enters into succession decisions: Leaders select new leaders who are like themselves or who conform to their preconceived notions or gut feelings about the candidates. Or they promote a leader with multiple recent successes without looking at a longer track record. This is known as hot-hand fallacy or recency bias.

Here are four practical steps to make your succession planning more scientific:

1. **Start with objective performance measures.** If succession is from manager to executive leader (manager of managers), look at objective performance measures over a significant amount of time — years if possible. Audit the success of the teams your prospects have led: sales, profit, employee turnover, customer ratings of service, absenteeism, safety and employee engagement.

2. **Analyze the key experiences that create success.** Evaluate the expectations for the new role. How is it evolving? Examine the key experiences your top performers have acquired and the experiences the role will need as it changes. Key experiences might include: taking on challenges that are beyond the individual's current expertise, leading teams through adversity, building high-quality partnerships across business segments, gaining international experience and engaging in deep customer learning. Bring objectivity to promotion decisions by using a method for quantifying these experiences.

3. **Tap in to innate tendencies.** As we discussed in the chapters on hiring, well-validated assessments can provide valuable guidance on individuals' natural tendencies as well as how they will do their job and partner with others. For example, prospects with an abundance of the five innate tendencies of motivation, workstyle, initiation, collaboration and thought process — calibrated for the position they are succeeding to — will have a higher probability of success. Ideally, your organization will have these metrics from before a prospect was hired so you can make informed succession decisions for as long as they stay with — and move up in — the company. Don't use this measure to replace the two on-the-job criteria above (performance and key experiences).

4. **Design highly individualized leadership development.** Leadership development programs should be strengths-based with an end goal of creating high self-awareness — targeted to the specific expectations for the role. Developing successful leaders — whether managers, executives or high-value individual contributors — is an ongoing process.

# CHAPTER 19

## THE EXIT

Today, 35% of workers report changing jobs in the past three years. And slightly more than half of employees say they are actively looking for a new job or watching for openings.

In this book, we outline practices that will substantially reduce turnover among your star employees. But inevitably, everyone will leave your organization. The exit is one of the most critical moments to get right in the employee life cycle.

Every company experiences good turnover and bad turnover. Good turnover, for example, is when an employee retires after a meaningful long-term contribution to the organization or changes jobs to pursue a new career path. Ideally, turnover is a positive experience for the employee and for the organization — the employee leaves on good terms and talks positively about your company. But that's easier said than done.

At the extreme other end of the scale, the most regrettable turnover is when exiting employees feel disrespected in any way, which we will discuss in other chapters.

Bad turnover also includes star employees who leave because they couldn't achieve or develop in your workplace. They join a competitor and trash your organization, which damages your reputation and makes it a lot harder to attract stars.

Our literature review estimates that the cost of turnover ranges from one-half to two times an employee's annual salary or more, depending on the complexity of the job. Cost estimates include hiring replacements, training and lost productivity — but don't include the skyrocketing cost of lawsuits. Even small gains in retention rates can equate to tens of millions of dollars in savings.

But perhaps an even bigger long-term cost of turnover is the risk to an organization's reputation if it's not handled effectively.

Taking a purposeful approach to the employee exit process will get you the right analytics to make future decisions about your culture and create ambassadors who can enhance your employment brand.

So what does a successful exit look like?

1. **The employee feels heard.** Exit interviews give you imperfect information. But that information can lead to insights that may prevent you from making the same mistakes again. You might also learn what your competitors are offering. Most importantly, exit interviews are a way for employees to be heard — to state their case for why they're leaving.

   There are now countless public forums on the internet where former or current employees can broadcast their dissatisfaction. Gallup recommends using a process that allows your employees to vent with you first. We have a large bank of exit interview questions that your organization can use.

   Gallup also recommends conducting ongoing interviews with star performers — while they're still with your company — so you can develop predictive analytics on their retention.

2. **The employee leaves feeling proud of their contribution.** Nearly everyone you hire will make some type of contribution to your organization that was meaningful to them and others. Except in cases of terminations due to unethical behavior, make sure everyone who leaves your organization knows what they contributed and that you appreciated it.

3. **You create a brand ambassador.** Of course, people often leave an organization due to a bad manager or some other negative situation. No company can turn around every disgruntled employee. Letting

people have their say and reviewing their contributions will increase the chance that each person who leaves can become an ambassador for your organization.

A loyal alumni network builds an organization's reputation like nothing else can. Check in with alumni to keep them in the loop about opportunities as your organization grows and as they continue to have work experiences outside your organization.

The experiences and interactions people have during their employee life cycle in your organization will determine your retention of star employees and ultimately, your employment brand. All this depends on how well your managers coach each person you hire.

# BOSS TO COACH

A CULTURE OF HIGH EMPLOYEE DEVELOPMENT IS THE MOST PRODUCTIVE ENVIRONMENT FOR BOTH YOUR BUSINESS AND YOUR EMPLOYEES.

# CHAPTER 20

## THREE REQUIREMENTS OF COACHING

1. Establish expectations.
2. Continually coach.
3. Create accountability.

The need for disruption in how employees are managed couldn't be more urgent. Gallup estimates that the cost of poor management and lost productivity from not-engaged or actively disengaged employees in the U.S. is between $960 billion and $1.2 trillion per year. Globally, that cost approaches $7 trillion — or 9% to 10% of GDP.

Let's take a look at the recent evolution of performance management. Your organization may be going through one or both of these changes:

- **Organizations have discovered that their performance management systems aren't yielding what they wanted.** Just one in five employees strongly agree that their company's performance management system motivates them. Large organizations spend tens of thousands of hours and tens of millions of dollars on activities that not only don't work, but that also drive out star employees and managers.
- **Extraordinary changes in technology, globalization and overwhelming information flow are shaping the future of work.** Today's workers, particularly millennials, are asking for something different. They want a coach, not a boss. They want clear expectations, accountability, a rich purpose — and they especially want ongoing feedback and coaching.

To help organizations everywhere tackle the problem of poor management, Gallup set out to learn everything we could about the current state of performance management. We reviewed and evaluated our own client databases of more than 60 million employees. We took a deep dive into other researchers' large-scale meta-analyses containing hundreds of studies on goal setting, feedback, engagement, individual differences and competencies. We interviewed top scientists, leaders, managers and employees.

We wanted to learn what the best science had to say as well as which insights were the most useful and actionable — from leadership to the front line.

On the positive side, the research reveals that there are better, newer ways to dramatically improve management and productivity — how to turn traditional performance management into performance *development*. Yet Gallup also found that organizations overlooked, or bypassed, established scientific findings. They appear to have been swept away by performance management fads over the years.

Specifically, organizations using traditional performance management systems have struggled to inspire and develop employees because their approach leads to unclear and misaligned expectations, ineffective and infrequent feedback, and unfair or missing evaluation practices.

When systems and processes make it difficult for people to get their work done, leadership loses credibility. But when employees can achieve what you ask them to achieve, you will start to see the culture you want.

To set your employees and culture up for success, you need to transform your managers into coaches by teaching them to meet these three requirements:

1. Establish expectations.
2. Continually coach.
3. Create accountability.

Why? Because Gallup's research revealed the following insights into performance development:

- **Employees whose manager involved them in setting goals were nearly four times more likely to be engaged than other employees.** Yet only 30% of employees experience this basic expectation.

- **Employees who receive daily feedback from their manager are three times more likely to be engaged than those who receive feedback once a year or less.** But the feedback needs to be meaningful. It has to be based on an understanding of the individual's strengths. As a rule, managers should give their employees meaningful feedback at least once a week. These coaching conversations can vary from daily Quick Connects to recurring Check-ins to Developmental Coaching. (See Chapter 21.)
- **While many organizations are changing their annual review systems, accountability is still important.** Managers should have progress reviews at least twice per year and focus on the employee's purpose, goals, metrics, development, strategy, team contribution and personal life. These reviews should be achievement-oriented, fair and accurate, and centered on development.
- **Performance measurement needs to be paired with individualized development.** If managers don't merge individual employee development with their performance measurement, employees can perceive performance measurement as a threat, and their development becomes disconnected from business goals.

# CHAPTER 21

## THE FIVE COACHING CONVERSATIONS

Almost half (47%) of employees report that they received feedback from their manager "a few times or less" in the past year. What's more, only 26% of employees strongly agree that the feedback they receive helps them do their work better.

Much of the criticism aimed at performance management focuses on annual reviews — and for good reason. Managers are asked to rely on them too heavily as their primary method for giving employees feedback. Employees need to hear from their managers more than once a year.

Many managers *want* to communicate with their teams regularly. Yet almost half (47%) of employees report that they received feedback from their manager "a few times or less" in the past year. And only 34% of employees strongly agree that their manager knows what projects or tasks they're working on.

What's more, only 26% of employees strongly agree that the feedback they receive helps them do their work better.

Multiple large-scale academic studies find that continual coaching has a powerful impact on performance. And goal setting has a stronger positive effect on performance when it is accompanied by feedback on progress.

Without effective ongoing conversations between managers and employees, the success of any goals and performance metrics is left to chance. In most companies, objectives change as business needs shift throughout the year, and change often creates anxiety and confusion. But with ongoing coaching, employees are more likely to have clear expectations that are aligned with the overall business, so they can better handle change with confidence and clarity.

Most companies don't require managers to provide frequent, ongoing performance coaching to their direct reports. On the contrary, managers' responsibilities — including budgeting, strategic planning and administrative duties — make it difficult to prioritize employee contact.

For leaders to dramatically change their performance management approach, they must give managers the resources and training they need to meet the new requirements for employee development and improved performance.

***If leaders were to prioritize one action, Gallup recommends that they equip their managers to become coaches.***

Preparing managers to coach goes beyond *telling* them to coach. Leaders need to:

- redefine managers' roles and expectations
- provide the tools, resources and development managers need to meet those expectations
- create evaluation practices that help managers accurately measure performance, hold employees accountable and coach to the future

Simply replacing or supplementing annual reviews with more frequent conversations isn't enough. Coaching discussions demand substance and purpose — without leaving employees feeling micromanaged.

Note that different performance scenarios will require different approaches. Employees who have complex jobs need coaching that's more focused on defining general outcomes for success and plenty of autonomy and support to achieve those expectations. Micromanaging doesn't work for those kinds of jobs. In contrast, employees in less complex roles can accomplish their jobs more effectively when they have specific goals and prescriptive steps for how to do their work. Some micromanaging may be OK in those types of roles.

Gallup has discovered a practical framework for how and when to establish expectations, continuously coach and create accountability using five coaching conversations.

## THE FIVE CONVERSATIONS THAT DRIVE PERFORMANCE:

1. **Role and Relationship Orientation.** Coaching starts with first impressions. The primary objective of this initial conversation is to get to know each individual and their strengths — and to establish expectations that align with the person's strengths and the organization's overall objectives.

   In this conversation, which typically lasts from one to three hours once a year or when a person's role changes, managers define what success looks like in the individual's role and how their work relates to their coworkers' expectations. This conversation should serve as a prelude to the semiannual Progress Review (the fifth conversation) and include discussion of the employee's purpose, goals, metrics, development, strategy, team and wellbeing.

2. **Quick Connect.** While it's important for employees to have the autonomy to "own" their work and how they do it, ongoing daily and weekly conversations serve many purposes. For one thing, employees hate feeling ignored — it's even worse than focusing on their weaknesses. *Some attention, no matter what form, is better than no attention.* Ongoing conversations that are rooted in the individual's strengths are the most engaging.

   In addition, it's best to discuss some business issues while they're happening so managers can make quick decisions and steer the employee in the right direction. For managers to become effective coaches, they need to develop the Quick Connect habit — either through email, phone calls, hallway conversations or other brief interactions (one to 10 minutes) at least once a week.

   When managers master the art of the Quick Connect conversation, employees always know if they're on the right track — and can proceed without unnecessary barriers. Also, managers can give employees timely recognition for a success, discuss anything that's getting in the way of their progress or just touch base. The cadence of Quick Connect conversations shouldn't feel forced and will vary, depending on the employee, their strengths and their job responsibilities.

3. **Check-In.** In Check-In conversations, managers and employees review successes and barriers and align and reset priorities. Managers should have Check-In conversations once or twice a month, and they should last from 10 to 30 minutes, depending on the employee's needs and job responsibilities. Check-In conversations are somewhat more planned than Quick Connect conversations. In Check-In conversations, the manager and employee discuss expectations, workload, goals and needs.

4. **Developmental Coaching** is a true art and arguably the most difficult type of conversation to master. A Developmental Coaching conversation can be as brief as 10 to 30 minutes, but it can have an impact on an employee's entire career.

   Developmental Coaching conversations are most effective when the manager knows the employee well and understands their unique personality. Managers should have these conversations based on project assignments and development opportunities. The purpose of this conversation is for the manager to give the employee direction, support and advice when they are exploring career, aspirational or developmental opportunities.

   Developmental Coaching conversations can lead to scheduled skills training or action-planning activities. And managers need to remember to focus on the employee's strengths and accomplishments during these conversations — rather than fixate on their weaknesses.

5. **Progress Reviews.** While the annual review has become the scapegoat for failed performance management, that is mainly because most managers haven't been using the other four conversations.

Annual reviews evolved into threatening and dreaded performance meetings with enormous implications for pay and promotion. Of course, effective ongoing coaching has to create accountability. Managers need to formally review performance progress and reset expectations as performance needs change.

Progress Review conversations are a powerful coaching tool when they focus on celebrating success, preparing for future achievements, and planning for development and growth opportunities. Managers should have formal Progress Review conversations at least twice a year for one to three hours. And the dialogue in these conversations needs to be consistent with the managers' other daily, weekly and monthly coaching conversations.

The best Progress Review conversations are not just a review of performance. Gallup recommends that managers use the following topics as a coaching guide to the Progress Review:

*My purpose.* Ask the employee to describe why they do what they do.

*My goals.* Ask the employee what they want to accomplish, and work with them to align their goals with organizational objectives.

*My metrics.* Generate measurements and scores to gauge the employee's progress on individual achievement, collaboration with team members and customer value.

*My development.* Talk to the employee about their future growth and development and what they want that future to look like.

*My strategy.* Think critically with the employee about their purpose, goals, metrics and development and how they will use their strengths to create an action plan.

*My team.* Identify the employee's best partners.

*My wellbeing.* Based on the employee's preferences and comfort level, open the door for discussions about their overall life, including finances, community involvement, social activities and health.

On the surface, it might seem like these five conversations are yet another burden on already overscheduled managers. *Who has time for all this?* But actually, these five conversations make managing employees more efficient. And ultimately, they will save managers significant time because with successful ongoing coaching, employees will put less energy toward misguided work efforts and unproductive politics that hurt the business.

Becoming an effective coach is the most important skill any manager can develop. How employees interpret their value to the organization, even their pay, will be a direct reflection on how they are coached.

By mastering the five coaching conversations, managers can focus more of their time and effort on the coaching moments that matter most.

# CHAPTER 22

## PAY AND PROMOTION

**To get pay and promotion right, they need to be grounded in:**

- a plan for development
- fair performance evaluation

As you probably noticed, the five coaching conversations don't address the elephant in the room: pay and promotion. Because these matters are such emotionally charged indicators of status and value, you need to treat them as seriously as employee development.

Yet pay and promotion also demand their own conversation.

Think about it. What's foremost in an employee's mind going into an end-of-year performance review, when managers try to address the employee's purpose, goals, metrics, development, strategy, team, wellbeing — and *pay and promotion*?

The question answers itself.

When the discussion of pay looms, consideration of other productive issues gets shoved aside. This is why we strongly recommend that you focus on pay and promotion in a different conversation — an entirely separate discussion.

Development should never take a back seat to pay and promotion. On the contrary, pay and promotion discussions need to be *consistent with* development and real career progress. But leaders and managers need to understand that primal psychological traits reflecting human nature and the need for equity, fairness, contribution, social comparison, autonomy and wellbeing are embedded in perceptions of pay.

An employee's perception of their pay is deeply ingrained into all their work experiences. In low-development work environments that don't have the five coaching conversations, pay and promotion have no clear business or career context. They simply become carrots that lead to dysfunctional behavior such as political maneuvering for higher pay and higher status positions.

This politicking and lobbying for higher pay and status imposes an inefficiency tax on organizations. If employees are spending their time playing politics, they're less productive. When these employees waste time and energy, they're getting a lot less work done, so organizations have to hire more people just to accomplish the same amount of work. And when you have to hire more people, everyone's individual pay goes down.

Employees in high-development environments have more favorable perceptions of their pay compared with workers in low-development workplaces. This is the case regardless of income.

The reason high-development environments have an advantage when it comes to pay is because everyone has an inherent need to see progress. And employees with managers who coach their development are much more likely to see that progress.

On the other hand, when employees don't have ongoing coaching about their development and feel like things never change, they turn to the most quantitative measure of their value and progress — pay.

It's worth noting that a competitor needs to pay an employee over 20% more to get them to switch jobs if that employee is engaged. If an employee is disengaged, they will leave for almost any increase in salary.

An effective compensation offering fuels employees' ownership of their individual performance as well as the organization's outcomes. Use the following guiding principles, grounded in science, to decide the approach to pay and promotion that best suits your organization and employees:

1. **While pay is a personal matter, criteria for pay increases and promotions should be transparent.** Research shows that a high percentage of employees who are paid equal to the market believe they are paid below the market for their type of work. Be clear with

employees about how their pay compares with what they could get somewhere else. If you don't lead this conversation, employees will fill the space with their own, likely negative, narrative. In many cases, they will formulate this narrative through stories or anecdotes that don't reflect reality.

And be especially clear about the criteria for making more money in a given job or for getting a promotion. Describe the opportunities, how the opportunities compare to the market, and what experiences and successes an employee needs to have to get a particular increase or promotion.

2. **Don't use forced rankings to determine pay or promotion for small groups.** As a means of determining pay and promotion, forced rankings assume that each team has high, middle and low performers. But some teams have all high performers, and in that instance, a forced ranking will penalize some employees. Other teams are made up of all low performers — in which case, a forced ranking will reward some of them for poor performance.

   The desire for fairness and equity is a basic human need. A performance system should have a clear definition of "exceptional" performance for each individual, given their job type and goals. The best way to do this is to combine multiple predetermined sources of the employee's performance with individualized key experiences they have that align with their career objectives. Also be prepared to describe how you measure performance and what below average, average, above average, outstanding and exceptional look like in each role.

3. **Most employees want some form of incentive pay.** People generally want autonomy and influence over their pay. Two-thirds of employees say they would like at least some form of incentive or variable pay. High performers can earn an equitable bonus through achievements that benefit the organization and that help them stand out.

   But leaders need to be mindful of the amount of total incentive or variable pay relative to base pay — and which negative behaviors variable pay can produce. High individual incentives create more individualistic behavior. Financial incentives shouldn't tempt employees to compromise customers or colleagues. Keep the incentives aligned with team and organizational goals. And keep performance grounded in individual achievement, collaboration and customer value.

4. **Make financial wellbeing an organizational responsibility.** When your employees have high wellbeing, they perform better. Implement support systems that give workers financial planning and investment advice. This means having internal financial experts on hand to help employees do what's in their own best interest. Financial experts can give advice that reduces short-term financial stress, increases long-term security and maximizes financial resources so employees can take care of their basic needs and build fulfilling experiences with their friends and family. A total compensation package that includes competitive benefits can also positively influence your employees' wellbeing.

# CHAPTER 23

## PERFORMANCE RATINGS: THE BIAS

Performance ratings reveal more about the supervisor than the employee.

Should your organization "rate" employees? Or do away with performance ratings altogether?

Many companies have opted for the latter — and with good reason. Getting rid of performance ratings is an understandable response to flawed performance management systems. Typically, performance ratings don't involve ongoing conversations, and they result in time-consuming year-end debates over who gets bonuses and promotions. These systems encourage political maneuvering to secure a high rating instead of inspiring higher performance.

The problem isn't the ratings themselves. Performance ratings and the systems around them were developed with the right intentions — to create accountability and reward high performers. The problem is that the ratings have been associated with biases in the system.

Even if you decide to eliminate performance ratings, that doesn't mean you have to transform your entire system. The three components that make a performance management system successful are: establishing expectations, ongoing coaching and accountability — and *accountability* still requires evaluation, with or without a rating.

Let's play this out. You remove the annual performance review and replace it with a system that includes more ongoing conversations. How then do you make fair decisions about promotion, succession and pay? You still need a system that accurately tells people how they're doing so everyone can benchmark their contribution and progress.

Traditionally, the annual review has filled this need.

The annual review was built on well-intended outcomes. But much like management development programs, annual reviews and the resulting performance ratings were executed based on flawed assumptions.

*The most flawed assumption is believing that a single manager can reliably rate an employee's performance through observation alone. In the end, the performance rating reveals more about the supervisor than it does about the employee.*

Regardless of how you adjust your rating scale and performance questions, individual raters have biases. These biases overwhelm any slight gains you might get from a new performance scale. Granted, some scales work better than others, and in the next chapter, we'll show you the scale that we found works best. But you need a system that corrects the idiosyncratic biases that come with individual raters.

## TYPES OF PERFORMANCE RATING BIAS:

- **Personal or idiosyncratic bias.** Managers are more likely to see the good in employees who they like and who do things the way the manager would do them.
- **Halo effect.** When employees usually perform well in one area the manager values, the manager may also rate substandard aspects of their performance favorably.
- **The middle default.** Managers have a natural tendency to give most people a "satisfactory" rating because they struggle to distinguish performance among workers. It requires more effort to justify why someone is performing substantially better or worse than other employees.
- **Leniency and strictness biases.** Though most managers tend to rate most people as at least satisfactory, some have a bias toward the extremes. Leniency bias is giving favorable ratings even though employees have notable room for improvement. Strictness bias is when a manager believes that "nobody is perfect" and tends to be overly critical of most employees.

- **Spillover effect.** As with the halo effect, managers are more likely to rate employees who were good performers in the past favorably in the future. Once managers set the bar for an employee and make up their mind, they need a compelling reason to modify their prior judgment.

Leaders have historically attempted to correct these biases by requiring a forced ranking. But forced rankings distort the data because they assume every team has high, middle and low performers. That isn't the case. (See Chapter 22.)

Some teams have all high performers, while others have mostly low performers. For example, a high-performing team's lowest rated performer may be more productive than the lowest performing team's highest rated performer. Who wants to punish a high performer or give too much credit to a slacker?

Here are two ways to improve the reliability of a performance metric:

1. Include information from multiple sources, such as coworkers, customers and as much performance data as you can get.
2. Have more frequent discussions with your employees.

No manager can know the full impact, day in and day out, of their employees without ongoing coaching conversations. Narrow metrics, especially without ongoing conversations, lead to narrow behavior — and pressure people to do whatever is necessary to improve the metric instead of contributing to the big-picture goals of the organization.

# CHAPTER 24

## PERFORMANCE RATINGS: THE FIX

### Three dimensions that define performance:

1. My work = individual achievement
2. My team = collaboration with team members
3. My customer = customer value

Gallup scientists studied behavioral job demands across more than 500 different roles to identify the responsibilities that matter most across all types of individual contributor jobs. We evaluated many different scales and more than 200 performance items.

Our analysis revealed three performance dimensions that provide the simplest and most comprehensive definition of performance that best statistically predicts overall success in a role:

1. **Individual achievement:** responsibilities that employees must achieve independently
2. **Collaboration with team members:** how effectively employees work with their teammates to achieve success
3. **Customer value:** the impact an employee's work has on customers; in this context, Gallup considers customers to be either external or internal to the organization

We can all name people who are exceptional individual contributors but who bring down other team members or don't consider the value of their work to customers. But for an engaged and productive workplace, leaders and managers should prioritize developing employees to achieve exceptional performance across *all three* dimensions.

After testing many variations of questions and scales with a sample of 3,475 managers and 2,813 peers, a five-category scale combined with the three job demands (individual achievement, collaboration with team members and customer value) provided the most reliable and valid indication of performance in response to this question:

"Please rate this person's performance in the past six months, based on the following key job responsibilities."

The scale was: Below Average — Average — Above Average — Outstanding — Exceptional

You will notice that the scale that worked best is imbalanced and does not have "average" as the middle response option. Gallup analytics found that an imbalanced scale produced more variance and reduced halo effect and leniency biases. (See Chapter 23.) This scale has more specific gradations toward the top of the scale to inspire exceptional performance over time.

Importantly, managers need to consider the metrics and observations that differentiate "exceptional" from "outstanding" and "above average" performance. This exercise alone is immensely valuable in developing managers. Generally speaking, Gallup recommends defining "outstanding" performers as one in 10 and "exceptional" performers as one in 100 in a typical workforce. The goal is to increase the number of outstanding and exceptional performers over time based on objective criteria.

Regardless of how you communicate performance levels and whether or not you use a scale explicitly in performance reviews, Gallup recommends going through the exercise of determining what "exceptional" individual achievement, collaboration with team members and customer value look like for each role in your organization. And during semiannual reviews and ongoing conversations, work with each employee to identify developmental experiences that move them toward "outstanding" and eventually "exceptional" performance in each dimension.

To substantially reduce idiosyncratic biases, Gallup recommends establishing performance measurement with these three types of data:

- **Performance metrics** that are within employees' control and that reflect key outcomes such as productivity, profitability, accuracy, safety or efficiency. These metrics should include peer and customer feedback systems.
- **Subjective observations** that allow a manager to qualitatively evaluate performance in the context of role expectations.
- **Individualized goals** that take into account each team member's expertise, experience and unique job responsibilities in conjunction with the general responsibilities of the job.

To view performance holistically, managers should use their qualitative observations and the quantitative objectivity of performance metrics. When managers take multiple sources of measurement into consideration, the results are much more reliable and accurate. If an employee receives favorable subjective ratings from a manager and demonstrates exceptional performance on key metrics, it is highly likely that they are performing well. However, when subjective ratings and performance metrics don't align, managers will have to review the employee's performance further.

To make general performance measures relevant to each employee, managers should individualize expectations and development. Individualized goals incorporate the unique capabilities, responsibilities, expertise, experience and aspirations of each team member.

Even the most technically sophisticated and well-intentioned system will fail if people do not think it is fair. For an accountability system to be perceived as fair, it must be achievement-oriented, accurate and developmental. It should inspire long-term thinking and behavior that contributes to the company's common good and aligns with its strategic goals and objectives.

Ultimately, measuring and managing performance takes practice. Managers need to compare notes with other managers and hold each other accountable for what they consider to be *exceptional*, *outstanding*, *above average*, *average* and *below average* performance. And managers should include top performers when defining what exceptional looks like. In most cases, they will push the definition to a higher level than the manager would have.

# CHAPTER 25

## MAKE "MY DEVELOPMENT" THE REASON EMPLOYEES STAY

**Three elements of career growth:**

1. Opportunity to make a difference
2. Success
3. Fit with career aspirations

Gallup discovered that the No. 1 reason people change jobs today is "career growth opportunities." And that reason is on the rise.

We found that 59% of millennials say that opportunities to learn and grow are extremely important to them when they apply for a job. Comparatively, 44% of Gen Xers and 41% of baby boomers say the same. And 87% of millennials rate "professional or career growth and development opportunities" as important to them in a job — far more than the 69% of non-millennials who say the same.

When Gallup asked people across generations why they left their last job, the most common words they used were "growth" and "opportunity." And 91% of U.S. workers say the last time they switched jobs, they left their company to do so.

### FROM CORPORATE LADDER TO CORPORATE MATRIX

The traditional career growth pattern has been "climbing the corporate ladder" — moving up through management with increasingly impressive titles and pay and more people to supervise.

But this model is radically changing because organizations are increasingly matrixed. Because of the growth of matrixed organizations, employees have many paths to career development and options to change teams, projects or managers.

Workers today are looking for a job that is customized to their individual life situation — an extremely attractive option that doesn't often fit the traditional corporate ladder model.

In response, organizational leaders need to expand their ideas about what "career growth opportunity" means for workers. Gallup's research and literature review on the topic suggests that these three elements are linked to employees' perceived growth: the opportunity to make a difference, success and fit with career aspirations.

Your managers can use these three elements as a guide to meaningful conversations with employees about their progress and potential. Here are eight questions to get you started:

1. What are your recent successes?
2. What are you most proud of?
3. What rewards and recognition matter most to you?
4. How does your role make a difference?
5. How would you like to make a bigger difference?
6. How are you using your strengths in your current role?
7. How would you like to use your strengths in the future?
8. What knowledge and skills do you need to get to the next stage of your career?

Employees develop through the discoveries they make *as they perform* — and *as they are coached*. Managers should ask themselves: How can I encourage individuals to make more discoveries about themselves?

Remember, different employees see growth and development differently. One may see winning internal awards as career growth, while another may think getting an advanced degree is more valuable. One employee may view travel and bigger client presentations as a step up, while another may want to be a mentor.

Unfortunately, many organizations still offer only one way "up": Become a manager, even if your strengths aren't in management. Some people who aren't really cut out to be managers may do an OK job, but they may never feel quite right managing. And this affects their wellbeing — and the wellbeing of those they manage.

Gallup recommends offering ambitious and productive employees these new paths for advancement — beyond becoming a manager:

- **Individual achievement.** Talented people should be able to advance in an organization either as a manager *or* as a high-performing individual contributor. We recommend having separate title and pay paths for individual contributors and managers.
- **Personalized development.** Managers should know their workers' aspirations. Career growth conversations need to be regular and informal — not merely an agenda item to discuss during an employee's performance review. Career paths should align with a person's strengths and be based on their experiences and successes.
- **Flexible career paths.** Your star employees should be part of a collaborative effort to design a career that works for them. This means different options for different stages of life, different circumstances outside of work, different interests and different personalities. For example, do career paths in your organization move at one speed, or do they allow people to slow down or speed up as their life changes? Having kids, caregiving, finishing a degree and other life events can alter the amount of time and energy employees have to focus on their career path. The right career path should meet your organization's objectives while being flexible enough to adapt to an employee's individual strengths and as circumstances in their lives change.

# CHAPTER 26

## MONEYBALL FOR WORKPLACES

**12 elements of team success:**

**Q01.** I know what is expected of me at work.

**Q02.** I have the materials and equipment I need to do my work right.

**Q03.** At work, I have the opportunity to do what I do best every day.

**Q04.** In the last seven days, I have received recognition or praise for doing good work.

**Q05.** My supervisor, or someone at work, seems to care about me as a person.

**Q06.** There is someone at work who encourages my development.

**Q07.** At work, my opinions seem to count.

**Q08.** The mission or purpose of my company makes me feel my job is important.

**Q09.** My associates or fellow employees are committed to doing quality work.

**Q10.** I have a best friend at work.

**Q11.** In the last six months, someone at work has talked to me about my progress.

**Q12.** This last year, I have had opportunities at work to learn and grow.

Whether you're in baseball or business, player decisions are tough to make.

That is why baseball's sabermetricians spend their lives compiling player statistics. Their goal is to make "Moneyball" decisions about players who will succeed in the game. They do this by gathering detailed statistical data on past performances, from batting averages and hitting locations to fielding percentages. They then combine these data to forecast individual and team success.

Some teams are effective at teaching their coaches and players how to use Moneyball data to make better decisions. The 2017 World Series champion Houston Astros, 2016 champion Chicago Cubs, the Boston Red Sox and the low-payroll Oakland Athletics have been particularly successful at using the statistically rigorous Moneyball approach in player development, recruiting, trades and in-game strategy.

Businesses face similar challenges when trying to forecast how much performance or profit various teams and business units will produce. Many organizations have developed systems to reduce the variability in team characteristics to maximize profit. They use everything from business unit size to location to marketing efforts and product availability, while providing extensive staff training to ensure quality performance.

Can businesses benefit from a Moneyball approach like Houston, Chicago, Boston and Oakland have in baseball?

Yes, according to Gallup. We have been collecting data on teams in businesses around the world for 50 years, including measuring employees' perspectives on the crucial elements of workplace culture, which Gallup calls employee engagement. Employee engagement is determined by factors such as role clarity, having the opportunity to do what you do best, opportunities to develop, strong coworker relationships, and a common mission or purpose. Importantly, these are all factors that managers can directly influence.

Gallup also collected performance measures for those same teams, ranging from absenteeism, turnover rates and customer perceptions of service to productivity and profit metrics. The problem is that each business has a limited set of teams or business units that researchers can study at any given time. Any one study might include both imperfect measurement and limited sample size, which increases the chance for errors in predicting outcomes.

Combining employee engagement and performance data for teams across many organizations results in a meta-analysis — a study of many studies. This method provides a more precise estimate of the influence of team engagement on performance than any one study can capture.

Gallup has completed nine meta-analyses of the relationship between team engagement and performance over the past two decades. The most recent study includes more than 82,000 teams in 230 organizations — including 1.8 million employees — across 49 industries and in 73 different countries. (See Appendix 3.)

Gallup assesses team engagement using the 12 statements listed at the beginning of this chapter. These 12 statements measure critical workplace elements with proven linkages to performance outcomes. Teams often vary widely in how engaged they are — even teams in the same organization — much as they vary in performance.

One of the central findings of this meta-analytic study is that the relationship between team engagement and performance is consistent across time and across different organizations. This is true despite wide variations in industries and nationalities and across different economic periods, with massive changes in technology during the decades we conducted the studies.

When Gallup researchers compared teams that ranked in the top quartile of their company to those in the bottom quartile on the measure of engagement, we found median differences in performance. (See graphic on the next page.)

## Engagement's Effect on Key Business Outcomes

When Gallup analyzed the differences in performance between engaged and actively disengaged business/work units, work units scoring in the top quartile on employee engagement significantly outperformed those in the bottom quartile on these crucial performance outcomes:

**41%**
lower absenteeism

**24%**
less turnover
(in high-turnover organizations)

**59%**
less turnover
(in low-turnover organizations)

**28%**
less shrinkage

**70%**
fewer
safety incidents

**58%**
fewer patient safety incidents

**40%**
fewer defects (quality)

**10%**
higher customer ratings

**17%**
higher productivity

**20%**
higher sales

**21%**
higher profitability

Combining these performance metrics into an overall composite performance metric, we found that teams ranking at the 99th percentile of their company had four times the odds of success (or above-average performance) compared with teams at the first percentile.

Team performance will never be perfectly predictable, of course. But these results provide strong evidence that it is possible to measure the cultural elements of a team that predict how well that team will perform.

Just as baseball teams apply Moneyball data to make better decisions, businesses that measure and manage the 12 elements of engagement can increase performance — and improve their chances of success.

# CHAPTER 27

## THE TEAM LEADER BREAKTHROUGH

One of Gallup's biggest discoveries is: The manager or team leader alone accounts for 70% of the variance in team engagement.

The single most important factor in building a successful team is the quality of the manager. Managers — through their strengths, their own engagement and how they work with their teams every day — account for 70% of the variance in team engagement.

Great managers learn the strengths of each member of their team, develop and position them, and make tough decisions about who can best perform each role as the team evolves and grows. Through their reputation, they are more likely to attract top performers and retain them longer. They build connections to the rest of the organization through their own networks and through the networks of key influencers on their team.

The best managers and team leaders shape team performance using the 12 elements of team success. (See Chapter 26.) A team's performance is also influenced by team members' connectedness to the rest of the organization, the composition of the team's strengths, experience working together and team size.

### CONNECTEDNESS TO THE REST OF THE ORGANIZATION

We know that social connections on a team matter. Teams with members who have deep respect for each other and friendships are more engaged and perform better. They serve customers more effectively because the "handoffs" between team members are seamless.

Likewise, in multiple studies, Gallup has found that teams that are highly socially connected to the rest of the organization are also more engaged and higher-performing. The *influencers* on a team are not just the team members who have more personal connections. They are also those who are connected to *other* influencers in the organization. Through these connections, the team can rely on others in the organization to support and complement their work. This is a *reputational resource* that makes the entire team more effective.

But not every member of a team needs to be highly connected. In one study, we found that at least one member of a customer service team needed to be highly connected to the rest of the organization for the team to be successful in serving customers.

## COMPOSITION OF THE TEAM'S STRENGTHS

Gallup has found that the 34 CliftonStrengths themes (See Chapter 15 and Appendix 1) fit into four broad domains of human behavior — Executing, Influencing, Relationship Building and Strategic Thinking. Gallup recently conducted a study of 11,441 teams across six industries in an effort to understand if particular compositions of strengths on teams — those with a balance or imbalance of the four domains of themes — predicted team success.

While it was rare to find teams with extreme imbalance in their collective strengths, Gallup found that *awareness* of team members' strengths was far more predictive of a team's engagement and performance than the *composition* of the team's strengths. Teams whose members know their own strengths and those of their teammates can more quickly and efficiently do what they do best. They understand and appreciate the idiosyncrasies of their teammates.

## EXPERIENCE WORKING TOGETHER

Studies in the academic literature suggest a collective team intelligence that accounts for much more than the sum of the individual team members' abilities.

Employees who have more tenure have a greater likelihood of doing what they do best. In short, experience matters. Individuals on teams who have worked together longer have a greater opportunity to learn their role, to anticipate what a teammate will do in response to something they do and to find efficiencies that lead to higher effectiveness.

The amount of collaborative experience team members need depends on the complexity of the work and the interdependency of tasks on the team. Generally speaking, Gallup finds a significant uptick in employees saying that they know what is expected of them and that they can do what they do best at the three-year mark. And for those who stay with their company for 10 years or more, there is an even greater increase in role clarity.

Does this mean teams need three to 10 years of tenure for people to clarify and perfect their roles on the team? No. Great managers speed up the *collaboration learning curve* through extreme individualization. And they *need* to speed up this learning curve in today's job-hopping environment.

While team stability is important, it is also crucial for teams to avoid groupthink by continually experimenting with new members. In one Gallup study of more than 100 business-to-business customer service teams, we found that teams with 100% retention of team members performed at lower levels than teams with 75% to 99% retention. *Teams benefit from the positive friction of new members.*

## TEAM SIZE

Gallup has studied the engagement levels of 3 million teams. The number of employees on the teams varied considerably. Teams with fewer than 10 members have the highest *and* the lowest levels of engagement. In essence, teams with fewer members can more easily be swayed in one direction or the other. Managers seem to have more opportunity for influence, good or bad, in these small teams.

While most engagement elements are weaker as team size increases, there are three exceptions. The *knowing what's expected* and *having the opportunity to do what you do best* elements are stronger in larger teams, while the *best friend at work* element is similar across various team sizes, though these trends vary by industry. Larger teams bring greater opportunity to clarify roles, specialize and meet a wider range of coworkers.

While team size — and these other team dynamics — can influence engagement, the most important factor is the quality of the manager or team leader.

# CHAPTER 28

## WHY EMPLOYEE ENGAGEMENT PROGRAMS HAVEN'T WORKED

Globally, 85% of employees are either not engaged or are actively disengaged at work.

Companies and leaders worldwide recognize the advantages of engaged employees, and most have instituted surveys to measure engagement. Yet employee engagement has barely budged in two decades.

Gallup has been tracking employee engagement in the U.S. since 2000. Though there's been some slight movement, two-thirds of U.S. employees have been either not engaged or actively disengaged in their jobs and workplaces during this time.

As of 2018, Gallup finds that 34% of employees in the U.S. are engaged — meaning they are involved, enthusiastic and committed to their team and organization. Worldwide, just 15% of employees who work for an organization are engaged.

On the positive side, U.S. and global numbers are on the rise — up from 28% in the U.S. and 11% globally at the start of this decade (2010). Doubling those numbers would change the world.

## Employee Engagement Historical Trend

*Percentage of engaged employees*

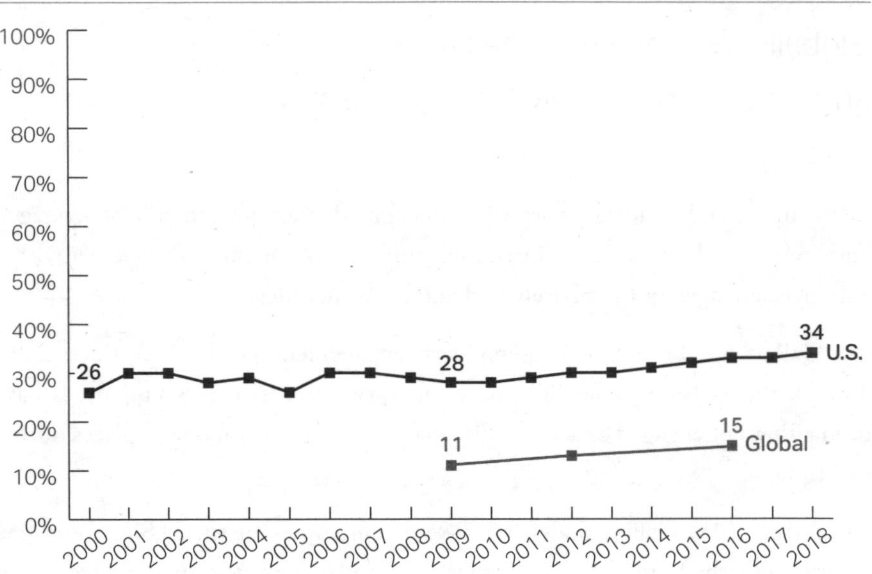


## WHY AREN'T THE NUMBERS MOVING FASTER?

With so many organizations focusing on engaging their employees, *why aren't engagement levels across the world increasing more rapidly?*

Many factors contribute to stagnant levels of engagement. One reason is how organizations measure and report employee engagement data.

It's not uncommon to see an organization with a report that says 60% to 80% of its employees are engaged — and no change in their results over several years. When we dig deeper into these results, we find the "percent engaged" these companies are using isn't a high-bar metric at all. They're just adding the 4s and

5s together (on a 5-point scale) for questions that measure advocacy with the organization, self-declared commitment or intentions to stay with the company.

Gallup research indicates that people who respond with a 4 are behaviorally very different from those who respond with a definitive 5 or "strongly agree." Do you want to celebrate the fact that a high percentage of your employees *sort of plan to be with you in the future* or are *sort of committed to your organization*?

And so, the company is touting that most of its employees are "engaged," but very few people in the organization actually feel that way. Instead, they're merely satisfied or content and will jump at the opportunity to work somewhere else when a better situation presents itself. Many employees are actively looking for another job.

Gallup sees a clear divide emerging in the engagement industry. On one end of the continuum are scientifically and experientially validated approaches that lead to changes in business performance. These approaches are supported by strategic and tactical development and performance interventions that transform cultures. Though these approaches require more investment, companies that use them are more likely to increase employee engagement and performance.

On the other end of the continuum are unfocused annual surveys and metrics. Much like a traditional employee satisfaction survey, these types of surveys usually measure an array of workplace dimensions that often don't have much to do with business objectives and that are hard to act on. These surveys are supposed to identify "unique drivers" of engagement. But this approach ignores the scientific fact that most foundational engagement elements — including clear expectations, doing what you do best, recognition and development — are consistently important in every organization and job. (See Chapter 26.)

And today's technology has made it extremely easy to create an employee survey and call it an "engagement program." Unfortunately, organizations can now use this tactic to fulfill their apparent need to check a box.

Companies can also continuously poll employees using "pulse surveys." But without a clear strategy and resulting actions based on the data they collect, pulse surveys can create more harm than good. Engagement is nearly three times higher when employees strongly agree with the statement: "My organization acts upon the results of surveys I complete."

A high-development workplace requires much more than just administering surveys. Measurement on its own doesn't inspire change or boost performance. Organizations put significant effort into *measuring* employee perceptions and providing metrics without actually *improving* their workplace or business outcomes.

The main reasons these approaches fail is because they:

- focus more on survey data or reports than on *developing* managers and employees
- view engagement as only a survey administration versus an ongoing, disciplined system to achieve high performance
- define engagement as the percentage of employees who are *merely content* with their employer versus those who are highly inspired and committed
- measure workers' satisfaction or contentment and subsequently cater to their desires — game rooms, fancy latte machines, bring your pet to work day, bowling parties — instead of treating employees as valued stakeholders in the company's future

These flawed approaches create barriers to improving employee development and achieving culture change. The result is that companies make false promises to employees — pledging change through intensive communication campaigns but providing little actual follow-through.

# CHAPTER 29

## CREATING A CULTURE OF HIGH DEVELOPMENT

**High-development cultures:**

- are CEO and board initiated
- educate managers on new ways of managing
- practice companywide communication
- hold managers accountable

Gallup has studied the factors that separate great workplaces from lousy ones.

A culture of high employee development is the most productive environment for both your business and your employees.

How can your organization create a culture where consistent high development is the norm rather than the exception? Unfortunately, your culture is not something you can just turn on or off. You need to start with an intentional, well-planned strategy.

To begin with, creating a culture of high development requires more than completing an annual employee survey and then leaving managers on their own — hoping they will learn something from the survey results that will change how they manage. You need to take a closer look at how critical engagement elements align with your performance management and human capital strategies.

The good news is that many organizations have successfully changed their culture. Gallup has partnered with 39 of the highest achieving organizations in the world. These organizations have nearly doubled their percentage of engaged employees and have attained a ratio of 14 engaged employees to every actively disengaged employee. This has resulted in resilient workforces that have endured extreme competition, market shifts, unfavorable regulatory conditions, recessions and other external threats.

High-development companies have a clear purpose behind their strategy for engaging employees. They know the specific behaviors they are trying to achieve and why those behaviors matter for success.

Here are four dominant patterns we see in organizations that have successfully built a high-development culture:

## 1. HIGH-DEVELOPMENT CULTURES ARE CEO AND BOARD INITIATED.

"Strategic alignment" sounds good to almost everyone. But the term has become watered-down consultant-speak. What does it really mean? *Strategic alignment is when managers and employees can see a seamless connection between what they are asked to do and what the organization stands for and is trying to get done.*

Anything you call "employee engagement" has no value unless it meets those criteria. Here's what the best do:

- The organization has a well-defined purpose and brand — why it exists and how it wants to be known. Everyone in the organization understands that employee engagement is a system for achieving unity of purpose and brand. Leaders explicitly connect engagement elements to their business issues. This means making engagement relevant to everyday work rather than an abstract concept.
- Top executives initiate the effort. They know that their attitudes, beliefs and behaviors have a powerful cascading effect on their organization's culture. Leaders of great workplaces don't just talk about what they want to see in the management ranks — they live it.
- Leaders map out a course for improvement. They identify where the company is today and where they want it to be in the future.

## 2. HIGH-DEVELOPMENT CULTURES EDUCATE MANAGERS ON NEW WAYS OF MANAGING.

- The best organizations have leaders who encourage teams to solve problems at the local level rather than using top-down commands. They focus their training and development programs on building local manager and team capability to solve issues on their own.
- Engagement, performance and training are all aligned. Training is strengths-based and grounded in the 12 elements of engagement. Managers learn how to identify the strengths of team members and how to use and build strengths as a way to achieve outcomes.
- Training is tailored to each manager's capability. Managers with high performance and high team engagement receive more advanced curricula than those with low performance and low team engagement.

## 3. HIGH-DEVELOPMENT CULTURES PRACTICE COMPANYWIDE COMMUNICATION.

- The best organizations have exceptional CHROs who build systems that teach managers how to develop employees in line with their innate tendencies.
- These organizations have a designated "champions network" that communicates, collects best practices and answers questions.
- The ongoing collection of best practice examples creates a vivid picture of what highly engaged teams look like.

## 4. HIGH-DEVELOPMENT CULTURES HOLD MANAGERS ACCOUNTABLE.

- The companies in our study with the highest engagement levels see employee recognition as a means to develop and stretch employees to new levels of success. Recognition of outstanding team leaders sends a strong message about what the company values.
- Tolerance of mediocrity is the enemy of the best organizations. They define high team performance based on a combination of metrics such as productivity, retention rates, customer service and employee engagement. It is clear to managers that their job is to engage their teams. The best companies have consequences for ongoing patterns of team disengagement — most importantly, changing managers.
- The best organizations believe that not everyone should be a manager, and they create high-value career paths for individual contributor roles. No one should feel like their progress depends on getting promoted to manager.
- The best organizations know there is no meaningful mission and purpose in the absence of clear expectations, ongoing conversations and accountability.

# CHAPTER 30

## THE FIVE TRAITS OF GREAT MANAGERS

1. **Motivation** — inspiring teams to get exceptional work done
2. **Workstyle** — setting goals and arranging resources for the team to excel
3. **Initiation** — influencing others to act; pushing through adversity and resistance
4. **Collaboration** — building committed teams with deep bonds
5. **Thought process** — taking an analytical approach to strategy and decision-making

Think back on the various managers you've had.

Chances are, for every 10 supervisors you've had throughout your career, you'd probably want to work for only two or three of them again. And that's if you're lucky. Some people have had maybe one manager they'd work for again — or none at all.

Whatever the case, most people have had at least some exposure to what a good manager can and should be like, either through their own experience or from what others have told them.

Consider everything you know about managing — what you've read, seen or experienced, including the best manager you've had. Take a moment to think about what makes someone a great manager.

You might also ask yourself *how* someone becomes a great manager. How do they acquire the characteristics you just thought about? Are they naturally gifted to manage others, or did they learn how to become great?

Behavioral genetics research suggests that people have individual traits such as those listed in Chapter 11 — predisposed patterns of thought, feeling and behavior that define who each person is — their personality and thought processes. Because of their genes and early-life developmental experiences, individuals have characteristics that make them unique. And that's a good thing. It means that everyone brings different abilities and qualities to organizations and teams.

Think about these traits as tendencies — your "default" in most situations. For example, in a social setting with lots of people, do you gravitate to the people you know best, or do you have an insatiable desire to introduce yourself to strangers?

At work, would you rather stay focused on completing a project or be involved in a lot of projects at the same time?

Do you enjoy the complexity of people, or do you love the complexity of ideas?

Gallup has conducted five decades of research into what makes a great manager — examining both hardwired tendencies and how managers intentionally improve over time.

*The most concise summary from this research is that about half of great managing is rooted in hardwired tendencies, and the other half comes from experiences and ongoing development.*

You can assess and predict hardwired tendencies before hiring a manager using scientific instruments — something few organizations do. To significantly improve the odds that someone will be successful in a managerial role, evaluate them on these five traits: motivation, workstyle, initiation, collaboration and thought process.

Unfortunately, the current practice of management promotes employees for the wrong reasons. When Gallup asked thousands of managers how they *became* managers, the top two reasons they gave were: success in a prior nonmanagement role and tenure.

On the surface, these reasons seem sensible. Those who are high performers or who have been with the company for a long time are rewarded with a higher-status position. And promotion to management comes with an increase in pay and status, which intensifies the desire to become a manager.

Gallup analytics finds that most current team leaders do not have the natural tendencies for managing people. When that is the case, they struggle in their role, and this makes them miserable — which is particularly discouraging when they were inspired in their previous role as an individual achiever.

The good news is that most organizations have the management talent they need *inside their companies*, and the right assessment system can find it.

So how can you build a system and culture that most effectively identifies the right people to become managers in your organization?

1. Use a scientifically designed and validated instrument to assess management prospects on the five traits of great managers: motivation, workstyle, initiation, collaboration and thought process.
2. Give talented individual contributors opportunities to lead projects and teams. Give them a shot. Watch them in action, and make note of who can lead winning teams.
3. Don't base your next manager decision solely on tenure or success in a nonmanagerial job. Becoming a manager shouldn't be an automatic rite of passage.
4. Make it desirable for highly successful individual contributors to continue to excel and gain status in their role. Look closely at the economic value of your most successful individual contributors. Your best should be able to make more income than many of your managers because of their value.

# CHAPTER 31

## HOW TO DEVELOP YOUR MANAGERS

Billions of dollars are spent each year on manager development. Yet Gallup finds that only one in three managers strongly agree that they have had opportunities to learn and grow in the last year.

Managing isn't a great experience for most people. Work is worse for them than for the people they manage. Managers report more stress and burnout, worse work-life balance, and worse physical wellbeing than the individual contributors on the teams they lead.

Managers' jobs are extremely difficult because they're caught between leadership and the front line. Market disruptions and opportunities that require sudden organizational change hit the organization at the point of the manager. They are less likely to know what's expected of them than the people they manage.

While the job of managing allows for greater autonomy and status than other jobs, it also comes with frequently shifting priorities and having to manage individual personalities on a team.

It's no surprise that organizations aren't getting the most out of their workforces. Less than 30% of managers strongly agree that someone at work encourages their development. According to the people receiving manager development training, the programs in place don't work.

One traditional approach to manager development is to identify the desired competencies of managing and then teach those competencies to each manager. Sounds reasonable. But Gallup finds that this approach doesn't work because it overlooks a critical principle of human nature — everyone develops differently based on their unique strengths.

While it's crucial for the managers of the future to know and develop the individual strengths of their employees, it's also essential that they know and develop *their own* strengths. No one can be expected to be good at all things in all situations.

Managers develop within the context of who they naturally are and can't be forced into a box that prescribes one style. Gallup finds that learning and development programs that acknowledge the strengths of individual managers outperform all others.

Managers and team leaders need to have the five coaching conversations with *their* manager, just like everyone else. (See Chapter 21.)

When considering exactly how to develop your managers, include the following Gallup recommendations:

1. Audit all current manager learning and development programs in your organization to ensure they are consistent with building a strengths-based culture. (See Chapter 16.)

2. Start with Gallup classroom learning that teaches managers the fundamentals of strengths-based leadership — including deep learning on strengths (See chapters 14 and 15), engagement (See Chapter 26) and performance coaching (See Chapter 20).

3. Deploy curricula that teach managers to shift from being a boss to being more like a coach.

4. Deploy ongoing e-learning experiences that advance the concepts taught during classroom learning.

5. Require executives to have strengths-based conversations once a week with each manager or team leader. (See Chapter 21.)

6. Make sure that an outcome of your Gallup strengths-based development courses is that each team leader or manager can strongly agree (give a 5 on a 5-point scale) with the following statements:
    - This course inspired me.
    - I have learned something that changes how I lead.
    - I am applying something I learned from this course every day.
    - I have substantially improved my performance after participating in this course.

# THE FUTURE OF WORK

**AMONG THE MANY CHALLENGES LEADERS AND MANAGERS FACE TODAY: MANAGING A DIVERSE WORKFORCE, REMOTE EMPLOYEES, THE RISE OF ARTIFICIAL INTELLIGENCE, GIG WORK, AND THE BLURRING OF WORK AND LIFE.**

# CHAPTER 32

## A QUICK REVIEW OF WHAT HAS CHANGED IN THE WORKPLACE

- Today's workforce has far more racial, cultural and gender diversity than prior generations.
- Remote working continues to increase.
- Most workplaces are now matrixed.
- Digitization is radically changing the nature of work.
- Mobile technology is blurring work and life.
- Contingent and "gig" jobs are here to stay.
- The most desired perk is workplace flexibility.

The workplace is changing at a dizzying pace, and it's hard for organizations and managers to keep up.

The question isn't *if* these changes are coming — it's how to deal with them.

Some aspects of engagement have become easier to achieve, while others have become far more challenging. For example, Gallup data indicate that in highly matrixed organizational settings, collaboration among employees is higher than in nonmatrixed settings, but expectations are not as clear. Team leaders need to connect regularly to clarify priorities as client needs change.

In remote work settings, it's just the opposite. Organizations are now much better prepared to set up remote workers with the right equipment and expectations — even giving them the autonomy to do what they do best. But remote workers can lose out on opportunities to collaborate or receive recognition. When remote workers become isolated from their colleagues and manager, they become a flight risk.

Today's leaders are managing in an environment where work and life are blurring. As an example, more than one-third of U.S. full-time employees say they frequently check their work email outside normal working hours. Most people carry around a smartphone that can tempt them to check in at least occasionally during nontraditional business hours. And more than three-fourths of full-time employees see the ability to do so as a strongly positive or somewhat to very positive development.

The catch is that almost half (48%) of workers who frequently check email outside normal working hours report having a lot of stress the day before. But checking work email before or after typical business hours doesn't increase stress significantly if the employee has the right manager who understands their situation, sets clear expectations, coaches them and creates accountability.

Think about what it's like for a highly engaged worker who wants to complete a project when they're away from the office, but their company has a policy that says they're not allowed to work outside normal working hours — such as the French law banning email during off hours. Policies like these assume that work outside of the traditional 40 hours in the office is bad for wellbeing.

However, most full-time employees consider the option to use mobile technology away from work an advantage rather than a hindrance, probably because of the flexibility it allows. With the help of great managers, engaged employees can take advantage of this flexibility without feeling extra stress. And though some organizations set blanket policies and assume indifference among employees, they might be better off engaging them first. Policies are important — but they shouldn't be any manager's starting point.

# CHAPTER 33

## THREE REQUIREMENTS FOR DIVERSITY AND INCLUSION

- "Treat me with respect."
- "Value me for my strengths."
- "Leaders will do what is right."

Diversity categories are expanding rapidly.

Here's a sampling: race, age, gender, religion, sexual orientation, socio-economic status, disability, lifestyle, personality characteristics, height, weight, other physical characteristics, family composition, educational background, tenure with the organization, political ideology, worldview and so on — essentially the full spectrum of human differences.

As a leader, how do you comprehend and address them all? The solution lies in how your employees feel about the three requirements listed above.

The topic of diversity and inclusion has emerged at the top of most leaders' list of priorities for a reason.

We've all seen the social unrest on college campuses and in our communities, and there are plenty of examples in business. In 2017, 42% of Americans said they worry a "great deal" about race relations — a record high in the U.S. Just three years prior, it was 17%. Black Lives Matter has become a national movement. On the other hand, there is pushback against political correctness.

Sexual harassment charges against leaders in Hollywood and entertainment, government, education, sports and business have exploded. Nearly seven in 10 Americans now say sexual harassment is a major problem, up from half of Americans two decades ago. The #MeToo movement has burst onto the scene.

Yet there is now no difference in Americans' preference for a male or female boss; it actually matters less to men. Most Americans believe that being gay or lesbian is morally acceptable and that same-sex orientation is something you're born with. These are dramatic changes in what people believe compared with past decades.

Demographics are also changing. For example, 42% of millennials are of a non-Caucasian race or ethnicity; this is double the percentage in the baby boomer generation.

As you attempt to build a culture of diversity and inclusion, think about how your employees would respond to these three statements:

- "At work, I am treated with respect."
- "My employer is committed to building the strengths of each employee."
- "If I raised a concern about ethics and integrity, I am confident my employer would do what is right."

Gallup found that focusing on these three requirements can move every organization in the right direction. The following three chapters will address these areas. But before we move on ...

**A note on diversity training:** Hundreds of studies have been conducted on diversity training effectiveness, including sensitivity training and unconscious bias training. The results are inconsistent and inconclusive. Diversity training often fails when it feels mandated and is not part of a culture built on respect, strengths and leadership commitment. An effective diversity intervention can't be just a one-day event.

# CHAPTER 34

## DIVERSITY AND INCLUSION: "TREAT ME WITH RESPECT"

Disrespect is toxic.

Disrespect may be one of the most intense feelings people experience. Everyone can remember times in their lives when they felt disrespected — it's hard to forget.

At the most basic level, respect starts with learning the name someone wants to be called and then learning something about who they are and what they value.

Employees who disagree or strongly disagree that they are treated with respect at work are a warning sign that you may have bigger issues in your organization; 90% of these employees say they have experienced some type of discrimination or harassment at work.

Gallup has found that the employee engagement elements most strongly linked to perceptions of inclusion are "My supervisor, or someone at work, seems to care about me as a person" and "At work, my opinions seem to count." These two elements also tell us something about respect.

Employees want to matter to the people they work with, and they want their ideas to count. If workers are shunned socially or feel like their ideas are dismissed, they feel disrespected, overlooked and rejected. And they will search for reasons for these feelings.

In some cases, employees' perceived disrespect may be due to outright discrimination. In other cases, it won't. But employees will look for something tangible to connect their sense of disrespect to: *Was it my race, my gender, my age or some other factor?* No organization can prevent all forms of unintended disrespect, but when people get to know and care about one another, they give each other the benefit of the doubt.

For example, a Gallup study published in the *Journal of Leadership & Organizational Studies* analyzed the effects of manager-employee race differences on intentions of workers to stay with or leave their current employer. Intentions to leave an organization were higher when the employee and manager were different races; being actively disengaged compounded this result.

However, when managers and employees were different races and worked in an engaging workplace, employees' intentions to stay were highest — even higher than when managers and employees of the same race worked in an engaging work environment. The engagement element most closely linked to an employee and manager of different races working well together is "My supervisor, or someone at work, cares about me as a person."

# CHAPTER 35

## DIVERSITY AND INCLUSION: "VALUE ME FOR MY STRENGTHS"

Only 21% of employees strongly agree that their organization is committed to building the strengths of each employee.

The best strategy to improve inclusion across your organization is to adopt a strengths-based approach to employee development and to build a strengths-based culture.

In one investigation, Gallup studied the relationship between using a strengths-based approach to development and subsequent changes in perceived inclusion for teams in an industrial organization. Teams with a higher proportion of employees who became aware of their strengths realized substantially higher improvement in perceived inclusion. The employees we surveyed said that learning about their strengths helped them feel a sense of value and belonging that they didn't have before.

A parallel stream of research in academia called the study of "interpersonal congruence" is an approach that quickly enables people to get to know one another by sharing something about themselves. This approach has been shown to improve the performance of diverse teams that otherwise had ineffective working relationships.

Not only does a strengths-based approach give people a shortcut for getting to know one another and for creating positive ongoing dialogue, but organizations with strengths-based cultures consistently outperform their competitors. (See Chapter 16.)

The CliftonStrengths assessment, which identifies a person's unique talent profile, is designed to generate productive conversations about individual talents and strengths. In these conversations, your managers can focus on employees' unique CliftonStrengths profile — or on their culture, background, or learned skills and knowledge. Let each individual define how they want to represent themselves.

Your employees, like everyone else, want to feel like they belong and have value regardless of who they are and where they come from. Strengths-based measurement and employee development can give you an in-depth look into the nuances of how your employees think, feel and respond to situations — not just what they look like.

# CHAPTER 36

## DIVERSITY AND INCLUSION: "LEADERS WILL DO WHAT IS RIGHT"

21% of employees disagree or strongly disagree that their employer would do what is right if they raised a concern about ethics and integrity.

You may have heard the cliché: "If you take care of inclusion, diversity will take care of itself." While you get the point — that building a great culture will naturally attract a diverse set of employees — it's not that simple.

*Organizations need strategies for how to hire and develop a diverse group of people and standards for what behaviors the culture will and will not tolerate.*

Leaders need to first recognize that diversity and inclusion are not the same thing. Diversity is the distribution of people you bring into your organization. Inclusion is how you involve and treat your employees.

Remember, your culture starts with a clear purpose and brand — what you want your reputation to be and what you stand for. Your leaders need to commit to zero tolerance of offensive and discriminatory behavior. And they have to formally and informally communicate and enforce this policy. Zero tolerance really does start at the top because leaders' behavior determines what's OK for the rest of the organization.

Your organization also needs to have a system for reporting ethics issues and a protocol for how you will handle them. Nothing else matters until you have cultural requirements and a strong system in place.

Your organization's principles are also evident in how you attract and hire employees. Clear criteria for defining success in a role is key to your recruiting strategy. The goal is to select qualified candidates using objective criteria such as experience, validated assessments and structured interviews that align with the job demands to reduce bias. (See Chapter 11.)

Gallup's research shows that innate ability exists in all demographic groups for every job we have studied. The key is to have a wide and diverse applicant pool and to hire based on valid criteria that predict performance. Doing what's right after someone is hired — with onboarding and promotions — needs to follow a similar discipline.

Finally, the single most important decision is who you name manager — and how you develop them.

*Great managers embody the integrity of your culture by naturally building relationships, connecting team members, being aware of what is happening on their team and resolving conflicts before they escalate.*

**A note on diversity and inclusion:** We realize that diversity and inclusion are complicated issues. Gallup's greatest contribution and best advice about this topic is that it begins with a culture where each person is treated with respect, is valued for their strengths and knows that leaders will do what is right.

# CHAPTER 37

## THE GENDER GAP

Organizations globally need a much higher proportion of women in the workplace — not just because it benefits women, but because it's good for business.

Gender equality remains a massive missed opportunity for companies around the world. Although women make up half of the world's population, the International Labour Organization (ILO) recently reported that only half of working-age women were participating in the global labor market compared with 76% of men.

While not all women want full-time work, Gallup has found that gender-balanced business units — those that are closer to 50-50 female/male — perform substantially better financially than those that are gender imbalanced. And when gender balance is coupled with a high-engagement culture, these positive results get even better.

Here are three reasons why gender balance improves financial performance:

- Gender-balanced workgroups have a greater capability to get work done and to meet customers' needs.
- On average, women are more engaged than men.
- Female managers tend to have more engaged employees than male managers.

Gallup has tracked a massive shift in boss-gender preferences in the U.S. Going back to 1953, when we first gathered data on this topic, Americans preferred male bosses over female bosses by a 61-percentage-point difference. Now, the majority of Americans report *virtually no difference* in gender preference for a boss.

However, only 32 CEOs of Fortune 500 companies are women — even though 45% of women say they would like to become a CEO or have a position in senior management or leadership.

## Majority of Americans Have No Gender Preference for Boss

*If you were taking a new job and had your choice of a boss, would you prefer to work for a man or a woman?*

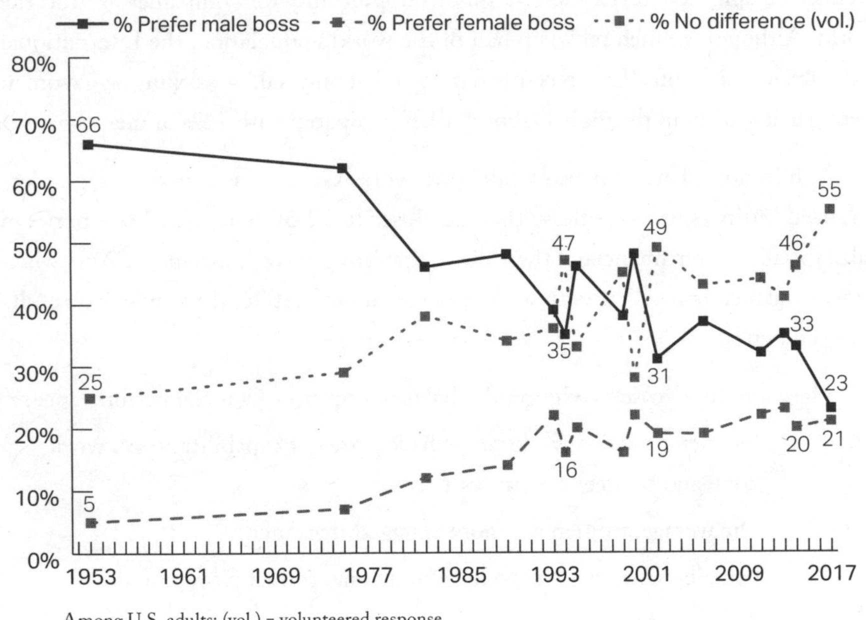


Among U.S. adults; (vol.) = volunteered response

## SO WHAT IS THE *BEST* WAY FOR YOUR ORGANIZATION TO ACHIEVE GENDER EQUALITY?

One answer is to have more women in leadership.

The small proportion of women in executive positions — and the pay gap we discuss in Chapter 39 — will continue to be issues unless your organization's leadership is transparent about how you tie promotion and pay to performance and legitimate qualifications. For example, when leaders set an expectation of working 40 hours per week, but the whisper for promotions is 60, they create confusion and potential perceptions of inequality.

The key is determining what constitutes high performance for any given job. In other chapters, we discuss methods to develop performance systems that reduce bias — accounting for *individual achievement, collaboration with team members* and *customer value.* You should also evaluate employees' institutional and industry knowledge.

Getting to the bottom of the disproportionate ratios of men to women in management and full-time work is complicated. No one has all the answers, but we can draw insights from the breakthroughs we find in the analytics.

As part of a global project with the ILO, Gallup asked men and women to name — in their own words — the top challenge facing women who work at paid jobs. Most of the challenges fall under these three areas:

- unfair treatment
- pay inequity
- work-life flexibility

We'll discuss these challenges in the next three chapters.

# CHAPTER 38

## WOMEN IN THE WORKPLACE: THE #METOO ERA

27% of working Americans report that they have been a victim of sexual harassment.

Unfair treatment at work is the most frequently mentioned concern in many developing economies and has recently come to the forefront in the U.S., with numerous harassment charges leveled at leaders in entertainment, politics, business and education. This has ignited the global #MeToo movement.

Currently, 63% of women and 54% of men say that people are not sensitive enough to the problem of workplace harassment. Both of these figures are up more than 20 percentage points since 1998. Further, 69% say sexual harassment is a *major problem*. Forty-two percent of U.S. women and 11% of U.S. men say they have been a victim of sexual harassment.

As we noted in Chapter 36 on diversity and inclusion, one of employees' foundational requirements when it comes to an organization's ethics and integrity is: "Leaders will do what is right."

Your organization's leaders must have a commitment to *zero tolerance* of harassment issues. Leaders can't allow rationalizations for harassment or use the excuse that "boys will be boys." This commitment includes formal and informal communication as well as enforcement. When male leaders are talking informally with other men in the organization and hear a disrespectful comment, do they say, "Knock it off" — or do they laugh it off? Your culture is built in those moments.

Every organization needs a confidential system for how to alert management to workplace harassment issues as well as a protocol for how to handle them. Some infractions will be "teachable moments" that stem from unintentional disrespect, while others will be grounds for immediate termination.

The devastation that can result from organizations sweeping harassment issues under the rug and attempting to self-protect leader infractions has been well-documented — "everybody knew" about most of the highest profile scandals. There is no worse characteristic of a high-risk culture than mistreatment everybody knows about and implicitly agrees to.

# CHAPTER 39

## WOMEN IN THE WORKPLACE: WHY THE PAY GAP?

83%: what women earn as a percentage of what men earn.

Unequal pay is the top concern of adults in North America and many developed economies; this is one of the powerful findings in the Gallup/ILO report on women and work. Comparing the wages of men and women across similar job types and other factors results in an unexplained wage gap. Some have attributed this gap to discrimination.

Claudia Goldin, professor of economics at Harvard, is a leading expert on this topic who has extensively studied the U.S. data. She compared 469 occupations, controlling for various life situation factors, time in role, hours worked and job types. Her findings suggest there is no strong evidence that the gender pay gap is due to discrimination in the aggregate.

Goldin found that the biggest disparities in pay are in jobs where the *career cost* of having "temporal flexibility" in work was greatest — jobs in the corporate world, financial sector, law and some health professions with high self-employment. In other words, jobs that have the greatest gender pay gap are those where it is more difficult to achieve high levels of success if employees need flexibility in where and when they work; these jobs traditionally require long hours of time in the office.

Jobs that have *less* difference in pay by gender are in science, technology and some health professions. These types of jobs naturally lend themselves to more flexibility in scheduling and, in many cases, location.

When men and women start jobs directly out of college, their pay is similar. The pay gap (and difference in titles) becomes substantial about 10 to 15 years later. The change starts to happen a year or two after a female employee has a child.

While the roles of men and women have increasingly converged over time, as a whole, women still assume the primary role of caregiver. Essentially, men have simply been freer to devote more time and effort to advancing their careers, particularly in jobs that traditionally require long hours of work to advance. And this explains, in large part, the pay gap. It's worth noting that women without caregiving obligations have incomes similar to men's.

Gallup data also indicate that children are the most influential factor keeping mothers out of the workforce. In fact, 54% of employed women with children younger than 18 indicate that they would prefer a homemaker role (40% prefer to work outside the home). For women without children younger than 18, 70% favor working outside the home.

The key to attracting female employees to your organization is making your workplace culture flexible enough to accommodate family and life obligations — while giving equitable credit and pay for performance and achievement.

# CHAPTER 40

## WOMEN IN THE WORKPLACE: WORK-LIFE FLEXIBILITY

1 in 3 working mothers say their employer is doing "very well" at allowing them to work from home when needed. The same proportion say their employer is doing "very poorly."

Almost universally, men and women mention "balance between work and family" as one of the top challenges that working women in their countries face.

Some businesses may struggle with meeting the needs of the new workforce, including working mothers. But to be competitive for the best and brightest, most industries will have to adapt. Many organizations will change organically over time and explore the aspects of wellbeing that attract female employees, specifically flexibility in work schedules.

Whether an organization offers flexibility and whether it actually *honors* flexibility are two different things. Some organizations have an explicit policy about flexibility, yet they implicitly pressure employees to be in the office or make them feel guilty for leaving work to take care of family matters during the day.

While for many jobs, technological advances make it easier for employees to work from wherever they need to, not every job lends itself to flexibility in where and when employees work. But every organization should examine its policies, benefits and performance management systems and be open to adjusting them to allow for more flexibility while maintaining high productivity.

For example, organizational leaders need to seriously consider whether more time in the office relates to better actual performance. Are your employees achieving the same outcomes — or could they — using nontraditional, individualized approaches?

As you think about how to address the challenge of work-life balance in your workplace and how to attract and retain female employees, consider what the best organizations do:

- **Some women want the C-suite but need support to get there while they raise their families.** The best organizations help women stay on their career path, but also give them the flexibility to focus on their families at certain points in their life (and do the same for men).
- **Some women want high-level positions and leadership responsibility, and putting in long hours does not deter them.** The best organizations listen for who wants advancement opportunities and encourage them to take the right steps to accelerate their development.
- **Some women want steady growth and career development while managing other parts of their lives.** The best organizations offer employees options for when and where they can work.
- **Some women don't want to be in leadership positions.** The best organizations help women find and do what they do best. Your performance system should empower your employees to work in a job they love where they can continue to grow without having to climb the corporate ladder.

Perhaps the most salient point is that each individual employee — women as well as men — defines what a good life and career means for them. Great managers know each person's aspirations and provide realistic paths of opportunity.

# CHAPTER 41

## ARE BOOMERS A BURDEN?

74% of Americans plan to work past age 65.

Millennials are eager to see their careers progress. And they may leave your company to grow elsewhere. Meanwhile, baby boomers and older workers are reaching or surpassing traditional retirement age. And given their tenure and experience, they can put substantial salary burdens on your organization.

Many older workers don't want, or can't afford, to retire. Still others pose organizational risk: If they retire, the organization loses their accumulated wealth of institutional knowledge and wisdom.

Among the five generations currently in the U.S. workforce, the traditionalists (one generation older than baby boomers) are the most engaged at work. It is likely that these employees, who are now in their 70s and older, are working by choice. They have found an occupation, whether part time or full time, that gives them meaning and purpose. They also love autonomy.

While 40% of employees age 50-64 expect to retire after age 65, this group includes those who *want* to continue working as well as those who are disengaged with their work but *have to* keep working for financial reasons.

All of this leaves CHROs to wrestle with tough questions: *How do I transition older employees to retirement or a reduced role? And how do I manage succession to prepare future generations to take over?*

Many older workers hold senior positions in the organization, which often doesn't make conversations about career transitions and retirement easy. Ideally, your organization laid the succession planning groundwork years in advance. (See Chapter 18.)

Here are three strategies for leaders to consider:

## 1. SET OLDER EMPLOYEES UP FOR SUCCESS.

Setting older workers up for success starts with asking them about their long-term plans. Give them a sense of autonomy about their future — and reassure them that no one is forcing them out. Help them see opportunities to use their strengths, either with your organization or elsewhere. Having a plan for using their strengths in the future will also improve their wellbeing.

For older employees who have been with your company for a long time, give them credit for their loyalty by enrolling them in a program where they can start thinking about the future they want *before it arrives*. For example, you could use a program that combines their age and tenure into a score that determines their eligibility for various educational, financial and retirement benefits. Through these types of programs, you can give older employees recognition for their service and let them know you will help them transition to the next stage of their life.

The goal is to empower older employees to make good decisions for their future wellbeing and to create a celebratory, graceful exit strategy for every individual.

## 2. KNOW OLDER EMPLOYEES' STRENGTHS AND POTENTIAL.

Baby boomers have shown a greater desire than workers in other generations to develop their colleagues, and they often outpace younger workers in their capacity to build a business. Some are outstanding mentors — a role many could continue to play in your organization even on a part-time or emeritus basis. And some may want to take on an advisory role in the launch of a new division or unit in your company.

Unfortunately, some older employees may have lost their energy and enthusiasm due to a lack of fit to their current role or progressively disengaging work. People's need for development doesn't stop as they progress in their careers or reach a certain age. Regrettably, older employees report substantially less developmental attention than younger employees — a clear failure of performance management.

Acknowledge the strengths, institutional knowledge and potential of your older employees, and look for opportunities for them inside or outside your company. Every person — regardless of their age or experience — wants to learn and grow.

## 3. USE ADVANCED ANALYTICS TO REPLENISH TALENT.

To keep your company's talent pool robust as older employees retire — and to put younger workers on a rewarding career path — study your top performers. Use strong, well-validated assessments that document who has been successful in the past — and why — and calibrate what type of employee will be successful in the future as the nature of your work and organization changes. Build and refine profiles of high performers so that you're systematically finding candidates and promoting younger people with the right innate traits for their roles.

Experience is also an important ingredient of success. Conduct *experience reviews* with your most successful older employees — especially those in leadership positions — to determine what experiences younger employees should invest in. Many organizations rarely discuss or document experience beyond a résumé, but it is important to have a record of the experiences that have shaped your top performers.

# CHAPTER 42

## BENEFITS, PERKS AND FLEXTIME: WHAT DO EMPLOYEES REALLY CARE ABOUT?

The likelihood of changing jobs for better benefits is substantially higher when employees are disengaged.

Employees in the new workforce aren't looking for amenities such as game rooms, free food and fancy latte machines. But they are looking for benefits and perks that will improve their wellbeing — those that offer them greater flexibility, autonomy and the ability to lead a better life.

Recently, Gallup conducted research on various benefits and perks to better understand which ones are differentiators for the workforce.

U.S. employees are the most likely to change jobs for health insurance — an expense that, for most, is increasing and cutting into their discretionary income. More than half would change jobs for bonuses, a retirement plan, paid vacation or flextime.

A majority of employees say that their company offers health insurance (91%), paid vacation (92%) and a 401(k) (68%). Less than half say that their employer offers bonuses and flextime.

In some cases, benefits are a matter of awareness rather than reality. For example, fewer employees claim that their company offers a 401(k) plan, an employee assistance plan and flextime than human resources professionals say offer them.

After examining the frequency of benefit offerings and their relationship to intentions to change jobs, engagement and workers' wellbeing, Gallup grouped common benefits into four categories:

- **Basics** — Retirement plans with employer match, health insurance, paid leave, paid vacation and other insurance coverage

- **Important to some** — Profit sharing, flexible work location, paid time to work independently on a project of the employee's choice and monetary bonuses
- **Differentiating** — Flextime
- **Added value** — Professional conferences and development programs, sponsorship of community organizations or events, opportunities to volunteer, hardware or software reimbursement, and financial planning or coaching

Benefits are just one of many factors that influence whether employees will join, stay with or leave an organization. But it's important to note that *the likelihood of changing jobs for a better retirement program, flexible working locations and profit sharing is substantially higher when employees are actively disengaged.*

Gallup recommends examining your organization's benefits and perks and then answering these two questions:

1. **Do you know the ROI analytics for each of your benefits and perks?** Estimating your return on investment (ROI) should include analyzing the use of benefits and improvement in wellbeing throughout your organization.
2. **Do your employees understand the purpose of your benefits and perks?** Your employees need to know how the benefits you offer can improve their physical, social, purpose, community and financial wellbeing.

# CHAPTER 43

## HOW FLEXTIME AND HIGH PERFORMANCE CAN GO HAND IN HAND

Less than half of employees say that
their organization offers flextime.

When it comes to workers' engagement and wellbeing, *flextime* is the perk or benefit they value most. Yet only 44% of employees say their organization offers some form of flextime.

Consider these Gallup findings:

- 53% of employees say greater work-life balance and personal wellbeing are very important to them when considering whether to take a job.
- 63% of millennials and slightly more than half of all employees would change jobs for flextime.
- Employees would trade some of their salary for flextime. They would take a job that offered flextime for 2% less of a raise in income compared with those who are offered a raise without flextime.

So why don't all organizations simply embrace flextime? What's holding them back?

Let's start with why flextime is so popular. Probably the biggest reason flextime has an impact on both engagement and wellbeing is that people deeply crave freedom. *People want to be in control of their own lives.* There are many life responsibilities that employees have to handle during the traditional work hours of 9-to-5. People also do their work differently depending on their lifestyle and circumstances.

Employers often need to ask people to respond to work issues during off hours. So one fair tradeoff is the ability to take care of personal matters — attending a child's game, caregiving, working out, appointments — during traditional work hours.

But how can flextime work in the real world? Can you really get work done when people come and go as they please? Is it even possible to give flextime to people in most roles, where they actually have to *be* at work to do their job?

Flextime isn't feasible in jobs that require employees to be physically present at scheduled times such as manufacturing, medical and direct customer service jobs. And even for industries where flextime is a good fit, *flexibility* does not have to be a one-size-fits-all benefit.

Here are some examples of different types of flexibility beyond just when and where people work:

- **Type of work.** Encourage employees to get involved in selecting the projects, teams and roles they want to be part of.
- **Organizational structure.** Consider a reduced hierarchy with a highly collaborative work environment.
- **Culture and work environment.** Design open floor plans with flexible work areas. Allow casual dress days, and encourage employees to make their own decisions about things like their lunch and break times.
- **Roles.** For front-line customer service roles that require employees to be at work at specific times, encourage them to swap shifts with their coworkers. Some organizations use advanced technology to make this easy for employees and offer rewards to those who pick up shifts for others.

Keep in mind the ultimate outcome of flexible work: *autonomy with accountability*. Here's how great managers make flextime a performance boost rather than a performance drain:

- They know each person they manage — their strengths, weaknesses and what's going on in their life — and they continuously coach them.
- They hold employees accountable for the outcomes they are responsible for — individual achievement, collaboration with team members and customer value.

Having a *real* flexible work environment starts with your leaders and how they respond to employees who use the flexible options your organization provides — and how they use flexibility in their own lives while getting their work done.

Ultimately, the key to flextime that is autonomous with high accountability is *the manager*.

# CHAPTER 44

## THE NEW OFFICE

43% of employees report working in a different location from their coworkers at least some of the time.

Today's employees demand autonomy and flexibility — right down to where they work and how their workspace is designed and arranged.

Slightly more than half of American workers say they would change jobs for one that offered them more flexibility. More than one-third would change jobs for one that allowed them to work where they want at least part of the time.

According to a 2016 Society for Human Resource Management (SHRM) benefits survey, 60% of companies offer their employees telecommuting opportunities — a threefold increase from 1996. Gallup has also found an increase in the percentage of employees who report working in a different location from their coworkers at least some of the time. And the percentage who work in a different location all the time has increased from 9% in 2012 to 13% in 2016.

At the same time, many organizations are changing the layout of their offices to feel more open and flexible. A survey by the International Facility Management Association found that about 70% of U.S. companies have some type of open floor plan.

Former New York City Mayor Michael Bloomberg famously redesigned part of city hall to make it an open workspace, with his cubicle right in the middle of the action. As recently as 2018, he tweeted, "I've always believed that open, collaborative workspaces make a difference — in businesses and city halls alike."

### ARE THESE TRENDS GOOD OR BAD FOR COMPANIES?

Gallup finds that those who work either 100% remotely or 0% remotely are less likely to be engaged and generally more likely to be actively disengaged. The highest engagement falls in a sweet spot of working remotely three to four days in a five-day workweek. This is up from 2012, when the sweet spot was about one day a week.

Some companies have chosen to scale back their remote work options, citing a need to improve collaboration and communication. They have a point. Gallup analytics finds that while remote workers tend to enjoy greater role clarity and other positive benefits, they lack strong relationships with colleagues who encourage their development.

The effectiveness of remote working depends on the role. It works better for employees who have jobs that rely on specific knowledge or educational background to complete tasks and projects as well as for employees who do not have to primarily respond to others' immediate needs. Yet active disengagement increases when service and support employees spend more than 40% of *their* time working remotely.

To maximize remote working, organizations need talented team leaders who practice *the five coaching conversations*. (See Chapter 21.) These managers need to have a strategy for approaching three key performance development outcomes: *clear expectations, ongoing coaching* and *accountability*. If there isn't a strategy with great coaches to execute it, remote working is a gamble. Some employees will be good at it on their own, and many won't.

Whether they are working at home or in the office, what do employees want from office space in general?

Most employees work in the same place as their coworkers 100% of the time, so their workspace matters to them. The three office features employees want most are:

- privacy when they need it
- personal workspace
- having their own office

Many organizations try to enhance office environments with amenities like free food, latte machines and rock-climbing walls. While these are all nice perks, they're no substitute for a great manager-coach — nor do they compensate for a poor one.

When Gallup asked millennials which factors are extremely important to them when applying for a job, amenities were at the bottom of the priority list. Only 18% of millennials said a "fun place to work" is extremely important to them when applying for a job. The most important things were opportunities to learn and grow and the quality of the manager.

Here are seven things to consider for *all* your employees:

- Does each person know what is expected of them?
- Can each person get their work done without distractions?
- Can you give people choices for when and where they work?
- Does everyone have a personal space they can call their own?
- Is it easy for employees to interact with their coworkers?
- Can you effectively coach and develop each employee using the five conversations?
- Can you hold every employee accountable?

Regardless of where your employees' workspace is and how it is designed — and regardless of their job — you need great managers who can inspire engagement and productivity while maintaining clear expectations, ongoing coaching and accountability for all your employees.

# CHAPTER 45

## CORPORATE INNOVATION: HOW TO MANAGE — AND NURTURE — CREATIVITY

30% of employees strongly agree that they are expected to be creative or think of new ways to do things at work.

Creativity in organizations is essential. This is especially true for companies adapting to an ever-changing marketplace — *and who isn't?* — and trying to build organic growth.

Innovation can no longer be the sole responsibility of R&D departments in a world where the competition is constantly rewriting the rules of the game and requiring exceptional agility.

Many organizations say they want their employees to be highly creative. Yet most employees don't believe that they're expected to be creative or think of new ways to do things. This is a problem, because all organizations face serious industry disruption.

You might counter with, "But many jobs aren't designed for creativity." True, there may not appear to be much creativity in driving a bus, greeting a customer, stocking shelves, hauling trash, completing a spreadsheet or writing code to spec. But *every* job has the potential for creativity, whether it's how to meet a customer's specific needs or how to improve a process to make work more efficient. And no one is closer to the job than the individuals doing it.

Yet it appears few organizations truly integrate creativity into their performance management systems. Even when employees strongly agree that they're expected to be creative, only half of them are given time each day to do so or believe they can take the risks required to be creative.

At face value, it might seem like creativity and performance management are incompatible — but they don't have to be. To have a creative workplace, your employees need *expectations, time* and *freedom to take risks*.

- **Expectations.** While "creativity" may be a word on your corporate values mural, it's only a priority when managers make it an expectation. As many employees know, there's a big difference between formal expectations and the everyday realities of the job. If creativity is important to your organization, you need to make it part of regular conversations and measurement and focused on clear outcomes that individuals are responsible for. When employees have well-defined expectations for creativity, they are three times more likely to believe they can take risks that lead to new products, services or solutions.
- **Time.** The important elements of an organization's long-term success are often at odds with its most urgent, short-term objectives. Creativity requires time — time for experimenting, time for sharing ideas with a team, time for learning new things — and room to learn from failure. Make sure your employees have the time they need to be creative.
- **Freedom to take risks.** Employees will quickly shut down if they think their employer won't really hear or implement new ideas and approaches. Clearly, managers have to take calculated risks, and they need to empower and support their employees to take risks too.

Here's how to put creativity into practice in any organization:

- **Make sure creativity is in the job description — and publicly recognize great innovation.** If creativity is a value and top priority in your organization, make sure that daily behaviors and the decisions leaders make support it. Give employees time every day for creative thinking and for sharing ideas. Successfully implemented creativity is focused and grounded in clear job expectations. And when you publicly recognize innovation that genuinely improves the team or organization, it sends a message to all employees that part of their job is to continuously improve on how things get done.

- **Define the outcomes, not the steps.** When managers overly legislate the steps that employees must take to reach a goal, they squelch innovation. For example, if the outcome you want is to create customer engagement, but the steps you put in place get in the way of serving customers, employees won't be able to provide true individualized service. Great team leaders set clear goals and expectations and allow workers flexibility for how to reach those goals. This gives employees the chance to try out new ways of doing things and to use their strengths. However, the freedom to be creative doesn't mean it's OK to cut corners. Make sure your employees know that their innovation has boundaries that are aligned with your organization's goals and standards.
- **Increase engagement to generate more ideas.** When employees show up to work wanting to go above and beyond, they generate significantly more ideas for their company. Engaged employees are 20% more likely than average employees to say they (or their team) had an idea. And they are 2.4 times more likely than average employees to say they had an idea that was successfully implemented.
- **Reinforce flexibility and autonomy in your organizational structure.** Employees who work on highly matrixed teams and who work remotely say that they have more time to be creative. As with so many aspects of the new workforce, increasing flexibility and autonomy for workers improves engagement and performance. Our research has found that a work schedule of 20% to 60% remote working is the most conducive to creativity.

# CHAPTER 46

## YOU CAN'T BE "AGILE" WITHOUT GREAT MANAGERS

Organizations that aren't agile and that don't have the capacity to adapt quickly will be overcome by their competitors — or put out of business.

The saying "adapt or die" has never been more relevant than it is today. Consider just three life-or-death problems threatening organizations:

- radically disruptive technology
- growth only through acquisitions
- old-style cultures that fail to attract stars

Organizations that aren't agile and that don't have the capacity to adapt quickly will be overcome by their competitors — or put out of business.

How can organizations effectively respond to the rapid-pace changes in today's marketplace and workplace?

They need to become far more *agile*. Agility, if it exists in an organization at all, is dictated by culture. Is your culture customer-focused and fast? Or is it inwardly focused and bogged down by bureaucracy and process?

Restructuring your organizational chart and creating a matrixed organization isn't enough. Gallup analytics finds that you can't have exceptional agility without great managers.

This is the case whether you use traditional single reporting lines or if you split your people management function among multiple roles in a matrix structure. The problem is, lousy managers are barriers to exceptional agility because they don't translate change effectively, they blame the company when change is uncomfortable, and they don't cooperate or share information with other departments.

On the other hand, great managers create an agile mindset because they engage your workforce, manage performance, coach and develop effectively, and work well with departments throughout the organization. They build agility into each stage of the employee life cycle — recruiting, hiring, onboarding, engaging, performance and development. They create opportunities rather than miss them.

But managers can't do it alone. Like their team members, they need development and support from the organization. For example, human capital management systems need to be easy to learn and use. High-performing team leaders should be spending their time developing strengths rather than wrestling with technology.

You can't have a culture of agility until you equip your managers with the right development, clear expectations, ongoing coaching and accountability.

# CHAPTER 47

## GIG WORK: THE NEW EMPLOYER-EMPLOYEE RELATIONSHIP

About one in four full-time and one in two part-time workers have a gig job.

Since the Great Recession, many observers have been fascinated with the rise of "gig workers," a term for independent laborers who don't have a traditional employer-employee relationship.

*So how many gig workers are there?*

Gallup finds that *36% of U.S. workers participate in the gig economy through either their primary or secondary jobs — jobs with short-term contracts or freelance work.* The gig economy encompasses everyone from self-employed graphic designers to nurses who work on contract during shortages and from on-call substitute teachers to Uber drivers.

Clearly, the ability to work remotely via the internet has radically changed the kinds of work relationships that are possible. The percentage of people who primarily work full time using online platforms (like Uber) and who are not employed by an employer is 6.8% of full-time workers (7.3% of all workers).

Some call this new free market system the "Uber economy."

Call it what you will, it's a radical departure from past employer-employee arrangements. Not long ago, companies were responsible for caring for employees, and employees were, in turn, loyal to their companies. Workers would stay with their company for many years, and their employer would reward them with a healthy pension. There was an understood *social contract* between employees and employers.

That concept would be unrecognizable to the many U.S. workers who now have a nontraditional relationship with an employer. Today's employees may have a traditional job plus one or more "side hustles." They may work for multiple online platforms, do contract work or work through a temp agency. What employees and employers expect from each other is drastically changing.

Many companies are already using a contingent workforce to maximize their human capital. Yet, it's unclear if gig work is beneficial for workers and organizations over the long term.

# CHAPTER 48

## GIG WORKERS: DESPERATE OR SATISFIED?

Nearly two in three gig workers say they're doing their preferred type of work.

Controversy over the gig economy has focused on what this trend means for today's labor market. Are gig workers taking on piecemeal work out of desperation and doing whatever it takes to make ends meet? Or are they choosing to opt out of the traditional 9-to-5 to gain flexibility and autonomy?

Previous research has suggested that those who actually work in the gig economy prefer it. McKinsey Global Institute found that 30% of independent workers were doing gig work out of necessity, while 70% said it was their preferred choice. An Upwork and Freelancers Union study found that 63% of freelancers choose gig work arrangements out of preference versus necessity.

Gallup analytics found that 64% of gig workers say they're doing their preferred type of work, compared with 71% of traditional employees working for an organization who say the same. Among gig workers, independent contractors are more likely to be doing their preferred type of work, while temporary and contract workers are less likely.

Older gig workers are more likely than younger gig workers to say they are doing their preferred type of work. And there are some workers who want part-time gig work only. Six in 10 gig workers who work less than 30 hours a week say they don't want to work additional hours.

### THE WORKER EXPERIENCE DEPENDS ON THE TYPE OF GIG WORK

As a whole, gig workers report similar engagement with their work and satisfaction with their employer as traditional workers. But that depends on the type of gig work. For example, freelancers and online platform workers are more engaged than contract, on-call and temporary workers.

Progress review discussions and coaching are less likely to occur for gig workers. Counterintuitively, social relationships with coworkers are *more* likely among gig workers — specifically for independent contractors and online platform workers. Technology appears to have closed a social gap.

The benefits and challenges of gig work can be a dilemma for gig workers. While they are less likely to report that they are paid on time and accurately for their work, they are significantly more likely to report that the flexible work schedule is right for their lifestyle.

Prospective gig workers no doubt weigh both sides of the balance. Companies should too as they design creative packages to attract, hire and retain workers. Some are competing *for* gig workers to fill a need, while others are competing *against* gig jobs to hire the best and brightest.

Optimists claim that the gig economy represents a movement toward increased entrepreneurship and worker empowerment. It may also give people who might not otherwise work, such as stay-at-home parents or primary caregivers for aging or disabled family members, opportunities to work. This may benefit the economy over the long term as new technology opens up untapped pools of productivity.

On the other hand, this trend could signal a deterioration in the social contract between employees and employers as some organizations hire more contingent workers to cut labor costs and overhead.

# CHAPTER 49

## ARTIFICIAL INTELLIGENCE HAS ARRIVED. NOW WHAT?

73% of Americans say the adoption of artificial intelligence (AI) will lead to net job loss.

Automation in the form of artificial intelligence is fast becoming a reality, and it will eventually have an impact on workers across all industries, jobs and sectors — from truck drivers to housekeepers and from surgeons to factory workers. Automation is already affecting call center employees, bank tellers and servers.

What science fiction has dreamed up for decades is happening in today's workplace. Nearly half (47%) of all jobs in the U.S. are at risk of automation.

Three-fourths of Americans (76%) agree or strongly agree that AI will change how people work and live in the next decade, and 77% say those changes will be mostly or very positive.

Yet Americans also fear future outcomes: 63% believe the adoption of AI will increase the gap between the rich and the poor.

*American workers are more worried about losing their jobs to AI than to immigrants.* Nearly six in 10 Americans think AI is the greatest threat to U.S. jobs, compared with about four in 10 who think immigration is the greatest threat.

Only 13% say the job they have now is somewhat or very likely to be eliminated due to automation in the next five years. Twice as many (26%) say their job is somewhat or very likely to be eliminated in the next 20 years.

While few Americans are worried about losing their job in the next couple of decades, they do see and fear big changes ahead.

## WHICH INDUSTRIES WILL LOSE JOBS?

The most common job in America — retail salesperson — is also the most likely to shrink dramatically in the coming decade, according to a report published by Carl Frey and Michael Osborne of the University of Oxford. Fast-food workers, laborers, cashiers, secretaries and administrative assistants are also jobs that are likely to be lost. And nurses and teachers could soon join the list.

Strong majorities of Americans who work in repair and manufacturing; clerical or office; service and transportation; and financial, insurance and real estate believe that AI will eliminate more jobs than it will create in their industry.

So what jobs are safe? Americans say the legal and public policy sector is the least vulnerable to replacement by automation, with only 9% saying cuts in jobs related to AI will occur first in these fields. Additionally, Americans believe jobs in the fields of arts, entertainment and sports as well as those in community and social services are safe from AI — with only 15% and 16%, respectively, saying these positions will be eliminated first.

Public perception and industry experts mostly align. Jobs that require social skills, creativity or higher education are less likely to be automated. Roles such as counselors, therapists and police officers will likely be filled by humans for the foreseeable future.

The cultural transition will take some time. For instance, most investors still prefer a human adviser relationship when making investment decisions — even as "robo-advisers" continue to make headlines. Many services will become "blended," meaning clients can receive the best of both worlds — technological tools and a personal relationship. Gallup finds that the most engaged customers use automated and human channels to get their services.

## WHICH INDUSTRIES WILL GAIN JOBS?

Automation, while highly disruptive, has historically been a great job creator. Technological advances in transportation and communication have spawned millions of jobs. Yet Erik Brynjolfsson and Andrew McAfee of MIT warn of the gradual decoupling of productivity and income such that technology advances will destroy low-skill jobs faster than creating them.

On the other hand, as demand for e-commerce grows, there will likely be a need for people to work alongside robots. For example, warehouse robots are doing things people don't want to do — such as high-physical-strain activities — but the robots are not yet as good at dealing with unpredictable tasks, so they need to be overseen. According to *Inc.* magazine, since 2014, Amazon has used 100,000 robots in 25 warehouses globally while nearly tripling its hourly human workforce from about 45,000 to almost 125,000.

An Accenture global study of 1,000 large companies identified three categories of jobs that AI will create:

- **Trainers** — those who need to teach AI systems how to interpret interactions and perspectives.
- **Explainers** — those who interpret AI to make it contextually useful in making decisions.
- **Sustainers** — those who evaluate the ethical and performance characteristics of AI.

Retraining is another new expectation. Notably, *most Americans (61%) believe that employers should be responsible for retraining due to technological disruption.*

In December 2017, Google expanded its total workforce to over 10,000 content moderators and other enforcement staff to spot objectionable content on YouTube. According to Google, it will use the data from those human moderators to create more powerful machine learning that can flag similar objectionable content. This is just one example of the interplay between machines and the human workforce.

While humans have been anxious about machines taking their work with the historical dawn of each new wave of technology, the jury is still out on whether this wave will take jobs faster than creating them. Experts are split.

One thing is certain — AI will continue to significantly change how work gets done.

# CHAPTER 50

## ARTIFICIAL INTELLIGENCE: PREPARING YOUR WORKPLACE

Automation plus people development will triumph over automation alone.

Where do all the mixed messages about AI — not to mention anxiety and uncertainty — leave employers?

Of this much we're sure: Automation will have an impact on the workplace more than on any other part of society. Although much of the *how* and *when* is unknown, there are two things that leaders can do now to prepare for the next 10 years:

1. **Invest in your people.** It may seem counterintuitive, but in an increasingly automated world, people will matter more than ever. The most important jobs of the future will require social skills, and human interactions will remain the most powerful way to build relationships with customers. When everything is automated, customers will have high expectations for face-to-face interactions — a current example is the Genius Bar inside Apple stores.

   The jobs of the future will also require creativity and the ability to learn quickly. In short, organizations need to get much better, and fast, at developing people.

   Gallup has found that only three in 10 U.S. workers strongly agree that there is someone at work who encourages their development. And four in 10 strongly agree that in the last year, they have had opportunities at work to learn and grow. These ratios gradually shrink as people get older. Simply put, leaders will need to do a much better job at developing their workforces for future needs. Automation plus people development will certainly win over automation alone.

2. **Communicate future opportunities.** If the most extreme predictions come true, there will be role changes and massive layoffs in the years ahead. This type of organizational disruption requires clear and caring communication. Leaders will need to be transparent about where their organization is headed and what skills their company needs to win in the future. When changes occur in the organization, people need to know what role they play. They need to see a future of opportunities, and leaders need to be ready to develop them.

# CHAPTER 51

## CAUGHT UP IN TECHNOLOGY — HCM SYSTEMS AND OTHER SOLUTIONS

The goal is to blend technology with human nature — not the other way around.

Human capital management (HCM) systems are designed to maximize insights using existing data for all sorts of activities in your organization, including: recruiting, applicant tracking, onboarding, time use, attendance, turnover, performance, benefits, succession planning, career development, learning and employee engagement.

But while humans continue to build systems and machines with increasing capability, humans still have to use them. *Technology changes in months. Human nature takes millennia.*

The goal is to blend technology with human nature — not the other way around.

It is important to understand the brains that gave birth to the machines. The human brain has some requirements if it is to use its own inventions effectively. Here are some of them:

- **Progress-oriented.** Being able to make progress and accomplish a goal is crucial, but if the metrics your technology provides are too narrow, vague or confusing, they can work against overall organizational objectives and frustrate users.
- **Trustworthy, predictable and dependable.** The human brain needs to trust the machine it is working with, just as humans need to trust other humans. *Predictability* and *dependability* determine trust in a system. Technology needs to provide the comfort of an anticipated benefit that it can reliably deliver (predictability). And the quality

of the data put into the system and its functionality will determine whether people come back to it (dependability).

- **Easy to work with.** Daniel Kahneman describes two systems in the brain. System 1 is fast and prone to bias. System 2 is slower and more deliberate. The brain can get lazy and easily default to System 1 when tasked with too many demands. The best technology can replace many System 2 demands. People need to be able to trust that technology will help solve their most complicated problems, such as those in recruiting and hiring.
- **Cool to use.** Nearly anything positive that people experience — including accomplishing something meaningful, a pleasant and familiar voice, or inspiring feedback — results in a dopamine surge, which feels good. Technology should make people want to come back because it's fun to use.
- **Individualized.** The most effective systems will consider individuals' strengths, weaknesses, circumstances and experiences — and will automate, learn and provide unique advice for each person.

HCM systems can fail for several reasons — legal missteps and data security mistakes; poor data quality; ineffective planning and change management; and misguided information that disengages leaders, managers and employees.

Here's an example: Aware of research showing that praise is an important factor in employee engagement, one company started using a digital team recognition tool for its employees. Any employee could recognize any other employee at any time. So far, so good.

But there was not much discretion about who received the recognition. Less productive employees were as likely as productive employees to be recognized. Since there was no training for how to effectively give recognition in the first place, the company's good intentions resulted in failure.

Companies can also use technology to understand how employees use their time — how much time they spend in meetings, with customers, with coworkers and on email. Analysts can study and determine the right ratio of time for doing various activities. However, legislating the amount of time people spend doing each part of their job restricts their behavior and autonomy and pulls them away from the broader purpose of the insights — such as having a positive impact on customers and performance.

One big benefit of emerging technology is machine learning built on top of HCM systems to provide valuable insights. Some of the insights are designed for executives while others provide capability for middle and front-line managers through ad hoc reporting and analytics.

Advanced machine learning can make it easy to click a button and obtain a result — and sometimes *too easy not to slow down and think* — increasing the probability of misapplication.

Here are some questions to consider when your organization is evaluating technology and HCM systems:

- What are you trying to achieve?
- Do users know what is expected of them?
- Do you know your return on investment?
- Are you selecting an HCM system because it is the same brand as your financial system, or are you selecting the best system for your organization overall?
- Are you using the flashiest software or the software with the best business processes and scientific foundation?
- Are you choosing software that will meet the needs of your future workforce or the one you have today?
- Can the system individualize, or is it one-size-fits-all?
- Most importantly, does the system raise the quality of management in your organization? Does it provide information and education that will make your managers' jobs more efficient?

The power of technology, when combined with the power of people, will have a tremendous impact on transforming the workplace of the future, as long as you use the best science. And having great managers in place will ensure that any measurement system you use with your technology will be productive.

# CHAPTER 52

## BETTER DECISION-MAKING WITH PREDICTIVE ANALYTICS: MONEYBALL FOR MANAGERS

There are millions of things you can measure in an organization, but what leaders really want to know is what handful of things *really count* when it comes to moving the needle.

Gallup has been in the field of big data and predictive analytics for over 80 years, leading to all the discoveries we've made about the global workplace. We have more data on the *will* of the world's 7 billion citizens than many other institutions.

Our data cover everything from global employee engagement to universal management competencies to our taxonomy of 34 strengths.

International Data Corporation estimates that global data doubles in size every two years and that by 2020, it will reach more than 44 trillion gigabytes — increasing tenfold from 2013. A growing digital economy and advances in data science dramatically amplify the analytic value of big data.

But what is the purpose of all these big data and predictive analytics? And what can organizations and leaders really gain from them?

Gallup's answer is: superior decision-making.

Leaders benefit from big data and analytics when they find breakthroughs and discoveries that help them build high-performance teams and create new customers.

The problem is, moving from gigabytes to insights is easier said than done. Most leaders don't need more data. They need help maximizing all the data they already have. According to one KPMG study, more than half of executives (54%)

say the top barrier to success is identifying what data to collect. *And 85% say they don't know how to analyze the data they have collected.*

## A CULTURE OF ANALYTICS-BASED DECISION-MAKING

According to an estimate from Gartner, *60% of big data projects will fail to go beyond piloting and experimentation due to culture issues.* The right culture starts with the C-suite. The best leaders support a data-driven culture by following a clearly defined strategy to build and sustain it.

A successful data-driven culture also requires high trust in how leaders use the data. With some sources of big data, there's a perceived risk of violation of employees' privacy — tracking email and calendar activity, for example, or worries that employee surveys aren't really anonymous.

Gallup has found that an important element to making predictive analytics a cultural success is turning complex analyses into simple, actionable insights that create instant wins.

## START WITH AN ANALYTICS AUDIT

After one global services company invested in new data and analytics technologies and created a new data-science business division, Gallup conducted a *data experience audit*. One finding from the audit: Three out of five leaders in the company said they still did not get the information they needed from the new data analytics system to make good decisions.

Leaders believed that the company's data science lagged behind industry standards. But the data experience audit showed that the company's more pressing problems were communication and process management. The company lacked the ability to manage the full analytics life cycle, from request to decision-making, to set its analytics work up for success.

To correct these problems, the company adjusted its focus and launched a change management initiative that better aligned its leaders' and data science team's expectations, capabilities, decision-making protocols and accountability systems. This resulted in higher-quality decisions.

Here are some business challenges that Gallup's predictive analytics can address:

- Manager development — assessing manager traits, performance and experiences — to maximize performance and build winning teams
- Attracting and recruiting star team members — analyzing and improving your sourcing strategy
- Succession planning — identifying high-potential leaders early
- Identifying causes of turnover — examining the causes and costs of employee turnover, specifically top talent, and how to fix them
- Refining performance metrics — designing appropriate performance metrics that are aligned with organizational performance, culture and brand
- Forecasting automation of roles — identifying roles that digitization will replace and planning for cross-training and the future workforce
- Defects and safety risks — combining multiple sources of data to identify high-risk teams
- Compensation and benefits — designing rewards that are equitable; market appropriate; and lead to higher engagement, wellbeing, performance and retention
- Evaluating internal programs — estimating the ROI of initiatives and policies
- Diversity and inclusion — analyzing recruitment, hiring and culture

# IN CLOSING
## Human Nature's Role in Business Outcomes

Gallup has outlined a definitive set of steps that follow the role human nature plays in any organization. We call those steps The Gallup Path.

Gallup identified and validated this set of elements from our database of employee and customer interactions, including 300,000 business units around the world. This is the most advanced meta-analytics ever on the subject of behavioral economics.

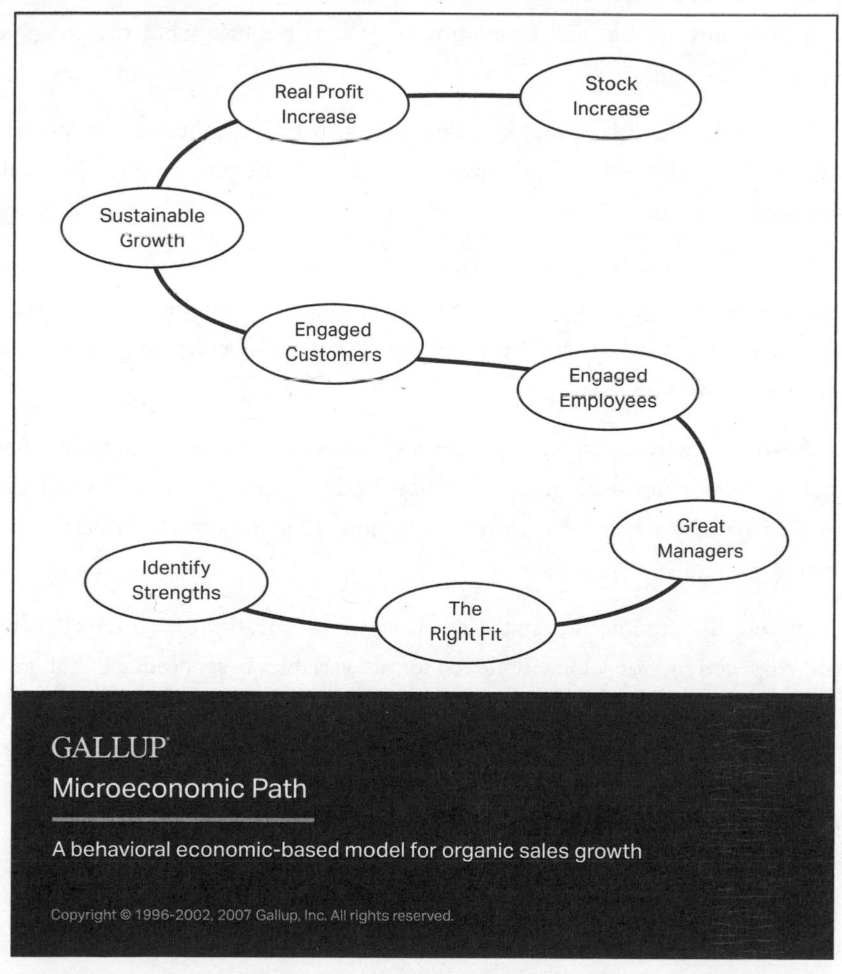

Let's walk through the path, starting at the top.

Publicly traded organizations aim for profit increase because it is the single biggest driver of stock increase. When companies have profit and stock increase, everything is wonderful. Everybody's job is safe. Leaders are heroes to shareholders and the press, and they get bonuses. The company can invest in growth activities, increase R&D, create products and internal startups, open offices around the world, acquire companies, make increased contributions to retirement and pension funds, spend time and money on community needs, and continually nurture the next generation of leaders because what the company does works and wins.

What role does behavioral economics play in this? Profit increase predicts share increase about 80% of the time. Real sales growth predicts profit increase about 80% of the time.

Keep in mind that there are many ways an organization can achieve profit increase: by implementing a huge cost-cutting Six Sigma/lean program, restructuring the balance sheet through amortization or redefining revenue, or simply selling off a division.

All these methods increase profit and therefore stock price. But authentic, sustainable profit and stock growth are most likely to occur as a result of real sales growth, especially when sales growth is organic. Organic growth is better than acquired growth.

If you like predictive statistics, your next question is surely: "What leadership activity or behavioral economic variable best predicts real sales increase?" The answer is high customer engagement. Gallup scientists call it customer *engagement* rather than customer *satisfaction* because feeling satisfied doesn't reliably predict buying more and buying more often. Being *engaged* is a better predictor of sales growth.

The big finding is that when customer engagement increases, sales increase. If customers rate their partnership with your organization as a 5 on a 5-point scale versus a 4 or lower (most executives believe a 4 is a good score, but it isn't), they'll do three things that less engaged customers won't:

1. buy more frequently
2. spend more per transaction
3. pay a higher margin

The next question is: "What causes a customer to become engaged?" Short answer: They have high trust in your organization. You treat them fairly and with respect. When a problem occurs, you quickly resolve it to their satisfaction. And they are emotionally attached to your organization. In a nutshell, they can't imagine a world without your organization's products or services.

For business-to-business companies, engaged customers will say that you are a trusted adviser, that you understand their business and that you have made a significant impact on their performance.

Working down The Gallup Path, as customer engagement drives sales growth and stock price increase, employee engagement drives customer engagement. You'll find the most powerful energy that you can push through your company at the intersection of employees and customers — not either one alone; the energy is in the intersection.

Business units that score above the median on both employee and customer engagement are, on average, 3.4 times more effective financially than units that rank in the bottom half on both measures.

You may have great products, great marketing and advertising, great traditional economics in general — but the most powerful behavioral lever to pull is increasing the number of your employees who are engaged. When you have engaged employees, you get a predictable domino effect: Engaged employees create customer engagement, which creates sales growth, which creates profit increase, which finally, creates stock increase. And then, everybody wins.

To make all this work perfectly, organizations must focus on the strengths — the ability to provide consistent, near-perfect performance in a given activity — of every employee.

There is one behavioral economic demand left, and it is the biggest. If you don't get this one right, everything else falls apart. Once you have carefully diagnosed an individual's strengths and given them a near-perfect job in which they have a natural capacity to perform, make sure they have one of the world's great managers.

*Everything else on The Gallup Path shuts down if an employee has a bad boss.*

If you give every team member in your company a great manager — a great *coach* — one who cares about their development and growth, you have successfully engineered an organization with unlimited potential.

It's the manager.

# APPENDIXES

# APPENDIX I

## Leading With Your Strengths: A Guide to the 34 CliftonStrengths Themes

As human beings, we have vast individual differences, and leaders are no exception. The best leaders have an acute awareness of their natural strengths — and their limitations. They understand where to invest their time to get the greatest return on their strengths. And they know the areas where they lack natural talent and need to reach out to others.

To help you build on your strengths and the strengths of the people around you, we have included access to the CliftonStrengths assessment with this book. You may be familiar with CliftonStrengths from the bestsellers *StrengthsFinder 2.0, Strengths Based Leadership* or a host of other popular books that feature the assessment. This assessment has helped more than 20 million people in over 100 countries discover and describe their strengths.

In the back of this book, you will find a packet with a unique access code you can use to take the CliftonStrengths assessment.

In this section, for each of the 34 CliftonStrengths themes, you will find a brief definition of the theme and tips for leading with that theme and for leading *others* who are strong in that theme. Use this appendix as a reference for building on the strengths of your team and the people around you.

# ACHIEVER

People exceptionally talented in the Achiever theme work hard and possess a great deal of stamina. They take immense satisfaction in being busy and productive.

## LEADING WITH ACHIEVER

- Others respect your work ethic and dedication. Hard work and productivity are visible signs that you are someone who can be trusted to do things right. Live up to that trust. Deliver when you say you will.
- Establish relationships with others by working alongside them. Working hard together can be a bonding experience. When others see that you're willing to put your shoulder to the wheel and work beside them, you'll make a connection. Showing people that you see yourself as an equal, not a superior, can inspire feelings of trust and respect.
- Because setting and achieving goals is of paramount importance to you, apply this way of living to more areas. Not spending enough time with the significant people in your life? Choose someone you care about, take on a project that both of you would like to accomplish and set a timeline. You'll feel good about what you get done and about the time you spend together.
- Every day, put at least one personal relationship goal on your list of things to do. You'll make people feel worthy of your time and investment — plus you'll have the satisfaction of checking the "done" box daily.
- Others can count on your belief in the importance of hard work and diligent effort, and they come to expect this from you. They see your consistency and effort as an example of what it takes to create a steady, secure life, and this gives them a sense of stability. Talk to people about how it feels to always give everything you have. Strive to help them see that the one thing they can control in life is their own effort.
- Your stamina causes others to see you as a rock. You are always working; you never seem to tire. People may even feel sorry for you

because you put in such long hours. Gently explain to them that while others may not work this way, it's what feels good to you. Ask them what makes them feel good about their approach to work. Strive to understand and support others by giving them confidence in their own work style.

- Your tremendous energy and desire to accomplish as much as possible is an inspiration to others. You can encourage people by knowing their goals and asking about their progress. By helping others put together timelines and checklists, you can help them achieve their plans and dreams.
- Setting goals and deadlines, so motivating for you, can also help others manage massive projects they undertake. You can make a large, complicated endeavor seem manageable by breaking it down and creating milestones along the way. When someone seeks you out for guidance about a colossal task, share your systems for managing the whole in a piece-by-piece manner.

## LEADING OTHERS WITH STRONG ACHIEVER

- When you have projects that require extra work, call on these people. Remember that the saying "If you want to get a job done, ask a busy person" is generally true.
- Recognize that these people like to be busy. Sitting in meetings is likely to be very boring for them. So either let them get their work done or arrange to have them attend only those meetings where you really need them and they can be fully engaged.
- Help these people measure what they get done. They may enjoy keeping track of hours, but more importantly, they should have a way to measure their cumulative production. Simple measures such as number of customers they served, customers they know by name, files they reviewed, prospects they contacted or patients they saw will help give them definition.

- Establish a relationship with these people by working alongside them. Working hard together is often a bonding experience for people with strong Achiever talents. And keep low producers away from them. They're annoyed by "slackers."
- When these people finish a job, a rest or an easy assignment is rarely the reward they want. They will be much more motivated if you give them recognition for the achievement and then a new goal that stretches them.
- These people may well need less sleep and get up earlier than most. Look to them when these conditions are required on the job. Also, ask them questions such as "How late did you have to work to get this done?" or "When did you come in this morning?" They will appreciate this kind of attention.
- You may be tempted to promote these people simply because they are self-starters. This may be a mistake if it leads them away from what they do best. A better course would be to pinpoint their other themes and strengths and look for opportunities for them to do more of what they already do well.

# ACTIVATOR

People exceptionally talented in the Activator theme can make things happen by turning thoughts into action. They want to do things now, rather than simply talk about them.

## LEADING WITH ACTIVATOR

- Action is what you are all about. Show people that you are someone whose ideals and principles are not just talk. Do something that promotes the values that are important to you. Make a difference. Demonstrate your integrity. Make your actions a reflection of your words.
- Action for action's sake is not enough. Honoring the desires of others is one way of demonstrating respect. Is this the direction they want to take? Are they willing to carry out what you start? Making certain that you are truly on their side, not merely promoting your own agenda, will build the trust and respect that allow you to lead.
- Activator talents can be a catalyst for creating one-on-one relationships and then taking them to the next level. Is there someone you can help? Reach out and offer. Make the first move, and you can boost the number of people in your network or deepen a connection that leads to an important friendship.
- Your rapid actions on behalf of another person send a powerful message. By showing that you care, you can create bonds much more quickly than you can using idle words.
- Stability may not be the first thing that comes to mind when thinking about Activators. However, consistency is part of stability — and you are consistently there to help others overcome hurdles and blast through resistance. Say it out loud: Let others know that you enjoy moving an objective forward and breaking bottlenecks. Knowing that you are there as a resource is a comfort to people who lack your talent for action.

- Perhaps courage is the part of stability you can offer. When others are reluctant to act and know they can count on you to help push them or their idea forward, they feel a sense of confidence that they do not have to go it alone. They can count on you to get them there faster.
- One way to lead others is by reducing their fear of failure. "You never know until you try" is an Activator attitude. Your ability to boost people's belief in a positive outcome and reduce their fear of a negative one can be very productive. "What's the worst case scenario?" you might ask. Showing others that even the downside isn't so terrifying helps them move toward attempting their dreams more quickly.
- Sometimes others simply need your energy to move them from fear to action. Getting started can be daunting, especially when uncertainty looms. Your "put one foot in front of the other" approach can help lessen the intimidation factor. Boost others' confidence that they can launch initiatives and new projects. Cheer them on by sharing your enthusiasm, and help them gain momentum.

## LEADING OTHERS WITH STRONG ACTIVATOR

- Give these people responsibility for initiating and organizing projects that fit within their areas of expertise.
- Tell these people that you know they can make things happen and that you will be asking them for help at key times. Your expectations will energize them.
- Assign these people to a team that is bogged down and that talks more than it performs. They will stir the team into action.
- When these people complain, listen carefully — you may learn something. Then get them on your side by talking about new initiatives they can lead or improvements they can make. Do this immediately, because unchecked, they can quickly stir up negativity when they get off track.

- Examine these people's other dominant themes. If they are strong in Command, they may have the potential to sell and persuade very effectively. If they are also strong in Relator or Woo, they may become excellent recruiters for you, drawing in potential employees and pressing them to commit.
- To prevent these people from running into too many obstacles, partner them with people who are strong in Strategic or Analytical to help them look around the corner. You may have to intercede for them in these partnerships so that their instinct to act is not stymied by their partners' desire to discuss and analyze.

# ADAPTABILITY

People exceptionally talented in the Adaptability theme prefer to go with the flow. They tend to be "now" people who take things as they come and discover the future one day at a time.

## LEADING WITH ADAPTABILITY

- Sometimes all you can do is help people learn to trust themselves and find their own ability to cope. When others feel like their power over a situation is lost, you can help them see that they still create the outcome by how they react. By trusting in their ability and helping them believe in what they can do, you give them confidence in themselves.
- You don't grab the reins and try to take control. Rather, you are a co-traveler on the road of life. Your lack of a personal agenda helps others trust that you are genuinely there to participate with them, rather than manipulate them. Ask questions about where people want to go, and help them get there. They will know that you are truly on their side.
- Others have such an appreciation for how you are "in the moment" when you are together. Make it a priority to focus on them — their feelings and their needs. Things may change in the future, but where they are right now is real. You can honor that and make them feel special by focusing your attention on what is important to them when you spend time together.
- Your ability to go with the flow creates a certain freedom from anxiety and allows frustrations to become more fleeting. This is good medicine for a number of other talent profiles. When others get stressed out, you can put things in perspective. Help people find the comfort that comes from releasing the need to control every aspect of life. Free them to be happier, whatever the circumstances might be.

- Responding to the task at hand is one of your great gifts. Your awareness of the immediate situation and attentiveness to others can't help but make them feel cared for. Sometimes you lead by responding to people's emotional states and helping them sort through what they require. This makes you an important partner when others are in need.
- Stability and flexibility — do they mix? Sure. Consider the jointed palm tree with a segmented trunk that makes it strong enough to withstand gale-force winds. In much the same way, you help others feel safe and secure by your lack of rigidity. When their plans have been carefully laid out, they may be thrown off course by a bump in the road or a detour. You can help them see that these "side roads" are sometimes the necessary, even preferred, paths to ultimate success. Help them persist when obstacles threaten their plans. Reassure them that they can navigate the next part of the journey.
- Patience is a virtue, but you may need to remind others of that from time to time. Those who need fast action and results may give up too easily and not persevere for the long haul. You can provide comfort and refuge by encouraging them to relax and let nature take its course. The resulting outcome may be better than anything they could have orchestrated.
- Give others the permission they may need to stop controlling and start living. Inspire them by sharing your perspective, experience and wisdom.
- Acceptance is very likely something you have to offer. Once an event, good or bad, is in the past, how can you help others cope and move beyond it? Think of the times you've come to terms with something you could not control. How did you feel? What did you do? How can you help others do the same?

## LEADING OTHERS WITH STRONG ADAPTABILITY

- These people live to react and respond. Position them so that their success depends on their ability to adjust to the unforeseen and then run with it.
- Let these people know about the plans you're making, but unless they are also strong in Focus, don't expect them to do the planning with you. They are likely to find preparation work boring.
- Examine these people's other dominant themes. If they also have strong talents in Empathy, you might try to position them in a role in which they can be sensitive to and accommodate the varied needs of customers or guests. If Developer is a strong theme for them, cast them in a mentor role.
- Be ready to excuse these people from meetings about the future, such as goal-setting meetings or career-counseling sessions. They are "here and now" people and will find these meetings rather irrelevant.

# ANALYTICAL

People exceptionally talented in the Analytical theme search for reasons and causes. They have the ability to think about all of the factors that might affect a situation.

## LEADING WITH ANALYTICAL

- Think about what you endorse. Because others trust your analytical mind, they may follow your recommendations without any investigation of their own. This may be just fine, but at times, others might need your help to realize that what's right for you may not be what's right for them. Help them sort out the factors that make an action or product likely to be successful for their individual needs and desires rather than allowing them to base their analysis on yours. When they know that you want what's best for them, they will trust you even more.
- You automatically uncover what's real, true and honest. Others will count on you to be the "truth finder" for any potentially conflicting or confusing information. Think of this as a way to support others, and don't wait for them to ask for help. Extend yourself; they will respect and trust your proactive analysis.
- Others who love to scrutinize ideas will be drawn to your analytical, truth-seeking approach. Stimulate debates — the tug-of-war of ideas that challenge one another. Make it fun to explore new ideas and to sort out fact from conjecture. When you find a kindred spirit, make a game out of discussion and debate, and forge a relationship you will both enjoy.
- Responding to people in crisis is an obvious way to extend compassion and caring. When others are overwhelmed by data and decisions, you can step in to help determine what's real and what can improve their odds in a difficult situation.
- Data are a source of security for many people; if the research backs it, then they are willing to accept a plan and its consequences.

Because you carefully examine all possibilities and non-possibilities, you provide the sense of security that many people seek. Do your homework carefully, and know that others are looking to follow your lead.

- Your endorsement can give others a sense of confidence that allows them to trust their own judgment. Thus empowered, they can move forward and make things happen. When you believe others are making good decisions, tell them. Your belief in their opinions and reasoning can give them the certainty and strength they need to proceed.
- Cheer for others when they are doing something difficult that you believe is right. They may be trying to guess how you feel or what you would do. Give praise for wise judgment, and offer encouragement that they can face what's ahead. If you believe they will be successful, tell them.
- If others seek you out for advice about making decisions, offer to break down your thought process, and show them how it helps you sort information. Be aware that many people may not be capable of following suit. However, some will want to be students of your approach. Though it may be so well-practiced that it's automatic for you, try to articulate the steps you use for analysis. If you have a willing student, teach.
- Guidance can be mutual. Partner with someone who has action-oriented talents. You can help them make wise, considered decisions. They can help you turn your analysis into action. Both of you will benefit and be inspired to grow.

## LEADING OTHERS WITH STRONG ANALYTICAL

- If you are explaining a decision that has already been made to these people, remember to lay out the logic of the decision very clearly. To you, it may feel as though you are overexplaining things, but for them, this level of detail is essential if they are to commit to the decision.
- Every time you have the opportunity, recognize and praise these people's reasoning ability. They are proud of their disciplined mind.
- Remember that these people have a need for exact, well-researched numbers. Never try to pass shoddy data to them as credible evidence.
- Discovering patterns in data is a highlight in these people's lives. Always give them the opportunity to explain the pattern in detail to you. This will motivate them and help solidify your relationship.
- You will not always agree with these people, but always take their point of view seriously. They have probably thought through their points very carefully.

# ARRANGER

People exceptionally talented in the Arranger theme can organize, but they also have a flexibility that complements this ability. They like to determine how all of the pieces and resources can be arranged for maximum productivity.

## LEADING WITH ARRANGER

- You want people to tell you the truth because you depend on honest feedback to make important midcourse corrections if necessary. Make sure people know that you expect the truth and that they will not be penalized for telling you exactly what they are thinking. Likewise, foster mutual respect by being honest with them.
- When you create new systems, plans or ways to execute, be extremely transparent. Being very open about your thought process will help people understand and follow your reasoning.
- When you invest your time considering what's right for other people and how to position them for success, they can't help but love you for it. You may see far more clearly than they do what they can do easily and well. Tell them what you see, and give them "permission" to be who they are and to do what they do best. You will free them to have a more satisfying life if you can minimize the frustrations and maximize the joys.
- Sometimes others simply need you to come to the rescue. Overwhelmed with confusion and dissonance, they may become emotionally helpless. When you see someone going into overload, step in and help them simplify their world. Show them how all the pieces can be arranged to fit together — and reduce the chaos.
- Your ability to deal with fluid complexity is a comfort to people who need a definitive agenda or plan. When you can keep the confusion as far away from them as possible and sort through myriad information to tell them what they need to know and do, they will feel safer and far more certain that all will be well.

- Sometimes the best laid plans spiral into chaos. By addressing problems before others even know any disruption happened; you help them stay in their comfort zone. Running a tight ship may not be so important to you, but running a steady one is. Many people need that kind of leadership to feel secure, and you provide it.
- Not only can you help people get involved in activities that are right for them, you can also help them figure out what they shouldn't be doing and encourage them to stop doing it. They may feel trapped by calendars and commitments; you can free them. Inspire them to think about how to rearrange their responsibilities to make their lives more satisfying and productive.
- Before people can reorganize their time and responsibilities for a more fulfilling future, they may need a clear and concrete view of their current situation. Encourage them to fill out a calendar that shows everything they do in a week. Have them account for every hour. Then help them find ways to combine, eliminate or add activities to enhance their quality of life.

## LEADING OTHERS WITH STRONG ARRANGER

- These people will thrive when they have a new challenge, so give them as many as you can according to their knowledge and skill levels.
- These people may well have the talent to be managers or supervisors. Their Arranger talents enable them to figure out how people with very different strengths can work together.
- Pay attention to these people's other top themes. If they also have strong Discipline talents, they may be excellent organizers who can establish routines and systems for getting things done.
- Understand that these people's modus operandi for team building is through trust and relationship. They may well reject someone who they believe is dishonest or does shoddy work.

# BELIEF

People exceptionally talented in the Belief theme have certain core values that are unchanging. Out of these values emerges a defined purpose for their lives.

## LEADING WITH BELIEF

- Ethical behavior is the foundation of respect and trust. Integrity is an expectation. To ensure fairness and promote unity, clearly communicate to others the behaviors you will and will not tolerate. Clarity on the front end can prevent misunderstandings and damage to relationships.
- The talent of Belief is more about an attitude of service than it is about a certain set of moral or spiritual beliefs. Show others what it means to be a servant leader. Get your team involved in doing something outside of themselves — something they do for the sole reason of helping another person or group. Demonstrate your Belief talents in actions that speak far louder than your words ever can. That level of integrity will earn you true respect.
- Your values are a deep source of meaning for you. Talk with others about what's most meaningful in their lives. Just being a sounding board about something as important as core values builds relationships. Learn what's most important to the people in your life, whether you've known them a long time or just met them. Recognize that we all come from different backgrounds and go through various stages in our lives, and be accepting. Relationships can always grow. Listening creates a connection.
- Some bonds will be almost instantaneous. Common values will bring you close to some people quite rapidly — and sometimes for life. This can be a source of great joy in your life and theirs. Explore beliefs together, ask questions and have conversations about what matters most in your lives. In these situations, relationships can grow surprisingly fast and remarkably deep.

- Take care not to create an "in" and an "out" crowd based on belief systems. Though you can never be values neutral, nor should you be, consider the messages you send with the judgments you make.
- Some of your beliefs are etched in stone. Even in an ever-changing world, they never sway. This firm foundation can be a cornerstone of relationships, activities and the work environment you create. Whether or not people believe as you do, they know where you stand and can be confident of the stability of those beliefs.
- Your passion equips you to fight. In these battles, strive to be a leader who is fighting for something rather than one who is fighting against something. Being seen in a positive light may help you enlist, engage and retain more support for your cause. People will trust that you will fight for what's right. They take confidence in the strength of your convictions.
- The meaning and purpose of your work will often provide direction for others, so talk about it; share its importance in your life. Remind people why their work is important and how it makes a difference in their lives and in the lives of others. Learn more about how they can live their talents and values through their work, and support them in finding those connections.
- Others may be less sure of their values than you are. If they are searching, ask them to take account of where they spend their time and money. The actual use of our time, talent and treasure speaks volumes about what we really value.

## LEADING OTHERS WITH STRONG BELIEF

- These people will have powerful bedrock values. Figure out how to align their values with those of the organization. For example, talk with them about how your products and services make people's lives better, or discuss how your company embodies integrity and trust, or give them opportunities to go above and beyond to help colleagues and customers. This way, through their actions and words, they will make visible the values of your organization's culture.

- Realize that these people may place greater value on opportunities to provide higher levels of service than on opportunities to make more money. Find ways to enhance this natural service orientation, and you will see them at their best.

# COMMAND

People exceptionally talented in the Command theme have presence. They can take control of a situation and make decisions.

## LEADING WITH COMMAND

- Because you're known for saying what you think, others trust that you won't play games. They can take what you say at face value, and they can be confident that you won't change your stripes once they've left the room. This directness builds trust, and trust builds relationships.
- Examine the correlations between your stated values and your actions. Are they consistent? Do they demonstrate integrity? Jot down the values that are most important to you. Can you think of recent examples of actions you have taken that confirm the integrity of your beliefs? Make this "walk the talk" checklist a regular part of your self-assessment, and ensure that others can trust what you say and respect your actions.
- You feel things intensely and are capable of expressing great emotion. Do what you do naturally. Tell people how you feel and why they are important to you. Express the connection that others may be too reserved to say out loud. Your saying it first may free them to acknowledge that the feeling is mutual. And even if they are not there yet, you can launch the opportunity for a meaningful relationship. An expression of genuine caring, affection or regard can be a powerful step toward initiating or deepening a bond between a leader and a follower.
- You use strong words. Express your sentiments to form a bond with others who will value what you stand for as a human being. Significant relationships are often formed on the basis of shared values, so stating your beliefs and passions can be a way for others to "find" you as a potential friend and champion. Invite them to join you — they may need the nudge.
- Sometimes others see the tough exterior of an individual with high Command and assume it's an impenetrable shell that protects you

from all hurt. They may feel vulnerable and see you as invulnerable. Yet relationships depend on mutual vulnerability. Be open. Share your pain and struggles. Letting others see the soft side of you gives them equal power in the relationship and demonstrates trust.

- People know where you stand. The security of understanding that your convictions are not built on sinking sand allows people to feel confident that you will always be there for them and always stick to what you believe.
- Others come to you when they need someone to be strong for them — perhaps to shore up their own flagging courage or to step in and be a spokesperson for them. When their courage falters, they seek to "borrow" yours. Be aware of this need you fulfill, and ask others if they would like you to intervene on their behalf or accompany them on a difficult mission. Your "take charge" attitude steadies and reassures others in times of crisis. When faced with a particularly trying challenge, use your Command talents to assuage others' fears and convince them you have things under control.
- Because you call it like you see it, others seek you out when they feel they can handle the truth. They might turn to others for support, but they go to you for an honest assessment of what they can and can't do or should and shouldn't do. You don't shy away from offering advice. Ask them how committed they are to their current plan. Ask if they want your honest opinion. If they say yes, give it gently but truthfully.
- Your powerful words inspire. Talk about the "why" of each mission without fearing to appear corny or sentimental. Your emotion allows others to rise to the occasion and give of themselves. They may be counting on you to give voice to the emotions that surround the cause. Paint an inspiring picture with your words.

## LEADING OTHERS WITH STRONG COMMAND

- As much as you can, give these people room to lead and make decisions. They will not like to be supervised closely.
- When confronting these people, take firm action. And if necessary, require immediate restitution. Then arrange for them to be productive as soon as possible. They will get over their mistakes quickly, and so should you.
- These people may intimidate others with their upfront, assertive style. You may need to consider whether or not their contribution justifies the occasional ruffled feathers. Rather than pushing them to learn how to be empathetic and polite, you'd make better use of your time by helping their colleagues understand that their assertiveness is part of what makes them effective — as long as they remain assertive rather than aggressive or offensive.

# COMMUNICATION

People exceptionally talented in the Communication theme generally find it easy to put their thoughts into words. They are good conversationalists and presenters.

## LEADING WITH COMMUNICATION

- You can use language to "spin" and to manipulate. But this is wearying over time. Remember that while spin can be persuasive in the short term, it exacts an emotional price. Make sure that you are not only effective, but ethical.
- Mutual respect is yours to build. Help people appreciate each other. Spend time "advertising" what they truly do well and what they are capable of contributing. Bear in mind that genuine praise encourages people, but false praise undermines them and is not taken seriously.
- Speak the same way about people to their faces as you do when they are not around. The consistency and honor of your words convey your integrity and shape the trust you build.
- You have the power to capture people's emotions and put words to what they feel — sometimes words they cannot find themselves. This naturally draws others to you. So ask questions. Try to pinpoint the key issues people are trying to communicate — what joys or struggles they want to convey. Then give voice to those feelings. Helping people find words to describe what they are feeling is a powerful way to get them to express and process their own emotions.
- Language is a clue to culture. In any group, from a family to a corporation, think about what the words you use suggest. Names convey expectations. Do you call your weekly meetings "department meetings," "staff meetings," "team meetings," "quality meetings"? Are they held in a "meeting room," a "conference room," a "break room," a "training center" or a "learning center"? Do you frame questions positively to help others see how much you care?

- Capture others' successes in words, and relate those words back to them, preferably in writing. Use your talent for finding just the right words to praise, give feedback and reassure. Your positive support of others' achievements will help them feel secure in their roles.
- Think about how you express time. Are we here for the long haul? Are we seeking immediate results or building a long-term reputation? As you choose your words, consider that stability is confidence in the long-term picture. Give people the sense that the big picture is what matters, and they will be free to experiment — even fail — to make things better for the future.
- Besides being the spokesperson, become the collector of your group's success stories. Create a brand for your group based on accumulated triumphs. This solid foundation will bolster your group's confidence for the future.
- In an organizational setting, offer to be the one who composes any "wrap-up" communication. After meetings, send a summary email to those who attended. Capture the key points, and outline the actions people must take. Summarize successes. Express kudos to those who have done good work. You can encourage and inspire positive activities and outcomes as well as future accomplishments.
- Your words influence the impressions and expectations that people form about individuals and groups. Are you enhancing or undermining their image? When you speak to or about others, consciously choose words that offer encouragement, inspiration and optimism.
- What terms and expressions do you use to paint pictures of the future? Your words can guide others. Consider the direction your words take people, and select them well. Those words may continue to inspire people longer than you imagine.

## LEADING OTHERS WITH STRONG COMMUNICATION

- Ask these people to learn the folklore and the stories of interesting events in your organization. Then give them the opportunity to tell these stories to their colleagues. They will help bring your culture to life and thereby strengthen it.
- Ask these people to help some of the specialists in your organization make more engaging presentations. In some situations, you could ask them to volunteer to make the presentation for the specialists.
- If you send these people to public-speaking training, make sure to place them in a small class with advanced students and a top-level trainer. They will be irritated if they're in training with beginners.

# COMPETITION

People exceptionally talented in the Competition theme measure their progress against the performance of others. They strive to win first place and revel in contests.

## LEADING WITH COMPETITION

- Cheaters never prosper. Remember that winning at all costs isn't winning; it's defeating yourself. The price of winning can be greater than the pain of losing, so make sure your integrity remains intact when you push for that ultimate victory.
- Protect the trust you have created with others. Sometimes you may need to "walk off the court" to keep your competitive emotions from damaging the respect you seek from others. Do it. Give yourself the release of an emotional reaction, but make sure you do it where the "judges" won't see you.
- Competitors recognize one another almost immediately. When you find someone who shares your desire to win, you might choose to compete and push each other, or you might combine forces to create a championship team. Either way, it's an opportunity to form a bond based on a shared outlook.
- Can you involve others in a weekly competitive activity they enjoy? This is one way to create a lasting connection based on mutual interests and a shared approach to life's challenges. Engage the competitor, and build on that relationship opportunity.
- Competition, despite all the effort it produces, can give many people a negative impression. Try to bring out the fun side of competition; use it to create emotional bonds rather than barriers. Remember that not everyone assigns the same emotional intensity to every activity, and remember to show that you accept and respect that they may have different reasons for being "in the game."

- A winning team promotes confidence. How can you help individuals or a team be their best? Position players so that they're building on their strengths; this gives them the best possible chance for success and security. Show people their capacity for peak performance based on their natural abilities.
- If you're in a losing battle, remember your ultimate goal. Keep in mind that you're in it for the long haul, and help others see that too. Give them the peace of mind that they are involved in an ongoing effort rather than experiencing a failure.
- Champion others. Verbalize your belief that they can be the best at something. You may see potential in them that they cannot see. Point out the talents you notice in them, and help them learn how to turn those talents into strengths.
- What are the measures to beat in your organization? Put them out there so everyone has a clear target.
- Number one is the only position that counts in your book, so you tend to confine yourself to areas where you know you can win. As a leader, identify the market niches in which your group truly excels, and define its strengths and competitive edge in specific terms. In doing so, you set the group and the organization up for unparalleled success, which naturally increases your group's optimism.
- You are naturally attuned to real-world measures that assess achievements. Use this talent to identify world-class performance within and outside your organization and to identify industry benchmarks that truly count. Evaluate your organization against these standards, and inspire others to exceed them.

## LEADING OTHERS WITH STRONG COMPETITION

- Measure these people's accomplishments against other people's — particularly other competitive people. You may decide to post the performance records of all your staff, but remember that only your competitive people will get a charge out of public comparison. Others may resent it or be mortified by the comparison.
- Set up contests for these people. Pit them against other competitors even if you have to find them in business units other than your own. Highly charged competitors want to compete with others who are very close to their skill level; matching them against modest achievers won't motivate them. Consider that one of the best ways to manage these people is to hire other competitive people who produce more.
- Talk about talents with these people. Like all competitors, they know that it takes talent to be a winner. Name their talents. Tell them that they need to marshal their talents to win. Do not "Peter Principle" these people by suggesting that winning means getting promoted.

# CONNECTEDNESS

People exceptionally talented in the Connectedness theme have faith in the links among all things. They believe there are few coincidences and that almost every event has meaning.

## LEADING WITH CONNECTEDNESS

- Your philosophy of life compels you to move beyond your own self-interests. Give voice to your beliefs. Take action on your values. When you move beyond yourself and give of what you have, others see the respect you have for every other human being, despite your differences. Respect is a natural byproduct of selfless acts.
- Look for global or cross-cultural responsibilities that capitalize on your understanding of the commonalities inherent in humanity. Build global capability, and change the mindset of those who think in terms of "us" and "them." Acting in the best interests of all parties is a sign of good faith and trustworthiness.
- You seek the mutual bond. Develop good questions to ask so you can quickly find common ground between you and each person you meet. Keep asking these questions until you find interests you share. Affirm and celebrate the connections you find, and start there to build a foundation for a relationship.
- Once you have discovered areas of commonality with someone, show that you care by remembering to ask about the belief or activity you share with them. Use this as a point of entry into deeper conversations about other parts of their life. Get to know them as a whole person, rather than limiting your connection to only one aspect of who they are.

- Your ability to bring people together around shared dreams and meanings is significant. You see the common thread in the greater whole. Take an active role in linking the lives of different individuals based on the connections you discover. Make others aware of the bonds they don't even know exist, and pave the road for friendship by helping strangers recognize what they have in common. You can help others make connections that influence the rest of their lives.
- Your sense of the bigger picture can bring calm in chaos. Point out the greater meaning you find in the events around you. Show others that a bump in the road is but a small part of a greater whole. Help them see the difference between what is constant in life and what is temporary. Put current difficulties in perspective.
- People feel safe when they are surrounded by comfortable familiarity. When others need that sense of security, remind them of what is constant, what is shared — and that a network surrounds them. Simply knowing that they are not alone during difficult times can bring peace and confidence.
- Faith can be a foundational strength when it is shared. If faith is part of your relationship with another person, your support may be very important in times of uncertainty or fear. Reach out when you know someone needs the assurance that shared faith can provide.
- It may surprise you when others are slow to discover the connections that you so easily see. Help them understand the interrelatedness you find in events and people. Broaden their worldview and get them thinking in new ways by helping them see a bigger picture. How could they take their own talents to a new level by applying them somewhere they've never thought about? How might they partner with someone they see as much different from themselves?

- You are aware of the boundaries and borders created by organizational structure, but you treat them as seamless and fluid. Use your Connectedness talents to break down silos that prevent shared knowledge across industry, functional and hierarchical divisions within or between organizations. Encourage different groups to work together toward their shared goals.
- Help people see the links among their talents, their actions, their mission, and the success of the larger group or organization. When people believe in what they are doing and feel like they are part of something bigger, they are more committed to achieve.

## LEADING OTHERS WITH STRONG CONNECTEDNESS

- These people are likely to have a spiritual orientation and perhaps a strong faith. Your knowledge and, at the very least, acceptance of their spirituality will enable them to become increasingly comfortable around you.
- These people may be receptive to thinking about and developing the mission for your organization. They naturally feel like they are part of something larger than themselves, and they will enjoy contributing to the impact of an overall statement or goal.

# CONSISTENCY

People exceptionally talented in the Consistency theme are keenly aware of the need to treat people the same. They crave stable routines and clear rules and procedures that everyone can follow.

## LEADING WITH CONSISTENCY

- Cultivate trust by subjecting yourself to whatever rules or programs you approve for your group or organization. When you live by the rules, it demonstrates your respect for principle, sets the tone for equality and encourages peaceful compliance.
- Though others may take advantage of the perks of their position, you likely reject them and prefer to live by the same set of expectations and standards as the larger population in your organization. Fully adapt this "equal footing" policy to win respect and solidify your constituency.
- Being able to predict how another person will act — and react — helps us confidently plot the course for a relationship. Think about how your Consistency influences the relationships others build with you. Are you always there in times of need? Do you reliably show compassion and caring? Analyze the foundations of your closest relationships, and see what you discover about the role your Consistency talents play. Then consider how you can use these patterns to expand the number of friendships in your life.
- When you show your appreciation for the value another person places on fairness and equity, you validate who they are and form a foundation of support and understanding. You may fare best in relationships with others who live their lives according to similar principles. Seek out opportunities to commend those whose values and ideals you admire. Tell them how they make the world a better place. By doing so, you show them that you notice what they do best and that you care about them.

- Others find comfort in knowing what is expected and what is not tolerated. Let people know the norms so that they do not unintentionally violate them.
- When others know your codes of behavior, they can count on you to be constant in your application of them. Verbalize the importance of consistency in your expectations of yourself and others. By doing this, people will not only know the rules but also their underlying principles. This will help them predict your behavior in situations the rules don't cover.
- When others come to you for help, it may be that they're seeking the comfort of your consistency. Your assurance that they can count on you to be there for them will be encouraging.
- You might find that you are a champion of the underdog. This should feel good to you. It means that your support is not destined only for those in the lead, but for all. Encourage those who struggle. Be sure to take into account their personal patterns of success. Perhaps they are striving to achieve in a way that does not suit them well and need some redirection. Help them make the most of their opportunities by finding a pattern that works for them.

## LEADING OTHERS WITH STRONG CONSISTENCY

- When you need to put consistent practices in place for your organization, ask these people to help establish routines.
- When these people are in an analytical role, ask them to work on group, rather than individual, data. They are likely to be more adept at discovering generalizations that can be made about the group rather than particulars about a certain individual.
- If, as a manager, you struggle with policies that require you to apply rules equally, absolutely and with no favoritism, ask these people to help you. The explanations and justifications will come naturally to them.
- In situations in which it is necessary to treat diverse people equally, ask these people to contribute to the development of the rules and procedures.

# CONTEXT

People exceptionally talented in the Context theme enjoy thinking about the past. They understand the present by researching its history.

## LEADING WITH CONTEXT

- Relate stories of your own life that you think will resonate with others. Being vulnerable enough to share a bit of your past can be a gateway to trust.
- Encourage mutual sharing of histories and life events if others are willing, and honor their trust when they confide in you.
- You're interested in the roots, the history and the formative moments in the lives of those around you. For you, a great conversation starter is "Tell me about a turning point in your life." Ask questions that elicit stories that will be as fun for you to hear as they are for others to tell. Showing your interest will demonstrate that you care.
- Remember the details of stories you've heard someone tell, and use them as ongoing connecting points with that person. Looking across a room and making eye contact when something you've heard holds meaning for the two of you shows that you listened, remembered and connected.
- Stability is linked to Context. The sense that nothing in the universe is new means that we have experienced these things before and will do so again. Remind others of their strength. Discuss previous trials they have survived, and point out that their fortitude and resilience can give them the confidence and courage to find new ways to triumph.

- History teaches patience, and putting things in perspective encourages understanding and security. Articulate the historical perspective on the issues people face today. Help them see the past as a teacher and find wisdom in its lessons.
- Ask others questions like "How did you come to that decision?" and "Have you ever dealt with an issue or situation like this in the past?" Your good questions and gentle guidance can help others get perspective on a situation and help them avoid recurring errors.
- Help people make sense of their lives and circumstances by showing them how to link their history to their present and future. Work with them to develop a timeline of their lives that includes significant decisions, trials, triumphs and turning points. Ask them what they learned at each juncture. And help them consider what they can do now as a result of what they learned.
- Boiling down complex ideas or proposals to their most basic elements helps you understand the original purpose or reasoning behind them. Trace the evolution of a plan or idea back to its inception, and clarify the purpose of its direction to those who may question it. You will strengthen your team's mission.
- Remind your colleagues that your organization's values and goals are based on wisdom derived from the past. Keep the history of your enterprise alive by retelling stories that capture its essence. These stories can offer guidance and inspiration in the present through understanding the insights of the past. Consider being the keeper of the wisdom — or at least initiate the collection and recording of the wisdom. Future generations will thank you.

## LEADING OTHERS WITH STRONG CONTEXT

- When you ask these people to do something, take time to explain the thinking that led to the request. They need to understand the background of a course of action before they can commit to it.
- No matter what the subject matter, ask these people to collect revealing stories, highlight the key discoveries from each one and perhaps build a class around them.
- Ask these people to collect anecdotes of people behaving in a way that exemplifies the cornerstones of your organization's culture. Their stories, retold in newsletters, training classes, websites, videos and so on will strengthen your culture.

# DELIBERATIVE

People exceptionally talented in the Deliberative theme are best described by the serious care they take in making decisions or choices. They anticipate obstacles.

## LEADING WITH DELIBERATIVE

- You inspire trust because you are naturally cautious and considerate regarding sensitive topics. Use these talents by taking on opportunities to handle delicate issues and conflicts.
- Others respect the time you dedicate to doing things right and to doing the right things. Let them know when you need time to think before making a decision. Trust them to appreciate that you have their best interests in mind.
- You understand the importance and weight of each relationship, and you take this responsibility seriously. Once you've chosen to add someone to your life, tend the relationship well. Invest in activities and conversations that keep you close, and reveal your heart to the people who matter most. Lifetime relationships are hard to find, as you know, and they deserve and require your attention and love.
- Understand that your praise is rare — and precious to many. So when you recognize others, consider marking the occasion with a tangible reminder. Giving someone a visible token of your appreciation will help the memory of your praise last for a long time.
- Rather than take foolhardy risks, you are likely to approach decisions cautiously. Trust your instincts when you believe something is too good to be true. Your deliberation and caution make others feel protected and secure about the conclusions you reach.
- Others will appreciate the careful thought that goes into each decision you make. Tell them about the options you have analyzed and why you have chosen a particular course. Consider that they have a stake in the decision too. Ask for and weigh their input as carefully as you do your own.

- Temper the tendency of others to move haphazardly into action by declaring a "consideration" period before making decisions. Your caution can serve to steer others away from impulsiveness and toward wise choices.
- When you know a great deal about a topic, offer others the benefits of the research and analysis you have done. Encourage them to try something if you believe it's the right thing for them to do. Show them the supporting evidence.

## LEADING OTHERS WITH STRONG DELIBERATIVE

- Do not position these people in roles that require snap judgments. They are likely to feel uncomfortable making decisions on gut instinct alone.
- When caution is required, such as circumstances that are sensitive to legal, safety or accuracy issues, ask these people to take the lead. They will instinctively anticipate where the dangers might lie and how to keep you protected.
- These people are likely to excel at negotiating contracts, especially behind the scenes. As far as you can within the confines of their job description, ask them to play this role.
- Do not ask these people to be greeters, rainmakers or networkers for your organization. The kind of effusiveness that these roles require may not be in their repertoire.
- In their relationships, these people will be selective and discriminating. Consequently, do not move them quickly from team to team. They need to feel assured that the people around them are competent and trustworthy, and this confidence takes time to build.
- These people will be known for giving praise sparingly. But when they do, keep in mind that it is truly deserved.

# DEVELOPER

People exceptionally talented in the Developer theme recognize and cultivate the potential in others. They spot the signs of each small improvement and derive satisfaction from evidence of progress.

## LEADING WITH DEVELOPER

- Doing something good for the sake of another is a sign of character and an invitation to trust. Extend yourself to others by helping them see their own potential and offering to work with them to develop it. This will increase the breadth and depth of your relationships, and you will enjoy watching them grow.
- Try not to be hurt when others look for an ulterior motive in your good deeds. It may take them time to trust you when you show interest in their personal development. Allow them to see you in action for weeks, months or even years before expecting their full confidence. They may not trust as easily as you do.
- You take genuine delight in people's growth and development. Your natural talent for focusing on others is a gift to those you nurture. Cheer for them, and let them know that you believe in them. Your compassionate caring touches their hearts and puts you squarely on their side. They will never forget the support you offer so easily.
- "We learn best from those we love" is a quote you understand and appreciate. Who loves you? Whom do you love? Be sure to get close enough to not only teach and guide, but to love. Communicate your feelings. Your impact will last forever.
- As you begin working with others on their development, first acknowledge the progress you've already seen. This provides a basis of confidence and security. You can make taking the next step less intimidating by reassuring others that you are confident they can do it because of what they've already proven they can do. Express your certainty that the next goal is within their reach.

- Developers help others step over comfort thresholds. You provide a "safe zone" where people have permission to strive and fail and strive again. Set others up for success by telling them that they will likely need to make more than one attempt at something before they reach ultimate success. Helping people set the right expectations gives them the security and the confidence to try again.
- Encourage people to dig deep into their talents and put them to the test. With you, they have a cushion for failure and will not feel the full force of it. You provide support so that they can take the risks necessary to make the most of their talents.
- Challenge others by asking good questions that stretch their imagination. What's the most they've ever done? How much do they imagine they could do? What do they dream of doing? What would they do if there were no obstacles or barriers to their choices?
- Your nurturing approach is your spontaneous response to those around you and makes you an inspirational mentor to many. Consider your best mentors' approaches and styles, and take a lesson from them. Adopt the ones that are right for you, and use them to encourage and champion those you are mentoring.
- You will be compelled to counsel more people than you possibly can. To fulfill this inner drive, consider being a "mentor for the moment." Many of the most poignant and memorable developmental moments occur in a mere instant when the right words are delivered at the right time — words that clarify understanding, re-ignite a passion, open eyes to an opportunity or change a life course.

## LEADING OTHERS WITH STRONG DEVELOPER

- Position these people so that they can help others in the organization grow. For example, give them the opportunity to mentor one or two people or to teach a class on a company topic, such as safety, benefits or customer service. If necessary, pay the fee for them to belong to a local training organization.
- These people might be good candidates for a supervisor, team leader or manager role. If they are already in a manager or executive role, look to their business unit for people who can be transferred to positions with greater responsibilities in the organization. People strong in this theme develop others and prepare them for the future.
- Be aware that these people may protect struggling performers long past the time when they should have been moved or terminated. Help them focus their instincts on setting people up to achieve success and not on supporting people who are enduring hardship. The best developmental action they can take with strugglers is to find them a different opportunity where they can truly excel.

# DISCIPLINE

People exceptionally talented in the Discipline theme enjoy routine and structure. Their world is best described by the order they create.

## LEADING WITH DISCIPLINE

- You never let yourself off the hook, and others will respect you for your uncompromising principles. Hold yourself to the standards you set, and your actions will reflect your integrity.
- Others can count on you to make sure every detail is executed exactly right. Your Discipline can become the basis for trust when people see that you meet their expectations time and time again. They will learn to respect your consistent delivery.
- Your powerful sense of order can make you a tremendous partner to those who rely on your discipline to supplement their own. Find and celebrate the positive traits others possess that you don't, and build a relationship based on mutual appreciation. When someone learns to rely on you, and you on them, a complementary partnership is at its best.
- Show others kindness by attending to the details that they are sure to miss. Adopt the mindset of a caring friend, and look for ways to free others from the details that bog them down. You can make their lives better — and gain their appreciation at the same time.
- You are predictable and consistent. You do what is required when it is required — if not before. Share your timelines with others, and let them see the consistent progress you make as promised. People will feel safe entrusting you with projects when they see that your actions always follow your words.
- Not everyone is blessed with your sense of order. Share with others the calmness and composure you get from orderliness by letting them know that you have things under control. Help them see that each step will be accomplished in its time, and the entire project will follow

according to plan. Others will be freed to do what they do well when they know that nothing important can slip through the cracks.

- Your performance objectives spur your efforts; you like to get things done each day and each week. Noticing your productivity, others may take their cue from your performance objectives as well. Detail your tasks, goals and timelines, and share them with interested teammates who may use your example to inspire their own work efforts.
- Trying to impose your systems and structures on those who lack strong Discipline talents simply won't work. Rather than trying to "convert" those who appear to need your sense of order, try to discover what they do well. Then support and encourage them in those areas.

## LEADING OTHERS WITH STRONG DISCIPLINE

- Give these people the opportunity to bring structure to haphazard or chaotic situations. Because they will not be comfortable in such shapeless, messy circumstances — and don't expect them to be — they will not rest until order and predictability are restored.
- When there are many things that need to get done in a set time period, remember these people's need to prioritize. Take the time to set priorities together, and once the schedule is set, stick to it.
- If appropriate, ask these people to help you plan and organize your own work. You might enlist them to review your time management system or even your ideas for re-engineering some of your department's processes. Tell their colleagues that this is one of their talents, and encourage them to ask for similar help.
- These people excel at developing routines that help them work efficiently. If they are forced to work in a situation that requires flexibility and responsiveness, encourage them to devise a set number of routines, each appropriate for a certain set of circumstances. This way, they will have a predictable response to fall back on, no matter what the surprise.

# EMPATHY

People exceptionally talented in the Empathy theme can sense other people's feelings by imagining themselves in others' lives or situations.

## LEADING WITH EMPATHY

- When others are faced with a worrisome situation, help them articulate and come to terms with their complex emotions. Respect their feelings, and allow them the freedom to express what they need to express, whether or not your feelings mirror theirs. Acknowledge and deal with these emotions honestly to build trust.
- Because trust is paramount to you, many of your associates are likely to feel comfortable approaching you to share their thoughts, feelings, concerns and needs. Encourage them. They will greatly value your discretion and desire to be genuinely helpful.
- Witnessing others' happiness brings you pleasure. Consequently, you are likely to notice opportunities to highlight people's successes and positively reinforce their achievements. At each opportunity, deliver a kind word of appreciation or recognition. By doing so, you are likely to make a profound and engaging impression on them.
- Sometimes you have the ability to understand what others are feeling before they've recognized it themselves. This uncanny awareness can be unnerving or comforting, depending on how you share it. Ask questions to gently guide people toward recognizing what you already suspect. Help them name their feelings and create their own path to self-discovery.
- Sensitive to the feelings of others, you readily gauge the emotional tone of a room. Use your talents to forge a bridge of understanding and mutual support. Your Empathy talents are especially important during trying times because they demonstrate your concern as a leader, thereby creating security and loyalty.

- Patience and understanding are your hallmarks. Take time to hear people out; don't rush to judgment. Giving people time and space to sort out their own thoughts and feelings in a safe environment promotes their sense of stability and tranquility.
- Others are likely to choose you as a confidante or mentor. Affirm that this is a satisfying relationship for you so they feel welcome to approach you. Encourage them by putting words to what you sense about their aspirations; inspire and guide their dreams by imagining with them.
- Your Empathy talents allow you to anticipate events and reactions. Because you are observant of how others are feeling, you are likely to sense what is about to happen in the organization before it becomes common knowledge. Help people be alert as positive emotions build, so as a group, you can capitalize on this anticipation to create hope.

## LEADING OTHERS WITH STRONG EMPATHY

- Pay attention, but don't overreact, if these people cry. Tears are part of their life. They may sense the joy or tragedy in another person's life more poignantly than even that person does.
- Help these people see their Empathy talent as a special gift. It may come so naturally to them that they think everyone feels what they feel, or they may be embarrassed by their strength of feeling. Show them how to use their talents to everyone's advantage.
- Test these people's ability to make decisions instinctively rather than logically. They may not be able to articulate why they think a certain action is right, but they will often be right nonetheless. Ask them "What is your gut feeling about what we should do?"
- Arrange for these people to work with positive, optimistic individuals. They will pick up on their feelings and be motivated. Conversely, steer them away from pessimists and cynics. They will depress people with strong Empathy talents.

# FOCUS

People exceptionally talented in the Focus theme can take a direction, follow through and make the corrections necessary to stay on track. They prioritize, then act.

## LEADING WITH FOCUS

- Others will respect you because you know what's important and you keep your attention there. Make sure that you're not delegating nonessentials. Before you ask someone to do something, ask yourself if it affects ultimate performance. If it's not worth your time, perhaps it's not worth anyone's time and you don't even have to ask. Others will trust your judgment.
- As a person with strong Focus talents, you know that life is about choices. Remember that everyone is responsible for their own decisions. Demonstrate to others that you understand and respect their choices in life.
- Take a step back and think about the priorities in your life. Use your Focus talents to target not only the projects that are important, but also the people. Set goals and strategies for giving those people the time and attention they deserve as partners in your life. Include these goals on your daily to-do lists, and check off what you accomplish.
- In whom should you be investing at work? Who makes your life better every day through their efforts on the job? Show appreciation to those who enable you to be so efficient. Acknowledge their role in your effectiveness, and don't forget to reach out when they need your help too.
- Expand the effects of your Focus talents by extending the period of time you usually plan in advance. For example, if you typically plan one year ahead, try planning three years out. Gradually increase the length of time that you forecast. Share your thoughts with others. Knowing that you are focusing on and thinking about the long term will give them security now.

- When you share long-term goals with your family and your work teams, tell them that they are part of your future projections. Give them the assurance that you value and need them and that they will be there with you.
- Over a lifetime, we accrue responsibilities and tasks that may have ceased to have meaning for us. Help others clear some of the accumulated clutter of their lives. Ask questions like "What are the most important priorities in your life and your work?" "What do you love about doing this?" and "What would happen if you stopped doing this?" By tackling these questions, you can help people focus — or refocus — their energy and offer them a fresh outlook on the future.
- Invest in your organization by guiding the career trajectories of your company's most promising protégés. When mentoring others, help them craft well-defined career paths and action plans to secure their aspirations.
- Having measurable, specific and tangible performance objectives is critical to your effectiveness. You enjoy setting regular "mini goals" for yourself because they keep your Focus talents sharp. Share your goals, measurement systems and performance objectives with associates. You will increase their sense of team and inspire them to track their personal progress in relation to the larger organizational objectives.

## LEADING OTHERS WITH STRONG FOCUS

- Set goals with timelines, and then let these people figure out how to achieve them. They will work best in an environment where they can control their work events.
- Check in with these people on a regular basis — as often as they indicate would be helpful. They will thrive on this regular attention because they like talking about goals and their progress toward them. Ask them how often you should meet to discuss goals and objectives.

- Don't expect these people to always be sensitive to the feelings of others; getting their work done often takes top priority. Be aware of the possibility that they may trample on others' feelings as they march toward their goal.
- These people do not thrive in constantly changing situations. To manage this, when describing a change to them, use language that they will be receptive to. For example, talk about it in terms of "new goals" and "new measures of success," giving the change trajectory and purpose. This is how they naturally think.
- Arrange for these people to attend a time management seminar. They may not naturally excel at this, but because their Focus theme pushes them to move toward their goals as fast as possible, they will appreciate the greater efficiency of effective time management.

# FUTURISTIC

People exceptionally talented in the Futuristic theme are inspired by the future and what could be. They energize others with their visions of the future.

## LEADING WITH FUTURISTIC

- When helping others imagine what could be, make sure that your visions are grounded in reality. Many people do not find it as easy as you do to envision what things will look like decades later, so provide as much detail as you can about what they can do to be a part of the future. A realistic attitude will help build trust and confidence in your visionary ideas.
- Given your natural ability to look ahead, at times you may see disturbing trends on the horizon. Even if you enjoy talking about possibilities more than problems, help others see and eliminate potential roadblocks before they cause difficulties. They will come to depend on you for this and trust what you see.
- One of the best ways to make a connection with another person is to listen. Ask the people you lead about their dreams. Have them describe their ideal future to you. Somewhere in their story, your Futuristic talents are likely to find a connection. Build on that connection by asking questions that will help them find clarity as they talk about their aspirations. They will feel closer to you simply because you took an interest in their hopes and dreams for the future.
- You see the future more clearly than others. Do a little dreaming for people. Tell them that dreams are possible if they set their sights on them. Perhaps you see talents in them that they are blind to or opportunities they have not considered. Investing your time and energy in thinking about possibilities and what is good for other people shows caring and friendship. It shows you are a leader.
- People sometimes exaggerate the fear of the present because they cannot see beyond to a future when "this too shall pass." You have

the gift of perspective; your thinking is not bound by present circumstances. Help others share the calm you possess — knowing that another day will come and their present worries will be behind them.

- As you think about the future, be sure to check in with the people you lead about their emotions. If the visions you have are too distant for them to imagine, or if too much seems uncertain, they may get worried or uncomfortable. Ask people how they see themselves in the scenarios you discuss, and help them know that these are "what if" pictures, not "must be" plans. They are the ones in control of their destiny.
- Because you have the gift of future thinking, it should come as no surprise that people choose you as their sounding board when they need direction and guidance. You may have been playing the role of a guide for others your whole life. Think through this role. Consider what questions you should be asking. What do others need from you? How do you find out? Having a set of questions to ask when others seek you out may help you match your advice to their expectations and aspirations.
- You inspire others with your images of the future. When you articulate your vision, be sure to describe it in detail with vivid words and metaphors so that others can better comprehend your expansive thinking. Make your ideas and strategies more concrete via sketches, step-by-step action plans or mock-up models so that your associates can more easily grasp what you see.

## LEADING OTHERS WITH STRONG FUTURISTIC

- Give these people time to think about, write about and plan for the products and services your organization will need in the future. Create opportunities for them to share their perspective in company newsletters, meetings or industry conventions.
- Put these people on your organization's planning committee. Have them present their data-based vision of what the organization might look like in three, five or 10 years. And have them repeat this presentation every six months or so. This way, they can refine it with new data and insights.
- When your organization needs people to embrace change, ask these people to put the changes in the context of the organization's future needs. Have them make a presentation or write an article that puts these new directions in perspective. They can help others rise above their present uncertainties and become excited about the possibilities of the future.

# HARMONY

People exceptionally talented in the Harmony theme look for consensus. They don't enjoy conflict; rather, they seek areas of agreement.

## LEADING WITH HARMONY

- You show others respect by valuing their input and helping them be heard. At times, you may need to point out that each person's point of view is valuable and deserves respect, if not agreement. Learn to briefly, yet effectively, communicate the value of listening.
- The loudest voices are not the only ones that should be heard. Sometimes you may need to stop a debate and help each person have a say. When you do, make sure the environment is one of trust and respect so that those with quieter voices feel comfortable sharing their opinions. By making it clear that decisions are better when every voice is heard, others will have faith in your motives and be more likely to share discussion time.
- Your Harmony talents make life more pleasant. You reduce stress by reducing conflict and friction. Invest some time in conceptualizing the greater purpose of your organization. When tensions mount, remind others of the overriding mission that binds you all together. In addition to cooling the conflict, you can help others rise to another level that is based on a shared purpose. Others will be drawn to you because you are considerate of everyone's opinions, and you honor their views.
- Seeking common ground comes naturally to you. Your quest for harmony between individuals and groups shows others that you care and enhances one-to-one and group relationships. How many points of commonality can you find per interaction on your team? Count them, and see if you can increase your average over time. The greater the number of connecting points, the greater the opportunity for establishing significant and lasting relationships.

- Your peaceful and understanding approach allows everyone to stay connected to the group, even when opinions differ. Remind others that the strength of a group is the ability to respectfully bring a variety of ideas to the table. Your knack for appeasing those with opposing views helps everyone in the group feel a sense of security that no matter what the issue, the group will remain intact.
- You calm others by smoothing the waters and helping everyone keep a level head. Make sure that no one is hurt by thoughtless words spoken in passion. Creating an atmosphere of dignity and respect helps others feel safe when it's their turn to share their views.
- Establish and encourage interactions and forums in which people feel that their opinions are truly heard. You will promote engagement, raise individual achievement levels and contribute to overall team performance. This will, in turn, create hope for the future.
- Polish your talent for resolution without agitation by gathering skills and knowledge. Become skilled in moving through the steps of conflict resolution, and invite someone to learn with you. Encourage and inspire each other to become experts in finding solutions through consensus. Learn and teach at the same time.

## LEADING OTHERS WITH STRONG HARMONY

- Find areas and issues on which you and these people agree, and regularly review these topics with them. Surround them with other people who are strong in Harmony. They will always be more focused, more productive and more creative when they know that they're supported.
- Don't be surprised if these people agree with you even when you are wrong. Sometimes, for the sake of harmony, they may nod their heads despite judging your idea a poor one. Consequently, you may need other people who instinctively voice their opinions to help keep your thinking clear.

# IDEATION

People exceptionally talented in the Ideation theme are fascinated by ideas. They are able to find connections between seemingly disparate phenomena.

## LEADING WITH IDEATION

- Knowing the purpose behind your pursuit of what's new can help others trust you to make good choices. Explain the "why" of what you do. Help people see that you are seeking to improve the status quo, to better explain the world and to make discoveries that ultimately serve humanity.
- Make things simple. All your ideas, possibilities and tangents can be confusing to some people. You see the simplicity of the underlying principles; articulate that to others so they can see it too. The clearer things are to people, the more certain they can be that you are doing what is right and what makes sense. Help people make connections between what is and what can be.
- Others have great appreciation for your creative imagination and your continual quest for new ideas. Invite them along for the ride. Ask them to dream with you. Shared excitement about ideas and possibilities, even from vastly different fields and approaches, can be a foundation for a mutually satisfying relationship.
- Partner with people who have a practical mindset — those who can make your ideas realistic and bring them to fruition. You can be their inspiration; they can help you realize your dreams. Your differences are what bind you together and make each of you more successful than you would be on your own. Show consideration and appreciation for what others bring to the table.

- Stability and Ideation might seem at odds. You are always searching for ways to break from convention and look at things from a new angle. Verbalize the fact that you're not seeking to destroy what is — rather, you want to make things better. You understand that security doesn't come from maintaining the status quo and doing things the way they've always been done. Security is about making sure you are prepared for the future.
- You must take risks. Still, you can calm others by educating them that those risks are calculated, not reckless. Build others' confidence by helping them see the logic behind your pursuit of what's new, and keep them informed along the way.
- You are a natural fit with people in research and development; you appreciate the mindset of the visionaries and dreamers in your organization. Spend time with imaginative staff members, and sit in on their brainstorming sessions. Invite people you know who have good ideas to join as well. As a leader with exceptional Ideation talents, you can contribute to inspirational ideas and make them happen.
- Find people in other walks of life who like to talk about ideas, and build mutually supportive and satisfying relationships. Their knowledge and dreams about an area that is foreign to you can inspire you. Feed one another's need for big thinking.

## LEADING OTHERS WITH STRONG IDEATION

- These people have creative ideas. Be sure to position them where their ideas will be valued.
- Encourage these people to think of useful ideas or insights that you can share with your best customers. From Gallup's research, it is clear that when a company deliberately teaches its customers something, their level of loyalty increases.

- These people need to know that everything fits together. When decisions are made, take time to show them how each one is rooted in the same theory or concept.
- When a particular decision does not fit into an overarching concept, be sure to explain to these people that the decision is an exception or an experiment. Without this explanation, they may start to worry that the organization is becoming incoherent.

# INCLUDER

People exceptionally talented in the Includer theme accept others. They show awareness of those who feel left out and make an effort to include them.

## LEADING WITH INCLUDER

- Your utter lack of elitism inspires respect and honor. Others can rely on you to find common ground and recognize the contribution each person makes to the team and to the entire organization.
- Automatic acceptance is part of your wiring. You don't debate the merits and drawbacks of including someone. If they are there, they should be welcomed and brought into the fold. Help others see past what's on the outside, and ask them to consider how others feel. They will realize that you are someone who deserves respect when they see the respect you give to others.
- Everyone needs an Includer as a friend. You help people feel welcome and immediately make them part of something larger than themselves. When others feel like outsiders looking in, you reach out and invite them to join. Never hesitate to include, even when you are rebuffed. Know that you are always doing the right thing.
- Nurture the new people in your organization. Be a first friend. Know their names, and introduce them to others to help them find connecting points. You will collect many best friends this way. It's hard to forget the person who first made you feel like you belonged in a new place where you felt uncertain.
- You foster stability and security when everyone knows that they will not be excluded. Being consistent with your invitations and open to a wide variety of people helps others know that they too find a welcome whenever they need it.
- Your attitude that "there's always room for one more" promotes inclusion rather than competition when someone new joins the group. When others see that the circle expands to accommodate all, they will

feel less territorial and more secure that they have a place in the fold. Make them feel even more confident by asking them to take on some of the orientation for new people.

- Be an "Includer coach." Share your ideas for helping people feel welcome. Others may require a caring nudge to get them to step outside their comfort zone and make the first move to add someone to their inner circle. When you offer that nudge, you give everyone more opportunity for growth.
- Consider that people will relate to each other through you. You are a conduit for information; you can connect with all of the people in a group and keep them effectively connected to each other. Watch as this network you have created multiplies by the day.

## LEADING OTHERS WITH STRONG INCLUDER

- These people are interested in making everyone feel like part of the team. Ask them to work on an orientation program for new employees. They will be excited to think about ways to welcome new recruits.
- Capitalize on these people's Includer talents by focusing them on your customers. Properly positioned, they may prove to be very effective at breaking barriers between customer and company.
- Because these people probably will not appreciate elite products or services made for a select category of customer, position them to work on products or services that are designed for a broad market. They will enjoy planning how to cast a wide net.
- If appropriate, ask these people to be your organization's link to community social agencies.

# INDIVIDUALIZATION

People exceptionally talented in the Individualization theme are intrigued with the unique qualities of each person. They have a gift for figuring out how different people can work together productively.

## LEADING WITH INDIVIDUALIZATION

- Sometimes you know more about people than they would like you to know. Keep strict confidences, and only share your insights with someone one-on-one. Each person should be the one to decide if they want you to relate your insights to others.
- Others trust your instincts about people's unique qualities. Continue to build on that trust by focusing on the positive as much as you can when you are asked to share your impressions about someone.
- Stand behind your tendency to treat each person individually according to their needs, strengths and style. Many may see this as playing favorites and distrust you. Be prepared to defend your Individualization from a performance-excellence standpoint, as well as from a humane perspective. This will give others confidence in your decisions.
- Others are often surprised at the depth of your insights about them, especially when you've known them only a short time. You've probably heard "How did you know that?" many times. As relationships develop, others will want to hear in greater depth your thoughts and insights regarding their actions, motivations and talents. You are a mirror for them, and you offer a valuable perspective. Ask them to tell you more about themselves, and test your insights. Accept and affirm what they tell you.
- You may have the gift of gifting — choosing the perfect gift for another person — even someone you don't know particularly well. Bring joy into others' lives with little surprises. Finding a small token and giving it unexpectedly can be a quick relationship builder. Give

yourself permission to reach out in this way, and enjoy the looks of surprise and delight. Who can resist a perfectly chosen gift?

- Your individualized awareness is essential to providing stability. Help others by using your natural attention to their desires and needs to position them in the right role. Their confidence and security will grow when they are doing what they do best.
- "All generalizations are false, including this one" is a phrase you might enjoy. Knowing that you are conscious of each person's special circumstances helps them feel understood and secure. Let people know that despite the rules or conventional wisdom, you will take their unique talents and needs into account when making decisions about opportunities they can pursue.
- Sometimes people are more predictable to you than they are to themselves. Use your talent to notice others' consistent behavior patterns to help them see things they can't. You might be able to help them capitalize on talents they seldom use or avoid pitfalls that repeatedly ensnare them. Give them feedback to help them streamline their dreams and aspirations.
- You are instinctively aware that individuals will be most productive when their environments are suited to their talents. Wherever appropriate, implement policies that allow your associates to work in their own style — policies that allow them to express their individuality through the clothes they wear, how they decorate their workspaces and the hours they work. Through these policies, you will engage and inspire your associates and empower them to produce their best work.
- You move comfortably among a broad range of styles and cultures, and you intuitively personalize your interactions. Consciously and proactively make full use of these talents by leading diversity and community efforts in your organization.

## LEADING OTHERS WITH STRONG INDIVIDUALIZATION

- Ask these people to serve on your selection committee. They will be good judges of each candidate's strengths and weaknesses. By figuring out the right people for the right roles using their Individualization talents, they can also help improve the organization's productivity.
- When appropriate, have these people help design pay-for-performance programs in which all employees can use their strengths to maximize their pay.
- Ask these people to teach an internal training class or mentor new employees. They may well have a knack for spotting how each person learns differently.
- Look at these people's other dominant themes. If their Developer and Arranger talents are also strong, they may have the potential to be managers or supervisors. If their talents lie in Command and Woo, they will probably be very effective at turning prospects into customers.

# INPUT

People exceptionally talented in the Input theme have a need to collect and archive. They may accumulate information, ideas, artifacts or even relationships.

## LEADING WITH INPUT

- Become a trusted authority by making sure that the information you provide is both current and accurate. Check multiple sources just to be sure, and help others distinguish between fact and opinion.
- You earn respect by doing your homework and providing others with the information they need to succeed. When they see that you have put in the time and taken the responsibility to do thorough research, they can't help but appreciate your desire to do good work and trust your comprehensive findings.
- People will be attracted to you as a leader because they see your resourcefulness and your awareness of recent developments and information. Let others know that you love to answer their questions and to research their most pressing issues. Use your Input talents to connect with others, and make yourself available as someone they can depend on for help.
- When you meet others who share your interests, think beyond the learning opportunity at hand, and consider the relationship possibilities. Could this be the start of a friendship? Invite this person along when you discover opportunities to pursue your mutual interest, such as an exhibit or an upcoming speech. Use your Input talents as a stepping stone to relationships, and extend the first invitation.
- Your knowledge base can be a foundation for stability. When others know that you have researched the topic at hand with your characteristic thoroughness and depth, they will feel confident that your decisions are well-thought-out. Share the extent of your research efforts with them.

- You don't merely collect information. You store it for a time when it might prove useful. By producing the backup and documentation for efforts that might seem risky to some, you assure them that they are moving in the right direction.
- Your mind is like a sponge — you naturally soak up information. But just as the primary purpose of a sponge is not to permanently contain what it absorbs, neither should your mind simply store information. Input without output can lead to stagnation. As you gather and absorb information, be aware of the individuals and groups that can benefit from your knowledge, and share it with them.
- Expose yourself to the written thoughts and ideas of other people. Then engage in serious discussion about them. Through this process, you will become a learner who also teaches.

## LEADING OTHERS WITH STRONG INPUT

- Focus these people's natural inquisitiveness by asking them to study a topic that is important to your organization. Or position them in a role with a heavy research component. They enjoy the knowledge that comes from research.
- Pay attention to these people's other strong themes. If they are also strong in Developer, they may excel as teachers or trainers by peppering their lessons with intriguing facts and stories.
- Help these people develop a system for storing the information they collect to ensure that they can find it when they and the organization need it.

# INTELLECTION

People exceptionally talented in the Intellection theme are characterized by their intellectual activity. They are introspective and appreciate intellectual discussions.

## LEADING WITH INTELLECTION

- When you carefully analyze others' thinking and then respectfully give your honest opinion, you can help them avoid pitfalls and mistakes. They will appreciate your forthright willingness to help them succeed, and they will come to depend on you for this.
- Your sheer intellectual capacity will cause some to respect and revere you. Prove yourself worthy by remembering that thought without action is not always particularly helpful. Use your gift of Intellection to make a difference, and your respect will be well-deserved.
- Engaging others in intellectual and philosophical debate is one way you make sense of things. It is also one way you build relationships. Channel your provocative questions to people who similarly enjoy the give and take of debate. They will seek you out as a friend and colleague who sharpens their thinking — and someone they want to spend time with again and again.
- Some people will want you to think with them, while others will want you to think for them. You may be able to build relationships with some people because you look at things from an entirely different angle than they do. For people who are single-minded and action-oriented, you may be the kind of thinking partner who improves their odds for success. Show that you truly care about them by sharing your thoughts with them.

- Remember to occasionally back up so others can follow the trail of your thinking. They may not be ready for your decisions until they have followed the path you took to get there. Share the mental steps you executed to arrive at your conclusions so people don't worry that your thinking lacks foundation.
- Help others understand your need for solitude and space to think. Let them know that this is simply a reflection of your intellectual style and that it results from a desire to bring the most you can to relationships and opportunities. Knowing that you think deeply about what's best for them and for the organization can be a great comfort.
- Encourage others to use their full intellectual capital by reframing questions for them and engaging them in dialogue. At the same time, recognize that there will be some who find this intimidating and who need time to reflect before being put on the spot. Help them engage their intellect in the way that is best for them. Then inspire them to use their own way of thinking to dream and meditate about the future.
- Others will seek out your opinion because they appreciate the wise scrutiny you give to ideas and efforts. Bear in mind that you are at your best when you have the time to follow an intellectual trail and see where it leads. Get involved on the front end of projects and initiatives so that your thinking can have a greater impact on long-term outcomes.

## LEADING OTHERS WITH STRONG INTELLECTION

- Encourage these people to find long stretches of time when they can simply muse. For some people, pure thinking time is not productive, but for those with strong Intellection talents, it most certainly is. They will emerge from quiet periods of reflection with more clarity and self-confidence.

- Have a detailed discussion with these people about their strengths. They will probably enjoy the introspection and self-discovery.
- Give these people the opportunity to present their views to other people in the department. The pressure of communicating their ideas to others will force them to refine and clarify their thoughts.
- Be prepared to team up these people with someone who has strong Activator talents. These energetic partners will push them to act on their thoughts and ideas.

# LEARNER

People exceptionally talented in the Learner theme have a great desire to learn and want to continuously improve. The process of learning, rather than the outcome, excites them.

## LEADING WITH LEARNER

- Be honest enough to admit that you're still learning. Being vulnerable and open about your own learning journey puts you on par with others and indicates mutual, not one-sided, expectations.
- Respect knowledge that is superior to your own. Some leaders feel the need to be more "advanced" than their followers in every area. This is unrealistic and unproductive, and it impedes progress. Show your respect through your interest and appreciation of what others know and are capable of knowing. Listen to them, and trust them to be experts in those topics.
- Learning with someone else creates mutual vulnerability and discovery. Always consider other people you can invite to learn with you. When you care enough to ask someone to join in your learning, you create a shared memory and a common opportunity that forges a bond.
- Appreciate and celebrate others' learning success, be it a completed project, a certification, a good spelling test or an improvement on a report card. Let others know that you understand the hard work and effort that goes into personal growth. Emphasize that the outcome is exciting, but recognize the merit of their journey as well. Affirm that learning has value, as does the learner.
- When you invest in another person's growth, you're saying, "You matter. You are here for the long term. You are worth my investment." This helps others know that you expect an enduring — not fleeting — relationship with them. Confirm that sentiment by saying it out loud. Tell people that you're committed to them for the long haul.

- Learning takes time. Your patience with others as they learn conveys to them that they're not disposable, but that you believe in them, value them and will support them as they grow.
- Your enthusiasm for learning may be shared by many in your organization. Ignite this passion by creating an ongoing organization-wide learning program.
- Research supports the link between learning and performance. When people have the opportunity to learn and grow, they are more engaged, more productive and loyal. Look for ways to measure whether people feel their learning needs are being met, to create individualized learning milestones and to reward achievements in learning. These rewards and seeing measurable progress can inspire others to even greater learning goals.

## LEADING OTHERS WITH STRONG LEARNER

- Position these people in roles that require them to stay current in a fast-changing field. They will enjoy the challenge of maintaining their competency.
- Regardless of their role, these people will be eager to learn new facts, skills or knowledge. Explore innovative ways for them to learn and stay motivated, or they may start hunting for a richer learning environment. For example, if they don't have opportunities to learn on the job, encourage them to take courses at the local college. Remember, they don't necessarily need to be promoted; they just need to be learning. The process of learning, not necessarily the result, energizes them.

- Encourage these people to become masters or resident experts in their field. Arrange for them to take the relevant classes to accomplish this. If necessary, help them secure financial support to continue their education. Be sure to recognize their learning.
- Have these people work beside experts who will continuously push them to learn more.
- Ask these people to conduct internal discussion groups or presentations. There may be no better way to learn than to teach others.

# MAXIMIZER

People exceptionally talented in the Maximizer theme focus on strengths as a way to stimulate personal and group excellence. They seek to transform something strong into something superb.

## LEADING WITH MAXIMIZER

- Admit that you do some things well and others not so well. Encourage others to disclose that they too have areas where they consistently struggle, and support them when they do. Simply being open can give people "permission" to be themselves in an honest way.
- Others might need to hear your message more than once before they believe that you sincerely expect them to shine where they shine and that you're avoiding their "dull spots." Repeat the message so they hear, understand and trust it. Some people may need to know that you're not going to surprise them later by telling them where they are weak or how they have failed. Continually focus on their excellence until they can truly trust that it will always be your emphasis.
- Use your Maximizer talents to set others free. Too often, people think they have to live up to the expectations of being a jack of all trades, a straight-A student or a well-rounded employee. But you don't expect all things from all people — you expect people to be more of who they already are. Make it clear that you appreciate their unique gifts and their personal brilliance. You may be the only one in someone's life who sees their talents this way.

- Point out the moments of excellence you notice in others' performance. Sometimes people don't recognize their own areas of greatness. Tell them that you see when and where they are truly gifted. We sometimes limit the notion of "talent" to obvious areas like sports or music. Broaden people's view of giftedness and of themselves. Tell them if they are a gifted friend, a gifted organizer or a gifted communicator. You can change lives and become a personal champion.
- The surest way to destroy other people's sense of security is to ask them to repeatedly do something for which they are not adequately equipped. Instead, allow others to do and build on what they do best, and watch their confidence grow.
- Support others in the areas in which they don't excel. Give them confidence by helping them find complementary partners or systems that free them from failure.
- Don't let your Maximizer talents be stifled by conventional wisdom, which says you should find what is broken and fix it. Identify and invest in the aspects of people and organizations that are working. Make sure that you spend most of your resources building up and encouraging the pockets of excellence you see.
- Explain Maximizer concepts to those who may not have ever considered pursuing only what they do well. Point out the advantages of a life lived by this principle: Capitalize on your natural talents and gifts. It is more productive. It sets higher expectations, not lower ones. It is the most effective and efficient use of energy and resources. And it's more fun.

- You will probably not have the opportunity to observe everything people do exceptionally well. So encourage others to be the keepers and tenders of their own talents. Ask them to study their successes: What did they do best in winning situations? How can they do more of that? Inspire them to dream. Tell them they can come to you for these kinds of discussions — and that this is one of your great pleasures in life.
- As a leader, you have a responsibility to make the most of your organization's resources — and talent is every company's greatest resource. You see talent in others. Use your authority to help your associates see their own talents and to maximize those talents by positioning people where they can develop and apply strengths. For every need, there is a person with a gift to match. Recruit and select carefully, and you'll have an organization full of opportunities for brilliance.

## LEADING OTHERS WITH STRONG MAXIMIZER

- Schedule time with these people to discuss their strengths in detail and to strategize how and where their strengths can be used to the organization's advantage. They will enjoy these conversations and offer many practical suggestions for how their talents can best be put to use.
- As much as possible, help these people develop a career path and a compensation plan that will allow them to keep growing toward excellence in their role. They will instinctively want to stay on a strengths path and may dislike career structures that force them off this path to increase their earning power.
- Ask these people to lead a task force to investigate the best practices in your organization. Also ask them to help design a program for measuring and celebrating the productivity of each employee. They will enjoy thinking about what excellence should look like across the organization as well as within each role.

# POSITIVITY

People exceptionally talented in the Positivity theme have contagious enthusiasm. They are upbeat and can get others excited about what they are going to do.

## LEADING WITH POSITIVITY

- Some people are so accustomed to hearing the negatives pointed out that initially, they will be suspicious of your continued positive remarks. Keep those remarks coming, and allow others to trust, over time, that you're always going to emphasize the positive — in your life and in theirs.
- Make sure that your praise is always genuine — never empty or false. Research shows that false praise does more damage than criticism. If you believe it, say it. If you don't, show your respect for others' intelligence and judgment, and don't yield to the temptation of false flattery.
- Your Positivity makes you naturally liberal with praise. You can't be too generous — precious few people believe that they are suffering from too much recognition in their lives. Give praise freely. Make it specific. Make it personal. Spread good feelings and genuine appreciation for others. Help people look forward to every interaction they have with you.
- In hard times, you may be one of the few bright spots in someone's life — a beacon. Never underestimate that role. People will come to you because they need the boost you consistently provide. Let them know that they can. Ask them what they need. You will refresh them.
- Be the person whose humor is always positive and encouraging. Because of your outlook, you don't resort to insulting, insensitive humor or sarcasm. This positive approach will surely rub off on others, and you'll influence the atmosphere around you.

- You have a natural talent to increase people's confidence. Look for ways to catch people doing things right or doing the right things. Affirm them. Watch them become stronger and more certain of themselves as a result of your praise.
- Your optimism allows you to live with solutions that are sometimes less than perfect. As a result, you encourage others to make progress rather than insisting on perfection. Continue to look for and describe to others the potential of less-than-ideal situations. By doing so, you encourage them to feel free to take risks to improve a situation, even when they don't have the entire solution.
- Play up the drama of moments. If everyone deserves 15 minutes of fame, perhaps you are the person to set the stage. Make each person's 15 minutes big enough to count and important enough to last.
- Your optimism helps others look ahead with anticipation. Talk about the future. Talk about what is possible. Ask others to share the opportunities and possibilities they see. Just saying them out loud helps them become expectations, and eventually, realities.
- Sometimes feelings are the result of action; other times, feelings are the cause for action. Insist on celebrations, employ the therapy of laughter, and inject music and drama into your organization. This positive impact on the emotional economy will influence productivity, mutual support and the bottom line.
- As you create positive environments, be sure to protect and nurture them. As much as possible, insulate yourself and others from chronic whiners, complainers and troublemakers. Their negativity is as contagious as your positivity. Intentionally spend time in highly positive environments that will invigorate and feed your group's optimism.

## LEADING OTHERS WITH STRONG POSITIVITY

- Ask these people to help plan events that your organization hosts for your best customers, such as new product launches or user groups.
- These people's enthusiasm is contagious. Consider this when placing them on project teams.
- These people like to celebrate. When others reach milestones of achievement, ask people with Positivity for ideas about how to recognize and commemorate the accomplishment. They will be more creative than most.
- Pay attention to these people's other top themes. If they also have strong Developer talents, they may prove to be excellent trainers or teachers because they bring excitement to the classroom. If Command is one of their strongest themes, they may excel at selling because they are armed with a potent combination of assertiveness and energy.

# RELATOR

People exceptionally talented in the Relator theme enjoy close relationships with others. They find deep satisfaction in working hard with friends to achieve a goal.

## LEADING WITH RELATOR

- Important relationships generate confidences. Maintain and build on the trust you have by keeping the confidences you are entrusted with. One breach empties a dam.
- You know that deepening a friendship carries inherent risk, but you're more comfortable than most in accepting that fact. Say so. Acknowledge it out loud, and tell the other person that the depth of the relationship has created trust on your part and makes you feel safe about disclosing more about yourself.
- Make sure you get enough one-on-one time with the key people in your life. Solidify relationships and create emotional energy to share with others. This is what endures. Don't miss opportunities to show that you care.
- As a strong Relator, you may get and give more love and friendship than most people. Tell others that your relationship with them creates happiness in your life. Ask them how it enhances their happiness. Show them that you care about the quality of their lives by extending compassion, thoughtfulness and interest in their wellbeing.
- Long-term close friendships are deeply fulfilling for you. Whether they are in your family, your personal circle or your organization, tell others that you expect these relationships to last your whole life. Set an expectation of ongoing mutual support, understanding and stability.
- You are more at home in situations that have informal, rather than formal, systems. But organizations that are growing in size and complexity are likely to require systems that are more formal. Even in the face of such workplace realities, you can help others understand

that the core importance of relationships remains constant. Create an informal island in the midst of the formal sea of your organization.

- You are a giver, not a taker. But for your generosity to continue, you must make sure that the inflow keeps up with the rapid outflow. Identify the people and events that really fulfill you, and schedule time for them. This will give you even more energy to share with those who look to you for hope.
- You build relationships that last, giving you a unique depth of perspective on other people's lives and triumphs. Help them see the big picture. Point out their achievements and patterns of success. Show them in as many ways as you can that their life has made a difference.

## LEADING OTHERS WITH STRONG RELATOR

- Help these people identify their colleagues' goals. They are more likely to bond with others when they understand their aims and aspirations.
- Think about asking these people to build genuine relationships with the critical people you want to retain. They can be key employees who can help keep good contributors in your organization through relationship building.
- Pay attention to these people's other strong themes. If they also show strong evidence of Focus, Arranger or Self-Assurance talents, they may have the potential to manage others. Employees will always work harder for someone who they know will be there for them and who wants them to succeed. Strong Relators can easily establish these kinds of relationships.
- These people may very well have the gift of generosity. Draw their attention to it, and show them how their generosity helps them influence and connect with those around them. They will appreciate your noticing, and your own relationship with them will be strengthened.

# RESPONSIBILITY

People exceptionally talented in the Responsibility theme take psychological ownership of what they say they will do. They are committed to stable values such as honesty and loyalty.

## LEADING WITH RESPONSIBILITY

- You may be the moral conscience for others. When a person or an organization is involved in something that seems wrong, an alarm in your head will go off, and you will feel compelled to address the issue. Go to the source first; ask questions to determine the reality and the motive. State your concerns honestly. Whenever possible and ethical, allow the person to correct the situation on their own. If necessary, take the next step to right the wrong and ease your conscience.
- It's important to appreciate and recognize moral strength and integrity. Make sure you acknowledge and affirm what's right at least as often — and preferably more often — than you point out what's wrong. Others will notice and respect you for this.
- You can't help but feel responsible for others, especially for the people you care about most. Check in with them frequently. How are they doing? How can you help? Show your compassion every day if you can, and know that you are adding warmth to their lives.
- When you make a mistake that affects someone else, go to that person as quickly as you can and try to make it right. Apologize, certainly, but go beyond apology to restitution. When you own your errors in relationships, you will find that others forgive you more easily and that intimacy is restored more quickly.
- Your sense of responsibility naturally creates a feeling of security in others. They know they can depend on you to make sure things get done properly and on time. Rather than shouldering all of the responsibility yourself, share some of it so that each team member contributes to the stability of the group.

- You're a leader who likes to serve. The service concept often applies to customers, members and patrons, but sometimes is overlooked when it comes to followers. Let your followers know about your desire to serve and support them — and that asking for your help is a form of recognition that you appreciate.
- You naturally take ownership of every project you're involved in. Share responsibility by encouraging others to do the same. Be their champion, and proactively guide them through the opportunity to experience the challenges of ownership. In doing so, you will contribute to their growth and development.
- Psychological ownership is a product of making choices. Rather than assigning responsibilities, invoke ownership by allowing people to choose what they will be responsible for contributing. Let them initiate true responsibility instead of merely accepting assignments.

## LEADING OTHERS WITH STRONG RESPONSIBILITY

- As much as possible, avoid putting these people in team situations with lackadaisical colleagues.
- Recognize that these people are self-starters and require little supervision to ensure that assignments are completed.
- Put these people in positions that require unimpeachable ethics. They will not let you down.
- Periodically ask these people what new responsibility they would like to assume. Volunteering motivates them, so give them the opportunity.
- These people may well impress you with their ability to deliver time and again, leading you to consider promoting them to management. *Be careful.* They may prefer to do a job themselves than be responsible for someone else's work, in which case they will find managing others frustrating. It might be better to help them find other ways to grow within the organization.

# RESTORATIVE

People exceptionally talented in the Restorative theme are adept at dealing with problems. They are good at figuring out what is wrong and resolving it.

## LEADING WITH RESTORATIVE

- People trust you because you close the loop, reinstate order and clean up messes. You restore integrity to systems and make sure that they perform reliably. Let people know that you're willing to do this whenever the need occurs, and they will come to depend on you.
- You're attracted to situations that others may deem impossible. Tell them that the more it seems like the odds are against you, the more motivated you are to resolve the problem and make things right. They will respect the intensity of your desire to tackle the tough jobs and learn to rely on you.
- People appreciate your willingness to jump in and solve problems. Your desire to put things right is a sign that you care. Solve problems before others are even aware they exist, and let people know that you did. It will show your concern and commitment.
- Perhaps people need you most when they feel broken themselves. Your instincts are to run to them and offer emotional support. Be a first responder. Reach people in need as quickly as you can, and offer your support and love. They will always remember that you helped them heal from physical or emotional pain, and they will count you among their closest supporters.
- You are naturally drawn to turnaround situations. Use your Restorative talents to devise a plan of attack to revitalize a flagging project, organization, business or team. Others will feel safer knowing you are on the case.

- Use your Restorative talents to think of ways to "problem proof" schedules, systems and efforts. Knowing that you have done the contingency analysis and taken precautions to prevent mistakes helps others feel secure.
- Use your Restorative talents to be the one who asks "How do we take it to the next level?" Done is never done because improvement is always possible. Be the instigator and inspiration for ever-higher levels of achievement and service.
- Make sure others don't think that flaws and shortcomings are all you can see. Appreciate people for their current levels of service and performance. And when they suggest a way to get even better, encourage their desire for excellence.

## LEADING OTHERS WITH STRONG RESTORATIVE

- Position these people in roles in which they are paid to solve problems for your best customers. They enjoy the challenge of discovering and removing obstacles.
- When these people resolve a problem, make sure to celebrate the achievement. Every wrong situation righted is a success for them, and they will need you to view it as such. Show them that others have come to rely on their ability to dismantle obstacles and move forward.
- Ask these people how they would like to improve. Agree that these improvements should serve as goals for the following six months. They will appreciate this kind of attention and precision.

# SELF-ASSURANCE

People exceptionally talented in the Self-Assurance theme feel confident in their ability to take risks and manage their own lives. They have an inner compass that gives them certainty in their decisions.

## LEADING WITH SELF-ASSURANCE

- Surprise others by admitting the mistakes, wrong turns and poor decisions you've made in the past. People may not expect someone who is so confident to willingly disclose failures. Actually, conquering your failures is what has made you certain that you can overcome whatever challenges you face. Be vulnerable, and show others that your strength springs from your vulnerability. It will help them trust that you are genuine.
- Share the fact that you sometimes face fears when you make decisions. It's not that you don't find decisions daunting — you simply ask yourself, "If not me, then who?" Once you have the best information you can gather, you know that it's time to take action. By better understanding how you approach decision-making, others can see that you are indeed trustworthy.
- Some people are drawn to you because your confidence bolsters theirs. They may not give themselves the credit they deserve for their ability to make good decisions, build solid relationships or achieve success in their lives. Your belief system says "Of course you can!" You remember their successes much more than their failures, and you can readily recall them in detail. With a cheering, supportive friend like you, they can venture out and try.
- You are undeniably independent and self-sufficient, and yet you need to give and receive love. You are human after all. When you build a relationship, consider what you can contribute to someone else's life. And consider what they can contribute to yours. Think about how

others make your life happier and more fulfilled, and let them know. Tell them you need them and value them. Tell them why.

- Confidence — you have it in spades. Share stories of previous successes to help others realize that your confidence is based in experience. That will calm people when you choose a huge goal and say, "We can do it."
- "If you must, you can." Use this adage to help people understand that when there are no options, they have the strength and wherewithal to do what is required of them. Inaction is not an option. The only choice is to make the best decision with the available facts and make a move.
- When considering a new task or venture, carefully reflect on the talents, skills and knowledge it will require. Assemble a solid team, and be prepared to give the helm to someone else if your talents aren't the best fit for the role. People will appreciate your capacity to defer to an expert and make sure they are in capable hands. This will give them comfort and security.
- Set ambitious goals. Don't hesitate to reach for what others see as impractical and impossible — but what you see as merely bold and exciting, and most importantly, achievable with some heroics and a little luck. Your Self-Assurance talents can lead you, your family, your colleagues and your organization to achievements that they would otherwise not have imagined.
- Ask others if they have set their goals high enough. They may not dare to dream as big as you do. If you can contribute to a loftier picture than they currently see, you can launch bigger lives.

## LEADING OTHERS WITH STRONG SELF-ASSURANCE

- Position these people in roles where persistence is essential to success. They have the self-confidence to stay the course despite pressure to change direction.

- Give these people roles that demand an aura of certainty and stability. At critical moments, their inner authority will calm their colleagues and their customers.
- Support these people's self-concept that they are agents of action. Reinforce it with comments such as "It's up to you. You make it happen," or "What is your intuition saying? Let's go with your gut."
- Understand that these people may have beliefs about what they can do that might not relate to their actual talents.
- If these people have strong talents in themes such as Futuristic, Focus, Significance or Arranger, they may well be potential leaders in your organization.

# SIGNIFICANCE

People exceptionally talented in the Significance theme want to make a big impact. They are independent and prioritize projects based on how much influence they will have on their organization or people around them.

## LEADING WITH SIGNIFICANCE

- Share your desire for achieving big goals. Be candid about what motivates you, and ask the same of others. This will lead to shared trust.
- Your impact on the world is almost entirely dependent on the number of people who believe in you as a leader. Always be true to who you are, on and off the stage, and people will see your authenticity.
- Your aspirations will usually be higher than other people's. During the long, steep climb toward the summit, be sure to reward yourself and others by recognizing and celebrating milestones. Reiterate the significance of the goal and the importance of each individual's contribution to it. Tell them what valued partners they are in this venture, and back up your words by giving them a stake in the prize. If your partnership is successful, you may be together for a long time.
- Applause, appreciation and affirmation from a valued audience will push you to ever-higher levels of performance. Whose approval you do most value? A parent, a sibling, a teacher, a boss? Your significant other? Have you told them how critical their approval is to you? Let them know how much you care about their opinions. Make sure that they understand the power of their perception and the valuable role they play in your motivation and in your life.

- Lasting impact matters to you. You want to build something that makes a difference beyond the immediate moment. Share that desire with others. Help them know that your vision is not for immediate glory but for the long haul. They will feel better knowing how deep your commitment goes.
- Leading crucial teams or significant projects brings out your best. Your greatest motivation may come when the stakes are at their highest. Let others know that when the game is on the line, you want the ball. They will be comforted by your confidence to take big risks and carry the responsibility on your own shoulders.
- You spend time thinking about the immensity of what you will achieve and what it will mean to the present as well as the future. Help others consider their legacy. Ask them what they are all about. What do they want to be known for? What do they want to leave behind? Show them a vision that looks past the moment and helps them assess the choices they make every day.
- Your Significance talents often put you in the spotlight. Use this opportunity to direct positive attention toward others. Your ability to champion others and set them up for success may be the best measure of your Significance.

## LEADING OTHERS WITH STRONG SIGNIFICANCE

- Arrange for these people to stand out for the right reasons, or they may try to make it happen themselves, perhaps inappropriately.
- Position these people so that they can associate with credible, productive, professional people. They like to surround themselves with the best.
- Encourage these people to praise other top achievers. They enjoy making other people feel successful.
- When these people make claims to excellence — and they will — help them picture the strengths they will have to develop to realize these claims. When coaching them, don't ask them to lower their aspirations; instead, suggest that they keep benchmarks for developing the relevant strengths.
- Because these people place such a premium on the perceptions of others, their self-esteem can suffer when people don't give them the recognition they deserve. At these times, draw their attention to their strengths, and encourage them to set new goals based on their strengths. These goals will help re-energize them.

# STRATEGIC

People exceptionally talented in the Strategic theme create alternative ways to proceed. Faced with any given scenario, they can quickly spot the relevant patterns and issues.

## LEADING WITH STRATEGIC

- When making decisions, discuss options candidly and thoroughly with those involved. Help them learn to trust your process of examining all alternatives and then working toward the optimal solution.
- Be aware of your own biases. Are you weighting possibilities objectively or leaning toward personal desires and comfort levels? Give each option its due. Enlist the help of a good thinking partner to ensure that you are making decisions for the right reasons. Others will respect your integrity and your desire for objectivity.
- Apply your strategic thinking to your relationships. Write down a list of the people who have the most positive influence in your life, and then map out specific things you can do to reinvest even more time and effort in each relationship.
- What are your goals for your family? Close friends? What are their goals? Turn your strategic thinking talents toward the important people in your life. Does someone have a dream but is seeing only obstacles? Does someone feel stuck with no options? You can help others circumvent a rocky path by pointing out alternate routes. Show that you care by helping them discover the possibilities.
- Take time to study the strategies that effective leaders you respect or admire employ. Input equals output. The insights you gather are likely to have a stimulating and resourceful effect on your strategic thinking. Make others aware that you are not bound by your own thinking and that your options and choices are supported by research. When they see the historical perspective and outside counsel you value, they will appreciate the stable foundation you build your ideas on.

- While others may consider only the tried-and-true route, you see the many possibilities that could result from taking a road less traveled. Set aside time specifically for considering "what ifs," and position yourself as a leader in that area. Explain your belief that focusing only on what has gone before may be more limiting than it is enlightening, and help others understand the benefits of carefully weighing all options. Your open-minded consideration will give others a sense of certainty that you are always on the lookout for the best path to take.
- Make sure that you are involved on the front end of new initiatives or enterprises. Your innovative yet methodical approach will be critical to the genesis of a venture because it will keep its creators from developing counterproductive tunnel vision. Broaden their view and increase their chances for success.
- Your strategic thinking keeps an achievable vision from deteriorating into a mere pipe dream. Lead people and organizations to fully consider all possible paths toward making a vision a reality. Wise forethought can remove obstacles before they appear and inspire others to move forward.
- Make yourself known as a resource for consultation with those who are stumped by a particular problem or hindered by an obstacle or barrier. By naturally seeing a way when others are convinced there is no way, you will encourage them and lead them to success.

## LEADING OTHERS WITH STRONG STRATEGIC

- Position these people on the leading edge of your organization. Their ability to anticipate problems and solutions will be invaluable. Ask them to sort through all of the possibilities and find the best way forward for your department. Suggest that they report back on the most effective strategy.

- Recognize these people's strong Strategic talents by sending them to a strategic planning or future-oriented seminar. The content will sharpen their ideas.
- These people are likely to have a talent for putting their ideas and thoughts into words. To refine their thinking, ask them to present their ideas to their colleagues or to write about their thoughts for internal distribution.

# WOO

People exceptionally talented in the Woo theme love the challenge of meeting new people and winning them over. They derive satisfaction from breaking the ice and making a connection with someone.

## LEADING WITH WOO

- You naturally charm others. Be sure to do it with integrity so they can trust you when it matters. Otherwise, you may have contacts but not followers.
- Others may share a good deal of information with you, even on a first meeting. How can you collect and store that information so people feel like their contributions are valued and, when necessary, protected? Invest in a system for maintaining contact with key people and logging important details of conversations. Make sure to exercise discretion when these details may be sensitive so others will trust you and keep in contact.
- You win friends and fans wherever you go. It's important to you that some of those contacts develop into long-lasting partnerships. Consider how to make those individuals feel a special connection with you — beyond the quick relationship you build with everyone you meet. How can you take important relationships to the next level? Invest the time and consideration necessary to do so.
- Leaders continuously build networks of trust, support and communication by contacting and relating with a wide range of people. By building a constituency, leaders make an impact across barriers of time, distance and culture. Create a map of your social network to define how broad you can go while still maintaining a genuine connection.
- Share the breadth and depth of your network with others. Knowing that you have contacts everywhere can help people feel sure that you

are in on the latest information and confident in the support you can expect when you need it.

- Get out and talk to your customers and your competitors, or get involved in the community. Effective leaders don't think their influence stops at their organization's walls. Rather, they recognize the larger network of connections and apply their influence within it. Having a broad base of support helps ensure the continued existence of organizations and opportunities for their expansion.
- Your Woo talents give you the ability to quicken the pulse of your organization. Recognize the power of your presence and how you can inspire an exchange of ideas. By simply starting conversations that engage your associates and bring talented people together, you will help dramatically improve individual and organizational performance.
- All of your meeting and greeting is sure to produce information that's valuable to those you are trying to help and guide — information from their customers, superiors and colleagues. Whenever you can, spread the good news and not the gossip. Let others know what they're doing well and how others perceive them. When you share the product of your wide-ranging influence with them, you validate the successes they have working with others.

## LEADING OTHERS WITH STRONG WOO

- Place these people at your organization's initial point of contact with the outside world.
- Help these people refine their system for remembering the names of the people they meet. Set a goal for them to learn the names of — and a few personal details about — as many customers as possible. They can help your organization make many connections in the marketplace.
- Unless these people also have strong talents in themes such as Empathy and Relator, don't expect them to enjoy a role in which they're asked to build close relationships with your customers. Instead, they may prefer to meet and greet, win over, and move on to the next prospect.
- These people's strong Woo talents will win you over and cause you to like them. When considering them for new roles and responsibilities, make sure that you look past your fondness to their genuine strengths. Don't let their Woo dazzle you.
- If possible, ask these people to be the builders of goodwill for your organization in your community. Have them represent your organization at community clubs and meetings.

# APPENDIX 2

## $Q^{12}$: The 12 Elements of Great Management

Gallup researchers have spent decades studying productive organizations, teams and individuals. The 12 engagement elements provide the most concise and comprehensive description of what it takes to build an engaging and productive workplace culture.

# Q01. I KNOW WHAT IS EXPECTED OF ME AT WORK.

Globally, one in two employees strongly agree that they know what is expected of them at work. By increasing that ratio to eight in 10, organizations could realize a 22% reduction in turnover, a 29% reduction in safety incidents and a 10% increase in productivity.

Clear expectations are the most basic and fundamental employee need. Employees who strongly agree that their job description aligns with the work they do are 2.5 times more likely than other employees to be engaged. The greatest pitfall of the first element is that managers assume the simplicity of the statement means the issue requires only a basic solution: "If people don't know what's expected, I'll just tell them."

But helping employees understand what their manager and organization expect from them requires much more than just telling them what to do. Employees need to grasp the fundamentals of their work, which are not limited to their job description. Unfortunately, less than half of employees (43%) strongly agree that they have a clear job description, and even fewer (41%) strongly agree that their job description aligns with the work they are asked to do. And, when leaders fail to articulate a clear strategy that aligns with managers' and employees' expectations, that further complicates this element of performance. In many cases, employees are held accountable for work that doesn't match their job description, which can confuse and frustrate them as they try to do their job and make decisions every day.

*What the best do:* Organizations and managers must get this right to optimize performance. The most effective managers define and discuss the explicit *and* implicit expectations for each employee's role and for the team. They paint a picture of outstanding performance and help employees understand how their work aligns with the success of their coworkers, their business area and the entire organization. The best managers involve employees in setting expectations and provide frequent formal and informal feedback to help employees meet and exceed those expectations. As priorities, roles and circumstances change, great managers continually assess and fine-tune expectations.

## Q02. I HAVE THE MATERIALS AND EQUIPMENT I NEED TO DO MY WORK RIGHT.

Globally, one in three employees strongly agree that they have the materials and equipment they need to do their work right. By doubling that ratio, organizations could realize an 11% increase in profitability, a 35% reduction in safety incidents and a 28% improvement in quality.

Of the 12 elements, the materials and equipment element is the strongest indicator of job stress. Despite the functional nature of this statement, this element measures both physical resource needs and potential barriers between the employer and employee. Employees get frustrated with their manager or organization for creating goals and expectations that seem impossible to achieve. But like expectations, materials and equipment are not just a checklist of tools organizations distribute to employees. They include the tangible and the intangible resources employees need to do their job. In today's workforce, information and empowerment are often as necessary as technology and office supplies.

*What the best do:* While there is a strong connection between this element and job stress, managers can take heart in this encouraging fact: People want to do their jobs well. They want to be productive. The secret to improving this element lies in managers' involvement, judgment and actions with their team. The most effective managers don't assume. They ask and listen to their employees' needs, advocate for those needs when they require organizational funds, and are transparent about what they can and cannot provide. The best managers are also resourceful.

They find ways to make the most of their team's ingenuity and talents when they cannot fully fund employee requests. From asking the best team members to share expertise, job tips and advice to finding time to learn from free educational sources, the best managers work with their employees and leaders to get their employees what they need.

## Q03. AT WORK, I HAVE THE OPPORTUNITY TO DO WHAT I DO BEST EVERY DAY.

### Globally, one in three employees strongly agree that they have the opportunity to do what they do best every day. By doubling that ratio, organizations could realize a 6% increase in customer engagement scores, an 11% increase in profitability, a 30% reduction in turnover and a 36% reduction in safety incidents.

One of the most powerful strategies for managers and organizations is giving their employees opportunities to apply the best of their natural selves (their talents) as well as their skills and knowledge. As the leading attribute employees look for in a new job — and its absence one of the main reasons employees leave a job — when people get to do what they do best every day at work, the organizations they work for get a boost in employee attraction, engagement and retention. Unfortunately, sometimes companies hesitate to put too much emphasis on an individual's abilities or accomplishments for fear others will feel hurt or left out. But individual differences give companies opportunities not just to advance business interests but to improve employees' careers and lives. And organizations that weave this element into their human capital strategy are more likely to attract and retain employees.

*What the best do:* Matching the right person with the right job is a complicated responsibility. Successful managers start by understanding what a job requires and then getting to know their employees as individuals. They build a performance development environment where there is ongoing dialogue, awareness and recognition of talents. They talk to each employee about their unique value and learn how each one contributes that value to the team, while making regular adjustments to align work, when possible, with team members' talents. They understand that, realistically, employees will have tasks and responsibilities that don't quite fall into the "do what I do best" category. But they ensure that each employee's overall role makes the most of their talents and strengths. And they look for career opportunities that empower employees to use their talents and strengths. Ultimately, the best managers know where their employees excel and position them so they are engaged as individuals who also provide value to the organization.

## Q04. IN THE LAST SEVEN DAYS, I HAVE RECEIVED RECOGNITION OR PRAISE FOR DOING GOOD WORK.

Globally, one in four employees strongly agree that they have received recognition or praise for doing good work in the last week. By moving that ratio to six in 10, organizations could realize a 28% improvement in quality, a 31% reduction in absenteeism and a 12% reduction in shrinkage.

Top performers are hard to find. And once an organization hires them, it needs to make sure these employees feel valued for their work and contributions, or they could be at risk of leaving. Employees who do not feel adequately recognized are twice as likely to say they'll quit in the next year. And given the low number of employees who strongly agree with this item, this element of engagement and performance might be one of the greatest missed opportunities for leaders and managers. Workplace recognition motivates, provides a sense of accomplishment and makes employees feel valued for the work they do. Recognition also sends a message to other employees about what success looks like. So beyond communicating appreciation, rewarding personal achievement and providing motivation, leaders and managers can use recognition to reinforce desired behaviors for other employees.

*What the best do:* The challenge of the fourth element lies in its specificity and immediacy. Many companies try to increase recognition by implementing technology-based recognition tools for immediate and peer-based feedback. While these tools can help reinforce a recognition-rich environment, organizations need to be cautious about relying on them too much. The best recognition is highly individualized. What is meaningful to one person may not be as valuable to another. In a Gallup study, employees revealed that public recognition or acknowledgement via an award is the most *memorable* form of recognition, followed by private recognition from a boss, peer or customer. The best managers learn how individual employees like to be recognized and praise them for doing good work and achieving their goals while emphasizing why their performance was important. In the same Gallup study, employees revealed that the most *meaningful* recognition came from their manager, leader or CEO. Technology alone should never replace face-to-face recognition. The most effective leaders and managers promote a recognition-rich environment with praise coming from multiple sources at multiple times.

# Q05. MY SUPERVISOR, OR SOMEONE AT WORK, SEEMS TO CARE ABOUT ME AS A PERSON.

Globally, four in 10 employees strongly agree that their supervisor, or someone at work, seems to care about them as a person. By doubling that ratio to eight in 10, organizations could realize an 8% improvement in customer engagement scores, a 46% reduction in safety incidents and a 41% reduction in absenteeism.

Employees need to know that they are more than just a number. They need to know that someone is concerned about them as people first and as employees second. The fifth element of engagement may seem like a "soft" aspect of management, but there are key payoffs when people work in an environment where they feel safe. They are more likely to experiment with new ideas, share information and support each other in their work and personal lives. They are prepared to give their manager and organization the benefit of the doubt, and they feel more equipped to strike a balance between their work and personal lives. In turn, they are more likely to be advocates for their employer.

*What the best do:* Because people cannot manufacture caring about someone else, it is not surprising that few managers and teams take defined actions to meet this employee need. This is one of the least likely elements a manager and team will focus on after receiving engagement results. But the very best organizations, managers and teams *do* focus on meeting this employee need by investing in employees through awareness, time and intention. They know employees as individuals, acknowledge achievements, have performance conversations, conduct formal reviews and, above all, respect their employees. The most successful managers create opportunities for development and career growth while also supporting an environment of team collaboration and cohesion. In doing so, they make employees genuinely feel valued and respected.

# Q06. THERE IS SOMEONE AT WORK WHO ENCOURAGES MY DEVELOPMENT.

Globally, three in 10 employees strongly agree that someone at work encourages their development. By moving that ratio to six in 10, organizations could realize a 6% improvement in customer engagement scores, an 11% improvement in profitability and a 28% reduction in absenteeism.

Gallup data show that lack of development and career growth is the No. 1 reason employees leave a job. Development is part of the unwritten social contract workers expect when they are hired. However, personal and professional development does not occur in a vacuum. It takes effort and attention. Employees need help navigating their career, whether that is through sponsorship, coaching, protection, exposure, visibility or challenging work assignments. One common misunderstanding about this element of engagement is that "development" means "promotion." But they are not the same thing. A promotion is a one-time event. Development is a process of understanding each person's unique talents and strengths and finding roles, positions and projects that allow employees to apply them.

*What the best do:* Development comes back to the manager-employee relationship, which should include defining goals, improving performance and assessing progress. Great managers discuss employees' professional growth and development with them more than once a year. They have ongoing conversations with employees and create opportunities for them to learn, grow, acquire new skills, try different ways of doing things and take on exciting challenges. The best managers don't look at development as a finished product. They coach their employees by identifying wins and misses, motivating them to go beyond what they think they can do, connecting them with potential mentors, and holding them accountable for their performance.

## Q07. AT WORK, MY OPINIONS SEEM TO COUNT.

Globally, one in four employees strongly agree that their opinions count at work. By doubling that ratio, organizations could realize a 22% reduction in turnover, a 33% reduction in safety incidents and a 10% increase in productivity.

The days of managers and leaders having to know it all are quickly vanishing as organizations accept the fact that they are facing unprecedented change, competition and stagnant organic growth. No leader or manager can survive alone, nor do they have all the answers. Asking for and considering individuals' input leads to more informed decision-making and better results. This element of engagement is powerful and measures employees' sense of value and contribution. It reveals if employees feel appreciated for their insights and have opportunities to make significant contributions to their work environment. Because they are on the front lines, employees want to know that their employer is considering their input when implementing changes, and they feel empowered when they have an opportunity and a channel to voice their opinions to someone who will listen without retaliation.

*What the best do:* The most successful leaders and managers frequently and sincerely harness the asset of their employees' knowledge to push through change, solve problems and innovate for growth. They listen to what is happening on the ground floor and ask for input along the way. How a manager listens to and processes an employee's thoughts and ideas can shape whether or not the employee feels valued for their contributions. The best managers promote open dialogue and encourage creativity and new ideas that can positively influence business results. They also provide open and honest feedback on employees' opinions and ideas — advocating for good ones and addressing unfeasible ones. Great managers create feedback loops so people feel like they are involved in the decision-making process, know what happens when they offer an opinion or suggestion, and understand why a recommendation may not be possible.

# Q08. THE MISSION OR PURPOSE OF MY ORGANIZATION MAKES ME FEEL MY JOB IS IMPORTANT.

Globally, one in three employees strongly agree that the mission or purpose of their organization makes them feel their job is important. By doubling that ratio, organizations could realize a 34% reduction in absenteeism, a 41% drop in patient safety incidents and a 19% improvement in quality.

The absence of many engagement elements — job clarity, proper equipment and resources, work that aligns with one's talents, consistent feedback — can create real obstacles to productivity. It's easy to see why employees need these elements to do their job well. The same cannot be said for the eighth element. It is a strictly emotional need, and a higher-level one at that, as if employees cannot energize themselves to do all they could do without knowing how their job fits into the grander scheme of things. The data say that is just what happens. If a job were just a job, it really wouldn't matter where someone worked. But employees want their job to have meaning. In fact, for millennials, this element was among the strongest drivers of retention. For reasons that transcend the practical needs that earning a living fulfills, people look for their contribution to a higher purpose. Employees want to believe in what their employer does. People like the feeling of belonging to a community, whether that community is their company, sports team or church. Yet, many leaders and managers think that putting the organization's mission statement on a wall is enough for employees to feel this connection. It is not.

*What the best do:* More than any other element, managers cannot be solely responsible for mission and purpose, but they do play a large role. Managers have to help employees understand how their role fits in with the bigger picture. The most effective managers cultivate a feeling of purpose among employees by clarifying the organization's mission and helping employees discover how their role contributes to attaining that mission by connecting it to their daily tasks. Great managers create opportunities for employees to share their mission moments and stories about how the organization is achieving its purpose. But leaders also play a large role in ensuring that the mission and purpose are clearly stated and aligned with the employee experience. Employees know when an organization's mission is just talk, and they need to be able to experience real mission in the culture and deliver on it when meeting customer needs.

## Q09. MY ASSOCIATES OR FELLOW EMPLOYEES ARE COMMITTED TO DOING QUALITY WORK.

Globally, one in three employees strongly agree that their associates are committed to doing quality work. By doubling this ratio, organizations could realize a 31% reduction in turnover and absenteeism, a 12% improvement in profit, and a 7% increase in customer engagement scores.

Trusting that one's coworkers share a commitment to quality is vital to excellent team performance. And as work is becoming more interconnected, interdependent and project-based, this element is critical. The worst performer on the team sets the team's standards. Employees need to be in an environment where there is mutual trust and respect for each other's efforts and results. This starts with a deep awareness of work standards and team expectations. By a 6-to-1 margin, people are more upset with a colleague who has the ability but does not try than with a colleague who tries hard but does not have much ability. For highly productive employees, there is a vast difference between being assigned to a team and actually identifying with that team. Employees want to know that everyone on their team is pitching in.

*What the best do:* Employees can become resentful when they have a coworker who is not contributing or being held accountable for subpar performance. Great managers do not sit idly by and let a team erode. They establish performance and accountability standards and ensure that all team members are held responsible for them. These managers foster an environment where employees can consistently produce high-quality work by outlining quality standards for each task or function, confirming that new team members know the importance of quality, recognizing employees who excel, and having each team member share their expectations for quality work during team meetings. And managers working in cross-functional or matrix environments have an additional duty. Though they may not have the authority to coach employees who don't report to them, they do have a responsibility to discuss expectations with project leaders, seek feedback on their employees' experience with other departments and work across functional lines to establish shared levels of quality. Cross-functional alignment is critical for applying quality standards in matrix structures.

## Q10. I HAVE A BEST FRIEND AT WORK.

Globally, three in 10 employees strongly agree that they have a best friend at work. By moving that ratio to six in 10, organizations could realize 28% fewer safety incidents, 5% higher customer engagement scores and 10% higher profit.

The 10th element of engagement is the most controversial of the 12. More than any other $Q^{12}$ statement, "I have a best friend at work" tends to generate questions and skepticism. But there is one stubborn fact: It predicts performance. Early research on employee engagement and the $Q^{12}$ elements revealed a unique social trend among employees on top-performing teams. When employees have a deep sense of affiliation with their team members, they take positive actions that benefit the business — actions they may not otherwise even consider.

The impact of friendships is context dependent — our social lives, and their effect on performance, don't exist in a vacuum. Likewise, the $Q^{12}$ elements are not isolated; they work together to create the employee's work experience. Having a best friend at work is particularly strong in predicting retention when people know what is expected of them and have the materials and equipment to do their work.

Beyond business outcomes or scientific validity, though, is a very simple premise: To ignore friendships is to ignore human nature. Yet, many organizations continue to abide by policies that dissuade or flat out discourage people from socializing or becoming friends.

*What the best do:* The best employers recognize that people want to build meaningful friendships and that company loyalty is built on these relationships. But friendships at work need to be put in the proper context. Managers should not try to manufacture friendships or to make everyone be friends. Rather, they should create situations where people can get to know each other. The best managers look for opportunities to get their team together for events, encourage people to share stories about themselves and plan for time to socialize at work when it will not disrupt customer service or other performance outcomes.

For most teams and organizations, the best friend item should not be their first priority. In fact, if organizations don't meet employees' basic needs (such as clear expectations, an opportunity to do what they do best, a manager who cares about them and opportunities to develop), then friendships can encourage gripe sessions. On the other hand, if basic needs are met, friendships can take on a powerful dynamic in which informal conversations turn into innovative discussions about how the organization can grow.

## Q11. IN THE LAST SIX MONTHS, SOMEONE AT WORK HAS TALKED TO ME ABOUT MY PROGRESS.

Globally, one in three employees strongly agree that someone at work has talked to them about their progress in the last six months. By doubling that ratio, organizations could realize 38% fewer safety incidents, 28% less absenteeism and 11% higher profit.

For all the complexity of performance appraisals — balanced scorecards, 360-degree feedback, self-evaluations and forced grading reports — the statement that reveals the best connection between perceptions of evaluations and actual employee performance is remarkably simple: "In the last six months, someone at work has talked to me about my progress." This statement does not specify that the discussion is an official review. What is most important to employees is that they understand how they are doing, how their work is perceived and what the future holds. There is nothing wrong with formal evaluations, and there are many reasons to recommend them. But success with the 11th element of engagement comes down to what happens *between* performance reviews. When a manager regularly checks in with their employees' progress, team members are more likely to believe they get paid fairly, more likely to stay with the company, less likely to have accidents and more than twice as likely to recommend the company to others as a great place to work.

*What the best do:* The best managers know that for employees to grow in their jobs, they must first know where they stand. The best managers know that feedback is essential to an employee's engagement and performance. They help employees see where they are in their professional journey and collaborate with them to set developmental goals. The most effective managers modify their feedback to fit each individual employee's personality, circumstances and potential. They regularly check in with employees and, without micromanaging, help them improve their performance by clarifying job expectations, developing and tracking performance metrics, learning about their goals, and finding creative ways to help them reach their goals. Above all, these managers serve as coaches — motivating, guiding and directing employees.

## Q12. THIS LAST YEAR, I HAVE HAD OPPORTUNITIES AT WORK TO LEARN AND GROW.

Globally, one in three employees strongly agree that they have opportunities at work to learn and grow. By doubling that ratio, organizations could realize 39% less absenteeism, 36% fewer safety incidents and 14% higher productivity.

The desire to learn and grow is a basic human need and one that is required to maintain employee momentum and motivation. This element is also critical in a time when companies are hungry for organic growth. When people grow, companies grow and are more likely stay in business. When employees feel like they are learning and growing, they work harder and more efficiently. But when they have to do the same thing every day without a chance to learn something new, they rarely stay enthusiastic or excited about their jobs. Many leaders and managers mistakenly attribute this element solely to *additional* training. But learning and growing can take many forms: finding a better way to do a job, earning a promotion or learning a new skill. The best employees are never quite satisfied. They always strive to find better, more productive ways to work. And where there is growth, there is innovation.

*What the best do:* For many people, progress in a role distinguishes a career from just a job. To improve and develop employees, successful managers challenge them. The best managers create individual learning opportunities that tie to a larger individual development plan and frequently check in on employees' progress by asking them what they are learning and how often they apply what they learn to their roles. Great managers understand that learning and growing is a never-ending process. They assess employee capabilities, look for ways to align these capabilities with long-term goals and aspirations, and develop short-term goals with each employee. Above all, these managers help employees see the value in new opportunities and willingly encourage them to take on new responsibilities or even new roles that can elevate their individual talents.

# APPENDIX 3

## The Relationship Between Engagement at Work and Organizational Outcomes

### Q[12]® Meta-Analysis: Ninth Edition

James K. Harter, Ph.D., Gallup
Frank L. Schmidt, Ph.D., University of Iowa
Sangeeta Agrawal, M.S., Gallup
Stephanie K. Plowman, M.A., Gallup
Anthony Blue, M.A., Gallup

# INTRODUCTION

## FOREWORD

In the 1930s, George Gallup began a worldwide study of human needs and satisfactions. He pioneered the development of scientific sampling processes to measure popular opinion. In addition to his polling work, Dr. Gallup completed landmark research on wellbeing, studying the factors common among people who lived to be 95 and older (Gallup & Hill, 1959). Over the next several decades, Dr. Gallup and his colleagues conducted numerous polls throughout the world, covering many aspects of people's lives. His early world polls dealt with topics such as family, religion, politics, personal happiness, economics, health, education, safety and attitudes toward work. In the 1970s, Dr. Gallup reported that less than half of those employed in North America were highly satisfied with their work (Gallup, 1976). Work satisfaction was even lower in Western Europe, Latin America, Africa and the Far East.

Satisfaction at work has become a widespread focus for researchers. In addition to Dr. Gallup's early work, the topic of job satisfaction has been studied and written about in more than 10,000 articles and publications. Because most people spend a high percentage of their waking hours at work, studies of the workplace are of great interest for psychologists, sociologists, economists, anthropologists and physiologists. The process of managing and improving the workplace is crucial and presents great challenges to nearly every organization. So it is vital that the instruments used to create change do, in fact, measure workplace dynamics that predict key outcomes — outcomes that a variety of organizational leaders would consider important. After all, organizational leaders are in the best position to create interest in and momentum for job satisfaction research.

Parallel to Dr. Gallup's early polling work, Don Clifton, a psychologist and professor at the University of Nebraska, began studying the causes of success in education and business. Dr. Clifton founded Selection Research, Incorporated (SRI) in 1969. While most psychologists were busy studying dysfunction and the cause of disease, Clifton and his colleagues focused their careers on the science of strengths-based psychology, the study of what makes people flourish.

Their early discoveries led to hundreds of research studies focused on successful individuals and teams across a broad spectrum of industries and job types. In particular, research on successful learning and workplace environments led to numerous studies of successful teachers and managers. This work included extensive research on individual differences and the environments that best facilitate success. Early in their studies, the researchers discovered that simply measuring employees' satisfaction was insufficient to create sustainable change. Satisfaction needed to be specified in terms of its most important elements, and it needed to be measured and reported in a way that could be used by the people who could take action and create change.

Further research revealed that change happens most efficiently at a local level — at the level of the front-line, manager-led team. For an executive, the front-line team is their direct reports, and for a plant manager, the front-line team is the people they manage each day. Studying great managers, Gallup scientists learned that optimal decision-making happens when information regarding decisions is collected at a local level, close to the everyday action.

Dr. Clifton's work merged with Dr. Gallup's work in 1988, when Gallup and SRI combined, enabling the blending of progressive management science with top survey and polling science. Gallup and Clifton spent much of their lives studying people's opinions, attitudes, talents and behaviors. To do this, they wrote questions, recorded the responses and studied which questions elicited differential responses and related to meaningful outcomes. In the case of survey research, some questions are unbiased and elicit meaningful opinions, while others do not. In the case of management research, some questions elicit responses that predict future performance, while others do not.

Developing the right questions is an iterative process in which scientists write questions and conduct analysis. The research and questions are refined and rephrased. Additional analysis is conducted. The questions are refined and rephrased again. And the process is repeated. Gallup has followed the iterative process in devising the survey tool that is the subject of this report, Gallup's Q[12] instrument, which is designed to measure employee engagement conditions.

The next sections will provide an overview of the many decades of research that have gone into the development and validation of Gallup's Q[12] employee engagement instrument. Following this overview, we present a meta-analysis of 339 research studies exploring the relationship between employee engagement and performance across 230 organizations and 82,248 business/work units that include 1,882,131 employees.

## DEVELOPMENT OF THE Q[12]

Beginning in the 1950s, Clifton started studying work and learning environments to determine the factors that contribute positively to those environments and that enable people to capitalize on their unique talents. It was through this early work that Clifton began using science and the study of strengths to research individuals' frames of reference and attitudes.

From the 1950s to the 1970s, Clifton continued his research of students, counselors, managers, teachers and employees. He used various rating scales and interview techniques to study individual differences, analyzing questions and factors that explain dissimilarities in people. The concepts he studied included "focusing on strengths versus weaknesses," "relationships," "personnel support," "friendships" and "learning." Various questions were written and tested, including many early versions of the Q[12] items. Ongoing feedback techniques were first developed with the intent of asking questions, collecting data and encouraging ongoing discussion of the results to provide feedback and potential improvement — a measurement-based feedback process. To learn causes of employee turnover, exit interviews were conducted with employees who left organizations. A common reason for leaving an organization focused on the quality of the manager.

In the 1980s, Gallup scientists continued the iterative process by studying high-performing individuals and teams. Studies involved assessments of individual talents and workplace attitudes. As a starting point for questionnaire design, numerous qualitative analyses were conducted, including interviews and focus groups. Gallup researchers asked top-performing individuals or teams to describe their work environments and their thoughts, feelings and behaviors related to success.

The researchers used qualitative data to generate hypotheses and insights into the distinguishing factors leading to success. From these hypotheses, they wrote and tested questions. They also conducted numerous quantitative studies throughout the 1980s, including exit interviews, to continue to learn causes of employee turnover. Qualitative analyses such as focus groups and interviews formed the basis for lengthy and comprehensive employee surveys, called "Organizational Development Audits" or "Managing Attitudes for Excellence" surveys. Many of these surveys included 100 to 200 items. Quantitative analyses included factor analyses to assess the dimensionality of the survey data; regression analyses to identify uniqueness and redundancies in the data; and criterion-related validity analyses to identify questions that correlate with meaningful outcomes such as overall satisfaction, commitment and productivity. The scientists developed feedback protocols to facilitate the feedback of survey results to managers and employees. Such protocols and their use in practice helped researchers learn which items were most useful in creating dialogue and stimulating change.

One outgrowth of a management research practice that was focused on talent and environment was the theory of talent maximization in an organization:

*Per-person productivity = Talent x (Relationship + Right Expectation + Recognition/Reward)*

These concepts would later become embedded in the foundational elements of the Q[12].

Over time, SRI and Gallup researchers conducted numerous studies of manager success patterns that focused on the talents of the manager *and* the environments that best facilitated success. By integrating knowledge of managerial talent with survey data on employee attitudes, scientists had a unique perspective on what it takes to build a successful workplace environment. Themes such as "individualized perception," "performance orientation," "mission," "recognition," "learning and growing," "expectations," and "the right fit" continued to emerge. In addition to studies of management, researchers conducted numerous studies with successful teachers, students and learning environments.

In the 1990s, the iterative process continued. During this time, Gallup researchers developed the first version of the $Q^{12}$ ("The Gallup Workplace Audit" or GWA) in an effort to efficiently capture the most important workplace attitudes. Qualitative *and* quantitative analyses continued. In that decade, more than 1,000 focus groups were conducted, and hundreds of instruments were developed, many of them with several additional items. Scientists also continued to use exit interviews; these revealed the importance of the manager in retaining employees. Studies of the $Q^{12}$ and other survey items were conducted in various countries throughout the world, including the United States, Canada, Mexico, Great Britain, Japan and Germany. Gallup researchers obtained international cross-cultural feedback on Gallup's core items, which provided context on the applicability of the items across different cultures. Various scale types were also tested, including variations of 5-point and dichotomous response options.

Quantitative analyses of survey data included descriptive statistics, factor analyses, discriminant analyses, criterion-related validity analyses, reliability analyses, regression analyses and other correlational analyses. Gallup scientists continued to study the core concepts that differentiated successful from less successful work units and the expressions that best captured those concepts. In 1997, the criterion-related studies were combined into a meta-analysis to study the relationship of employee satisfaction and engagement (as measured by the $Q^{12}$) to business/work unit profitability, productivity, employee retention and customer satisfaction/loyalty across 1,135 business/work units (Harter & Creglow, 1997). Meta-analysis also enabled researchers to study the generalizability of the relationship between engagement and outcomes. Results of this confirmatory analysis revealed substantial criterion-related validity for each of the $Q^{12}$ items.

As criterion-related validity studies are ongoing, the meta-analysis was updated in 1998 (Harter & Creglow, 1998) and included 2,528 business/work units; in 2000 (Harter & Schmidt, 2000), when it included 7,939 business/work units; in 2002 (Harter & Schmidt, 2002), when it included 10,885 business/work units; in 2003 (Harter, Schmidt, & Killham, 2003), when it included 13,751 business/work units; in 2006 (Harter, Schmidt, Killham, & Asplund, 2006), when it included 23,910 business/work units; in 2009 (Harter, Schmidt, Killham, & Agrawal, 2009), when it included 32,394 business/work units; and in 2013 (Harter, Schmidt, Agrawal, & Plowman, 2013), when it included 49,928 business/work units. This report provides the ninth published iteration of Gallup's $Q^{12}$ meta-analysis focusing on the relationship between employee engagement and performance.

As with the 2013 report, this report expands the number of business/work units and increases the total composition of different industries and countries studied.

Since its final wording and order were completed in 1998, the $Q^{12}$ has been administered to more than 30 million employees in 198 different countries and 72 languages. Additionally, a series of studies has been conducted examining the cross-cultural properties of the instrument (Harter & Agrawal, 2011).

## INTRODUCTION TO THE STUDY

The quality of an organization's human resources is perhaps the leading indicator of its growth and sustainability. The attainment of a workplace with high-caliber employees starts with the selection of the right people for the right jobs. Numerous studies have documented the utility of valid selection instruments and systems in the selection of the right people (Schmidt, Hunter, McKenzie, & Muldrow, 1979; Hunter & Schmidt, 1983; Huselid, 1995; Schmidt & Rader, 1999; Harter, Hayes, & Schmidt, 2004).

After employees are hired, they make decisions and take actions every day that can affect the success of their organizations. Many of these decisions and actions are influenced by their own internal motivations and drives. One can also hypothesize that the way employees are treated and the way they treat one another can positively affect their actions — or can place their organizations at risk. For example, researchers have found positive relationships between general workplace attitudes and service intentions, customer perceptions (Schmit & Allscheid, 1995) and individual performance outcomes (Iaffaldano & Muchinsky, 1985). An updated meta-analysis has revealed a substantial relationship between individual job satisfaction and individual performance (Judge, Thoresen, Bono, & Patton, 2001). Before 2000, the vast majority of job satisfaction research and subsequent meta-analyses had collected and studied data at the individual employee level.

There is also evidence at the workgroup or business unit level that employee attitudes relate to various organizational outcomes. Organizational-level research has focused primarily on cross-sectional studies. Independent studies found relationships between employee attitudes and performance outcomes such as safety (Zohar, 1980, 2000), customer experiences (Schneider, Parkington, & Buxton, 1980; Ulrich, Halbrook, Meder, Stuchlik, & Thorpe, 1991; Schneider & Bowen, 1993; Schneider, Ashworth, Higgs, & Carr, 1996; Schmit & Allscheid, 1995; Reynierse & Harker, 1992; Johnson, 1996; Wiley, 1991), financials (Denison, 1990; Schneider, 1991) and employee turnover (Ostroff, 1992). A study by Batt (2002) used multivariate analysis to examine the relationship between human resource practices (including employee participation in decision-making) and sales growth. Gallup has conducted large-scale meta-analyses, most recently studying 49,928 business and work units regarding the concurrent and predictive relationship of employee attitudes (satisfaction and engagement) with safety, customer attitudes, financials, employee retention, absenteeism, quality metrics and merchandise shrinkage (Harter et al., 2013; Harter et al., 2009; Harter et al., 2006; Harter et al., 2003; Harter, Schmidt, & Hayes, 2002; Harter & Schmidt, 2002; Harter & Schmidt, 2000; Harter & Creglow, 1998; Harter & Creglow, 1997). This meta-analysis, repeated across time, has found consistently that there are positive concurrent and predictive relationships between employee attitudes and various important business outcomes. It has also found that these relationships generalize across a wide range of situations (industries, business/

work unit types and countries). Additional independent studies have found similar results (Whitman, Van Rooy, & Viswesvaran, 2010; Edmans, 2012).

Even though it has been much more common to study employee opinion data at the individual level, studying data at the business unit or workgroup level is critical because that is where the data are typically reported (because of confidentiality concerns, employee surveys are reported at a broader business unit or workgroup level). In addition, business-unit-level research usually provides opportunities to establish links to outcomes that are directly relevant to most businesses — outcomes like customer loyalty, profitability, productivity, employee turnover, safety incidents, merchandise shrinkage and quality variables that are often aggregated and reported at the business unit level.

Another advantage to reporting and studying data at the business unit or workgroup level is that instrument item scores are of similar reliability to dimension scores for individual-level analysis. This is because at the business unit or workgroup level, each item score is an average of many individuals' scores. This means that employee surveys reported at a business unit or workgroup level can be more efficient or parsimonious in length, i.e., because item-level measurement error is less of a concern. See Harter and Schmidt (2006) for a more complete discussion of job satisfaction research and the advantages of conducting unit-level analyses.

One potential problem with such business-unit-level studies is limited data as a result of a limited number of business units (the number of business units becomes the sample size) or limited access to outcome measures that one can compare across business units. For this reason, many of these studies are limited in statistical power, and as such, results from individual studies may appear to conflict with one another. Meta-analysis techniques provide the opportunity to pool such studies together to obtain more precise estimates of the strength of effects and their generalizability.

This paper's purpose is to present the results of an updated meta-analysis of the relationship between employee workplace perceptions and business unit outcomes based on currently available data collected with Gallup clients. The focus of this study is on Gallup's $Q^{12}$ instrument. The $Q^{12}$ items — which were selected because of their importance at the business unit or workgroup level — measure employee perceptions of the quality of people-related management practices in their business units.

## DESCRIPTION OF THE $Q^{12}$

In short, the development of the $Q^{12}$ was based on more than 30 years of accumulated quantitative and qualitative research. Its reliability, convergent validity and criterion-related validity have been extensively studied. It is an instrument validated through prior psychometric studies as well as practical considerations regarding its usefulness for managers in creating change in the workplace.

In designing the items included in the $Q^{12}$, researchers took into account that, from an actionability standpoint, there are two broad categories of employee survey items: those that are reflective measures of attitudinal outcomes (satisfaction, loyalty, pride, customer service perceptions and intent to stay with the company) and those that are formative measures of actionable issues that drive these outcomes. The $Q^{12}$ measures the actionable issues for management — those predictive of attitudinal outcomes such as satisfaction, loyalty, pride and so on. On Gallup's standard $Q^{12}$ instrument, after an overall satisfaction item, are 12 items measuring issues we have found to be actionable (changeable) at the supervisor or manager level — items measuring perceptions of elements of the work situation such as role clarity, resources, fit between abilities and requirements, receiving feedback, and feeling appreciated. The $Q^{12}$ is a formative measure of "engagement conditions," each of which is a contributor to engagement through the measure of its causes.

More detailed discussion of the practical application of each of the $Q^{12}$ items is provided in Wagner and Harter (2006) and in various articles posted on Gallup.com.

As a total instrument (sum or mean of items Q01-Q12), the Q[12] has a Cronbach's alpha of 0.91 at the business unit level. The meta-analytic convergent validity of the equally weighted mean (or sum) of items Q01-Q12 (GrandMean) to the equally weighted mean (or sum) of additional items in longer surveys (measuring all known facets of job satisfaction and engagement) is 0.91. This provides evidence that the Q[12], as a composite measure, captures the general factor in longer employee surveys. Individual items correlate to their broader dimension true-score values, on average, at approximately 0.70. While the Q[12] is a measure of actionable engagement conditions, its composite has high convergent validity with affective satisfaction and other direct measures of work engagement (see Harter & Schmidt, 2008, for further discussion of convergent and discriminant validity issues and the construct of "engagement").

As previously mentioned, this is the ninth published iteration of the Q[12] business-unit-level meta-analysis. Compared with the previous meta-analysis, the current meta-analysis includes a larger number of studies, business units and countries. The current meta-analysis includes nearly three times more business units with patient safety data, 81% more business units with productivity data, 68% more with safety data, 48% more with profitability data, 42% more with turnover data, 34% more with quality or defects data, 39% more with absenteeism data, 27% more with customer data, and 16% more with shrinkage data. As such, this study provides a substantial update of new and recent data.

The coverage of research studies includes business units in 73 countries, including Asia (Bangladesh, Cambodia, China, Hong Kong, India, Indonesia, Japan, Korea, Malaysia, Nepal, Pakistan, the Philippines, Singapore, Sri Lanka, Taiwan, Thailand and Turkey), Australia, New Zealand, Europe (Austria, Belgium, France, Germany, Greece, Ireland, Italy, Netherlands, Spain, Sweden, Switzerland and the United Kingdom), former communist countries (Czech Republic, Hungary, Lithuania, Poland and Russia), Latin America (Argentina, Bolivia, Brazil, Chile, Colombia, Ecuador, El Salvador, Guatemala, Honduras, Mexico, Nicaragua and Peru), the Middle East (Bahrain, Brunei Darussalam, Egypt, Jordan, Oman and United Arab Emirates), North America (Canada and the United States), Africa (Botswana, Burkina Faso, Ethiopia, Gambia, Ghana, Kenya, Nigeria, Rwanda, Tanzania, Togo, Uganda, Zambia and Zimbabwe) and the Caribbean (Barbados, Bermuda, the Dominican Republic and Haiti). Thirty-eight companies included in the present meta-analysis operate exclusively in countries outside the U.S.

This meta-analysis includes all available Gallup studies (whether published or unpublished) and has no risk of publication bias.

# META-ANALYSIS, HYPOTHESIS, METHODS AND RESULTS

## META-ANALYSIS

A meta-analysis is a statistical integration of data accumulated across many different studies. As such, it provides uniquely powerful information because it controls for measurement and sampling errors and other idiosyncrasies that distort the results of individual studies. A meta-analysis eliminates biases and provides an estimate of true validity or true relationship between two or more variables. Statistics typically calculated during meta-analyses also allow the researcher to explore the presence, or lack, of moderators of relationships.

More than 1,000 meta-analyses have been conducted in the psychological, educational, behavioral, medical and personnel selection fields. The research literature in the behavioral and social sciences fields includes a multitude of individual studies with apparently conflicting conclusions. Meta-analysis, however, allows the researcher to estimate the mean relationship between variables and make corrections for artifactual sources of variation in findings across studies. It provides a method by which researchers can determine whether validities and relationships generalize across various situations (e.g., across firms or geographical locations).

This paper will not provide a full review of meta-analysis. Rather, the authors encourage readers to consult the following sources for background information and detailed descriptions of the more recent meta-analytic methods: Schmidt and Hunter (2015); Schmidt (1992); Hunter and Schmidt (1990, 2004); Lipsey and Wilson (1993); Bangert-Drowns (1986); and Schmidt, Hunter, Pearlman, and Rothstein-Hirsh (1985).

## HYPOTHESIS AND STUDY CHARACTERISTICS

**The hypotheses examined for this meta-analysis were:**

*Hypothesis 1:* Business-unit-level employee engagement will have positive average correlations with the business unit outcomes of customer loyalty, productivity and profitability and negative correlations with employee turnover, employee safety incidents (accidents), absenteeism, shrinkage (theft), patient safety incidents (mortality and falls) and quality (defects).

*Hypothesis 2:* The correlations between engagement and business unit outcomes will generalize across organizations for all business unit outcomes. That is, these correlations will not vary substantially across organizations. And in particular, there will be few, if any, organizations with zero correlations or those in the opposite direction from Hypothesis 1.

Gallup's inferential database includes 339 studies conducted as proprietary research for 230 independent organizations. In each $Q^{12}$, one or more of the $Q^{12}$ items was used (as a part of standard policy starting in 1997, all items were included in all studies), and data were aggregated at the business unit level and correlated with the following aggregate business unit performance measures:

- customer metrics (referred to as customer loyalty)
- profitability
- productivity
- turnover
- safety incidents
- absenteeism
- shrinkage
- patient safety incidents
- quality (defects)

That is, in these analyses, the unit of analysis was the business or work unit, not the individual employee.

Correlations (r values) were calculated, estimating the relationship of business/work unit average measures of employee engagement (the mean of the $Q^{12}$ items) to each of these nine general outcomes. Correlations were calculated across business/work units in each company, and these correlation coefficients were entered into a database. The researchers then calculated mean validities, standard deviations of validities and validity generalization statistics for each of the nine business/work unit outcome measures.

As with previous meta-analyses, some of the studies were concurrent validity studies, where engagement and performance were measured in roughly the same time period or with engagement measurement slightly trailing behind the performance measurement (because engagement is relatively stable and a summation of the recent past, such studies are considered "concurrent"). Predictive validity studies involve measuring engagement at time 1 and performance at time 2. "Predictive" validity estimates were obtained for 50% of the organizations included in this meta-analysis.

This paper does not directly address issues of causality, which are best addressed with meta-analytic longitudinal data, consideration of multiple variables and path analysis. Issues of causality are discussed and examined extensively in other sources (Harter, Schmidt, Asplund, Killham, & Agrawal, 2010). Findings of causal studies suggest that engagement and financial performance are reciprocally related, but that engagement is a stronger predictor of financial outcomes than the reverse. The relationship between engagement and financial performance appears to be mediated by its causal relationship with other outcomes such as customer perceptions and employee retention. That is, financial performance is a downstream outcome that is influenced by the effect of engagement on shorter-term outcomes such as customer perceptions and employee retention.

Studies for the current meta-analysis were selected so that each organization was represented once in each analysis. For several organizations, multiple studies were conducted. To include the best possible information for each organization represented in the study, some basic rules were used. If two concurrent studies were conducted for the same client (where $Q^{12}$ and outcome data were collected concurrently, i.e., in the same year), then the weighted average effect sizes across the multiple studies were entered as the value for that organization. If an organization had a concurrent *and* a predictive study (where the $Q^{12}$ was collected in year 1 and outcomes were tracked in year 2), then the effect sizes from the predictive study were entered. If an organization had multiple predictive studies, then the mean of the correlations in these studies was entered. If sample sizes varied substantially in repeated studies for an organization, the study with the largest of the sample sizes was used.

- For 94 organizations, there were studies that examined the relationship between business unit employee perceptions and customer perceptions. Customer perceptions included customer metrics, patient metrics and student ratings of teachers. These metrics included measures of loyalty, satisfaction, service excellence, customer evaluation of quality of claims, net promoter scores and engagement. The largest representation of studies included loyalty metrics (e.g., likelihood to recommend/ net promoter or repeat business), so we refer to customer metrics as customer loyalty in this study. Instruments varied from study to study. The general index of customer loyalty was an average score of the items included in each measure. A growing number of studies include "customer engagement" as the metric of choice, which measures the emotional connection between the customers and the organization that serves them. For more information on the interaction of employee and customer engagement, see Fleming, Coffman, and Harter (2005) and Harter, Asplund, and Fleming (2004).
- Profitability studies were available for 85 organizations. The definition of profitability typically was a percentage profit of revenue (sales). In several companies, the researchers used — as the best measure of profit — a difference score from the prior year or a difference from a budgeted amount because it represented a more accurate measure of each unit's relative performance. As such, a control for

opportunity (location) was used when profitability figures were deemed less comparable from one unit to the next. For example, a difference variable involved dividing profit by revenue for a business unit and then subtracting a budgeted percentage from this percentage. Or, more explicitly, in some cases a partial correlation (r value) was calculated, controlling for location variables when they were deemed to be relevant to accurate comparison of business units. In every case, profitability variables were measures of margin, and productivity variables (which follow) were measures of amount produced.

- Productivity studies were available for 140 organizations. Measures of business unit productivity consisted of one of the following: financials (e.g., revenue/sales dollars per person or patient), quantity produced (production volume), enrollments in programs, hours/labor costs to budget, cross-sells, performance ratings or student achievement scores (for three education organizations). In a few cases, this was a dichotomous variable (top-performing business units = 2; less successful units = 1). The majority of variables included as "productivity" were financial measures of sales or revenue or growth in sales or revenue. As with profitability, in many cases, it was necessary for the researchers to compare financial results with a performance goal or prior-year figure to control for the differential business opportunity because of the location of business units, or to explicitly calculate a partial correlation (r value).

- Turnover data were available for 106 organizations. The turnover measure was the annualized percentage of employee turnover for each business unit. In most cases, voluntary turnover was reported and used in the analyses.

- Safety data were available for 53 organizations. Safety measures included lost workday/time incident rate, percentage of workdays lost as a result of incidents or workers' compensation claims (incidents and costs), number of incidents, or incident rates.

- Absenteeism data were included for 30 organizations. Absenteeism measures included the average number of days missed per person for each work unit divided by the total days available for work. This included either a measure of sick days or a measure of hours or total absenteeism.
- Eleven organizations provided measures of shrinkage. Shrinkage is defined as the dollar amount of unaccounted-for lost merchandise, which could be the result of employee theft, customer theft or lost merchandise. Given the varying size of locations, shrinkage was calculated as a percentage of total revenue or a difference from an expected target.
- Nine healthcare organizations provided measures of patient safety. Patient safety incident measures varied from patient fall counts (percentages of total patients), medical error and infection rates, and risk-adjusted mortality rates.
- Sixteen organizations provided measures of quality. For most organizations, quality was measured through records of defects such as unsaleable/returned items/quality shutdowns/scrap/operational efficiency/rejections per inspection rate (in manufacturing), forced outages (in utilities), disciplinary actions, deposit accuracy (financial) and other quality scores. Because the majority of quality metrics were measures of defects (where higher figures meant worse performance), measures of efficiency and quality scores were reverse coded so that all variables carried the same inferential interpretation.
- The overall study involved 1,882,131 independent employee responses to surveys and 82,248 independent business/work units in 230 organizations, with an average of 23 employees per business unit and 358 business/work units per organization. We conducted 339 research studies across the 230 organizations.

- Table 1 provides a summary of organizations sorted by industry. It is evident that there is considerable variation in the industry types represented, as organizations from 49 industries provided studies. Each of the general government industry classifications (via SIC codes) is represented, with the largest number of organizations represented in services, retail, manufacturing and financial industries. The largest numbers of business units are in the financial and retail industries. Of the specific industry classifications, these are the most frequently represented (based on number of business units): Finance — Depository, Services — Health, Retail — Pharmaceutical, Retail — Food, Transportation/Public Utilities — Communications, Finance — Insurance, Manufacturing — Pharmaceutical and Retail — Miscellaneous.

## Table 1: Summary of Studies by Industry

| Industry Type | Number of Organizations | Number of Business/ Work Units | Number of Respondents |
|---|---|---|---|
| Finance — Commercial Banking | 2 | 996 | 7,419 |
| Finance — Credit | 2 | 59 | 581 |
| Finance — Depository | 21 | 16,320 | 176,430 |
| Finance — Insurance | 6 | 4,219 | 53,581 |
| Finance — Mortgage | 1 | 27 | 985 |
| Finance — Nondepository | 1 | 94 | 2,038 |
| Finance — Security | 4 | 797 | 25,833 |
| Finance — Transactions | 1 | 73 | 1,530 |
| Manufacturing — Aircraft | 1 | 3,411 | 37,616 |
| Manufacturing — Building Materials | 1 | 8 | 1,335 |

## Table I: Summary of Studies by Industry *(Continued)*

| Industry Type | Number of Organizations | Number of Business/ Work Units | Number of Respondents |
|---|---|---|---|
| Manufacturing — Chemicals | 1 | 928 | 8,203 |
| Manufacturing — Computers and Electronics | 3 | 239 | 27,002 |
| Manufacturing — Consumer Goods | 4 | 235 | 7,077 |
| Manufacturing — Food | 5 | 300 | 21,317 |
| Manufacturing — Glass | 1 | 5 | 1,349 |
| Manufacturing — Industrial Equipment | 1 | 89 | 639 |
| Manufacturing — Instrument | 7 | 105 | 2,112 |
| Manufacturing — Miscellaneous | 3 | 396 | 12,478 |
| Manufacturing — Paper | 1 | 60 | 17,243 |
| Manufacturing — Pharmaceutical | 5 | 4,103 | 39,575 |
| Manufacturing — Plastics | 1 | 133 | 938 |
| Manufacturing — Printing | 2 | 35 | 716 |
| Manufacturing — Ship Building | 3 | 882 | 134,297 |
| | | | |
| Materials and Construction | 4 | 1,270 | 29,932 |
| | | | |
| Personal Services — Beauty Salons | 1 | 424 | 3,226 |
| | | | |
| Real Estate | 3 | 199 | 5,964 |

## Table I: Summary of Studies by Industry *(Continued)*

| Industry Type | Number of Organizations | Number of Business/ Work Units | Number of Respondents |
|---|---|---|---|
| Retail — Automotive | 4 | 261 | 13,614 |
| Retail — Building Materials | 3 | 1,158 | 65,001 |
| Retail — Clothes | 4 | 1,055 | 28,937 |
| Retail — Department Stores | 2 | 816 | 6,594 |
| Retail — Eating | 6 | 736 | 37,191 |
| Retail — Electronics | 6 | 1,483 | 104,273 |
| Retail — Entertainment | 1 | 106 | 1,051 |
| Retail — Food | 5 | 6,204 | 97,049 |
| Retail — Industrial Equipment | 1 | 11 | 484 |
| Retail — Miscellaneous | 10 | 4,076 | 157,602 |
| Retail — Pharmaceutical | 2 | 7,321 | 138,428 |
| Services — Business | 3 | 645 | 10,309 |
| Services — Education | 7 | 459 | 10,746 |
| Services — Government | 4 | 240 | 8,336 |
| Services — Health | 61 | 12,619 | 281,995 |
| Services — Hospitality | 8 | 958 | 156,678 |
| Services — Nursing Home | 1 | 353 | 26,582 |
| Services — Recreation | 1 | 14 | 288 |
| Services — Social Services | 2 | 1,525 | 16,920 |
| Transportation/Public Utilities — Communications | 7 | 4,234 | 45,506 |
| Transportation/Public Utilities — Electric, Gas and Sanitary Services | 5 | 1,740 | 20,318 |

## Table 1: Summary of Studies by Industry *(Continued)*

| Industry Type | Number of Organizations | Number of Business/ Work Units | Number of Respondents |
|---|---|---|---|
| Transportation/Public Utilities — Nonhazardous Waste Disposal | 1 | 727 | 28,600 |
| Transportation/Public Utilities — Trucking | 1 | 100 | 6,213 |
| **Total Financial** | **38** | **22,585** | **268,397** |
| **Total Manufacturing** | **39** | **10,929** | **311,897** |
| **Total Materials and Construction** | **4** | **1,270** | **29,932** |
| **Total Personal Services** | **1** | **424** | **3,226** |
| **Total Real Estate** | **3** | **199** | **5,964** |
| **Total Retail** | **44** | **23,227** | **650,224** |
| **Total Services** | **87** | **16,813** | **511,854** |
| **Total Transportation/ Public Utilities** | **14** | **6,801** | **100,637** |
| **Total** | **230** | **82,248** | **1,882,131** |

Table 2 provides a summary of organizations sorted by business/work unit type. There is also considerable variation in the types of business/work units, ranging from stores to plants/mills to departments to schools. Overall, 23 different types of business/work units are represented; the largest number of organizations had studies of workgroups, stores or bank branches. Likewise, workgroups, stores and bank branches have the highest proportional representation of business/work units.

## Table 2: Summary of Business/Work Unit Types

| Business/Work Unit Type | Number of Organizations | Number of Business/ Work Units | Number of Respondents |
|---|---|---|---|
| Bank Branch | 19 | 16,276 | 183,926 |
| Call Center | 3 | 1,120 | 19,667 |
| Call Center Department | 4 | 120 | 2,409 |
| Child Care Center | 1 | 1,499 | 14,302 |
| Cost Center | 15 | 3,589 | 73,929 |
| Country | 1 | 26 | 2,618 |
| Dealership | 4 | 261 | 13,614 |
| Department | 12 | 1,347 | 33,275 |
| Division | 3 | 714 | 134,703 |
| Facility | 2 | 1,080 | 55,182 |
| Hospital | 6 | 782 | 53,307 |
| Hotel | 6 | 563 | 149,158 |
| Location | 8 | 163 | 8,904 |
| Mall | 2 | 166 | 3,790 |
| Patient Care Unit | 8 | 2,399 | 49,122 |
| Plant/Mill | 8 | 776 | 47,920 |
| Region | 2 | 113 | 13,520 |
| Restaurant | 5 | 373 | 21,183 |
| Sales Division | 6 | 391 | 21,722 |
| Sales Team | 6 | 420 | 27,543 |
| School | 6 | 409 | 10,496 |
| Store | 35 | 22,228 | 605,728 |
| Workgroup | 68 | 27,433 | 336,113 |
| **Total** | **230** | **82,248** | **1,882,131** |

## META-ANALYTIC METHODS USED

Analyses included weighted average estimates of true validity; estimates of standard deviation of validities; and corrections made for sampling error, measurement error in the dependent variables, and range variation and restriction in the independent variable ($Q^{12}$ GrandMean) for these validities. An additional analysis was conducted, correcting for independent-variable measurement error. The most basic form of meta-analysis corrects variance estimates only for sampling error. Other corrections recommended by Hunter and Schmidt (1990, 2004) and Schmidt and Hunter (2015) include correction for measurement and statistical artifacts such as range restriction and measurement error in the performance variables gathered. The sections that follow provide the definitions of the previously mentioned procedures.

Gallup researchers gathered performance-variable data for multiple time periods to calculate the reliabilities of the performance measures. Because these multiple measures were not available for each study, the researchers used artifact distribution meta-analysis methods (Hunter & Schmidt, 1990, pp. 158-197; Hunter & Schmidt, 2004) to correct for measurement error in the performance variables. The artifact distributions developed were based on test-retest reliabilities, where they were available, from various studies. The procedure followed for calculation of business/work unit outcome-measure reliabilities was consistent with Scenario 23 in Schmidt and Hunter (1996). To take into account that some change in outcomes (stability) is a function of real change, test-retest reliabilities were calculated using the following formula:

$$(r_{12} \times r_{23})/r_{13}$$

*Where $r_{12}$ is the correlation of the outcome measured at time 1 with the same outcome measured at time 2; $r_{23}$ is the correlation of the outcome measured at time 2 with the outcome measured at time 3; and $r_{13}$ is the correlation of the outcome measured at time 1 with the outcome measured at time 3.*

The above formula factors out real change (which is more likely to occur from time period 1-3 than from time periods 1-2 or 2-3) from random changes in business unit results caused by measurement error, data collection errors, sampling errors (primarily in customer and quality measures) and uncontrollable fluctuations in outcome measures. Some estimates were available for quarterly data, some for semiannual data and others for annual data. The average time period in artifact distributions used for this meta-analysis was consistent with the average time period across studies for each criterion type. Artifact distributions for reliability were collected for customer, profitability, productivity, turnover, safety and quality measures. But they were not collected for absenteeism, shrinkage and patient safety because they were not available at the time of this study. Therefore, the assumed reliability for absenteeism, shrinkage and patient safety was 1.00, resulting in downwardly biased true validity estimates (the estimates of validity reported here are lower than reality). Artifact distributions for these three variables will be added as they become available in the future.

It could be argued that, because the independent variable (employee engagement as measured by the $Q^{12}$) is used in practice to predict outcomes, the practitioner must live with the reliability of the instrument they are using. However, correcting for measurement error in the independent variable answers the theoretical question of how the actual constructs (true scores) relate to each other. Therefore, we present analyses both before and after correcting for independent variable reliability.

In correcting for range variation and range restriction, there are fundamental theoretical questions that need to be considered relating to whether such correction is necessary. In personnel selection, validities are routinely corrected for range restriction because in selecting applicants for jobs, those scoring highest on the predictor are typically selected. This results in explicit range restriction that biases observed correlations downward (i.e., attenuation). But in the employee satisfaction and engagement arena, one could argue that there is no explicit range restriction because we are studying results as they exist in the workplace. Work units are not selected based on scores on the predictor ($Q^{12}$ scores).

However, we have observed that there is variation across companies in standard deviations of engagement. One hypothesis for why this variation occurs is that companies vary in how they encourage employee satisfaction and engagement initiatives and in how they have or have not developed a common set of values and a common culture. Therefore, the standard deviation of the population of business units across organizations studied will be greater than the standard deviation within the typical company. This variation in standard deviations across companies can be thought of as indirect range restriction (as opposed to direct range restriction). Improved indirect range restriction corrections have been incorporated into this meta-analysis (Hunter, Schmidt, & Le, 2006).

Since the development of the $Q^{12}$, Gallup has collected descriptive data on more than 30 million respondents, 3.4 million business units or workgroups, and 1,165 organizations. This accumulation of data indicates that the standard deviation within a given company is approximately 8/10 the standard deviation in the population of all business/work units. In addition, the ratio of standard deviation for a given organization relative to the population value varies from organization to organization. Therefore, if one goal is to estimate the effect size in the population of all business units (arguably a theoretically important issue), then correction should be made based on such available data. In the observed data, correlations are attenuated for organizations with less variability across business/work units than the population average and vice versa. As such, variability in standard deviations across organizations will create variability in observed correlations and is therefore an artifact that can be corrected for in interpreting the generalizability of validities. Appendixes in Harter and Schmidt (2000) provide artifact distributions for range-restriction/variation corrections used for meta-analysis. These artifact distributions were updated substantially in 2009, and this meta-analysis includes these updates. We have included a randomly selected 100 organizations in our current artifact distributions. Because of the increased size of these tables, they are not included in this report. They resemble those reported in the earlier study, but with a larger number of entries. The following excerpt provides an overview of meta-analysis conducted using artifact distributions:

> In any given meta-analysis, there may be several artifacts for which artifact information is only sporadically available. For example, suppose measurement error and range restriction are the only relevant artifacts beyond sampling

error. In such a case, the typical artifact distribution-based meta-analysis is conducted in three stages:

- First, information is compiled on four distributions: the distribution of the observed correlations, the distribution of the reliability of the independent variable, the distribution of the reliability of the dependent variable and the distribution of the range departure. There are then four means and four variances compiled from the set of studies, with each study providing whatever information it contains.
- Second, the distribution of observed correlations is corrected for sampling error.
- Third, the distribution corrected for sampling error is then corrected for error of measurement and range variation (Hunter & Schmidt, 1990, pp. 158-159; Hunter & Schmidt, 2004).

In this study, statistics are calculated and reported at each level of analysis, starting with the observed correlations and then correcting for sampling error; measurement error; and finally, range variation. Both within-organization range-variation corrections (to correct validity generalization estimates) and between-organization range-restriction corrections (to correct for differences in variation across organizations) were made. Between-organization range-restriction corrections are relevant in understanding how engagement relates to performance across the business/work units of all organizations. As alluded to, we have applied the indirect range-restriction correction procedure to this meta-analysis (Hunter et al., 2006).

The meta-analysis includes an estimate of the mean sample-size-weighted validity and the variance across the correlations — again weighting each validity by its sample size. The amount of variance predicted for weighted correlations based on sampling error was also computed. The following is the formula to calculate variance expected from sampling error in "bare bones" meta-analyses, using the Hunter et al. (2006) technique referred to previously:

$$S_e^2 = (1-\bar{r}^2)^2 / (\bar{N}-1)$$

Residual standard deviations were calculated by subtracting the amount of variance due to sampling error, the amount of variance due to study differences in measurement error in the dependent variable, and the amount of variance due to study differences in range variation from the observed variance. To estimate the true validity of standard deviations, the residual standard deviation was adjusted for bias due to mean unreliability and mean range restriction. The amount of variance due to sampling error, measurement error and range variation was divided by the observed variance to calculate the total percentage variance accounted for. Generalizability is generally assumed if a high percentage (such as 75%) of the variance in validities across studies is due to sampling error and other artifacts, or if the 90% credibility value ($10^{th}$ percentile of the distribution of true validities) is in the hypothesized direction. As in Harter et al. (2002), Harter et al. (2006), Harter et al. (2009) and Harter et al. (2013), we calculated the correlation of engagement to composite performance. This calculation assumes that managers are managing toward multiple outcomes simultaneously and that each outcome occupies some space in the overall evaluation of performance. To calculate the correlation to the composite index of performance, we used the Mosier (1943) formula to determine the reliability of the composite measure (as described in Harter et al., 2002), using reliability distributions and intercorrelations of the outcome measures. Patient safety was combined with the more general "safety" category because patient safety is an industry-specific variable. The reliability of the composite metric is 0.91. Composite performance was measured as the equally weighted sum of customer loyalty, turnover (reverse scored as retention), safety (accidents and patient safety incidents reverse scored), absenteeism (reverse scored), shrinkage (reverse scored), financials (with profitability and productivity equally weighted) and quality (defects reverse scored). We also calculated composite performance as the equally weighted sum of the most direct outcomes of engagement — customer loyalty, turnover (reverse scored as retention), safety (accidents/patient safety incidents reverse scored), absenteeism (reverse scored), shrinkage (reverse scored) and quality (defects reverse scored). The reliability of this composite variable is 0.89.

In our research, we used the Schmidt and Le (2004) meta-analysis package (the artifact distribution meta-analysis program with correction for indirect range restriction). The program package is described in Hunter and Schmidt (2004).

## RESULTS

The focus of analyses for this report is on the relationship between overall employee engagement (defined by an equally weighted GrandMean of $Q^{12}$) and a variety of outcomes. Table 3 provides the updated meta-analytic and validity generalization statistics for the relationship between employee engagement and performance for each of the nine outcomes studied. Two forms of true validity estimation follow mean observed correlations and standard deviations. The first corrects for range variation within organizations and dependent-variable measurement error. This range-variation correction places all organizations on the same basis in terms of variability of employee engagement across business/work units. These results can be viewed as estimating the relationships across business/work units within the average organization. The second corrects for range restriction across the population of business/work units and dependent-variable measurement error. Estimates that include the latter range-restriction correction apply to interpretations of effects in business/work units across organizations, as opposed to effects expected within a given organization. Because there is more variation in engagement for business/work units across organizations than there is within the average organization, effect sizes are higher when true validity estimates are calculated for business/work units across organizations.

For instance, observe the estimates relative to the customer loyalty criteria. Without the between-organization range-restriction correction (which is relevant to the effect within the typical organization), the true validity value of employee engagement is 0.21 with a 90% credibility value (CV) of 0.14. With the between-organization range-restriction correction (which is relevant to business/work units across organizations), the true validity value of employee engagement is 0.28 with a 90% CV of 0.19.

As in prior studies, findings here show high generalizability across organizations in the relationships between employee engagement and customer metrics, profitability, productivity, employee turnover, safety, shrinkage and quality (defects) outcomes. Most of the variability in correlations across organizations was the result of sampling error in individual studies, and for each of these seven outcomes, more than 75% of the variability in correlations across organizations can be attributed to artifacts (sampling error, range variation and measurement error). In other words, the true validity is very similar and in the hypothesized direction for each organization studied. For the remaining two outcomes (absenteeism and patient safety), results indicate high generalizability across the organizations studied, as indicated by the 90% credibility value in the hypothesized direction. However, the validities vary somewhat more than with other outcomes, although the distribution of validities is in the hypothesized direction. The direction of the effect is predictable, but the size of effect across companies varies somewhat. Artifacts do not explain all of the variance in correlations of employee engagement and these latter two outcomes. It is possible that this is because of a lack of reliability estimates for these outcomes. Unfortunately, we have yet to acquire reliability estimates for these two outcomes. Once reliability estimates become available and as more studies are added to the meta-analysis, future research may shed light on this. Regardless, the 90% credibility values indicate substantial evidence of generalizability for all nine outcomes studied (Schmidt & Hunter, 1977). What this means is that the $Q^{12}$ measure of employee engagement effectively predicts these outcomes in the expected direction across organizations, including those in different industries and in different countries.

## Table 3: Meta-Analysis of Relationship Between Employee Engagement and Business Unit Performance

| | Customer Loyalty | Profitability | Productivity | Turnover | Safety Incidents | Absenteeism | Shrinkage | Patient Safety Incidents | Quality (Defects) |
|---|---|---|---|---|---|---|---|---|---|
| Number of Business Units | 20,679 | 31,472 | 45,328 | 43,987 | 9,746 | 11,460 | 4,514 | 1,378 | 2,320 |
| Number of r's | 94 | 85 | 140 | 106 | 53 | 30 | 11 | 9 | 16 |
| Mean Observed r | 0.16 | 0.10 | 0.14 | -0.10 | -0.12 | -0.16 | -0.09 | -0.42 | -0.16 |
| Observed SD | 0.09 | 0.07 | 0.08 | 0.06 | 0.08 | 0.09 | 0.06 | 0.14 | 0.10 |
| True Validity[1] | 0.21 | 0.10 | 0.16 | -0.15 | -0.14 | -0.16 | -0.09 | -0.42 | -0.16 |
| True Validity SD[1] | 0.05 | 0.04 | 0.04 | 0.01 | 0.03 | 0.05 | 0.03 | 0.08 | 0.04 |
| True Validity[2] | 0.28 | 0.14 | 0.21 | -0.20 | -0.19 | -0.22 | -0.12 | -0.53 | -0.22 |
| True Validity SD[2] | 0.07 | 0.05 | 0.05 | 0.01 | 0.04 | 0.07 | 0.04 | 0.08 | 0.05 |
| % Variance Accounted for — Sampling Error | 51 | 59 | 48 | 62 | 75 | 34 | 60 | 23 | 69 |
| % Variance Accounted for[1] | 80 | 76 | 78 | 98 | 92 | 60 | 75 | 71 | 88 |
| % Variance Accounted for[2] | 80 | 77 | 78 | 98 | 92 | 60 | 75 | 71 | 88 |
| 90% CV[1] | 0.14 | 0.06 | 0.10 | -0.13 | -0.11 | -0.09 | -0.05 | -0.32 | -0.12 |
| 90% CV[2] | 0.19 | 0.08 | 0.14 | -0.18 | -0.14 | -0.12 | -0.06 | -0.42 | -0.16 |

r = Correlation
SD = Standard Deviation
CV = Credibility Value
[1] Includes correction for range variation within organizations and dependent-variable measurement error
[2] Includes correction for range restriction across population of business/work units and dependent-variable measurement error

In summary, for the composite measure of engagement shown in Table 3, the strongest effects were found for customer loyalty metrics, productivity, employee turnover, safety, absenteeism, patient safety and quality. Correlations were positive and generalizable relative to profitability and shrinkage criteria, but of slightly lower magnitude. In the case of profitability, it is likely influenced indirectly by employee engagement and more directly by variables such as customer loyalty, productivity, employee turnover, safety, absenteeism, shrinkage, patient safety and quality. Remember, the productivity variable includes various measures of business/work unit productivity, the majority of which are sales data. Of the two financial variables included in the meta-analysis (sales and profit), engagement is most highly correlated with sales. This is probably because day-to-day employee engagement has an impact on customer perceptions, turnover, quality and other variables that are in close proximity with sales. In fact, this is what we have found empirically in our causal analyses (Harter et al., 2010). In the case of shrinkage, correlations may be somewhat lower because many factors influence merchandise shrinkage, including theft, attentiveness to inventory and damaged merchandise. The next section will explore the practical utility of the observed relationships.

As in Harter et al. (2002), we calculated the correlation of employee engagement to composite performance. As defined earlier, Table 4 provides the correlations and d-values for four analyses: the observed correlations; correction for dependent-variable measurement error; correction for dependent-variable measurement error and range restriction across companies; and correction for dependent-variable measurement error, range restriction and independent-variable measurement error (true score correlation).

As with previous meta-analyses, the effect sizes presented in Table 4 indicate substantial relationships between engagement and composite performance.

Consistent with the 2013 meta-analysis, business units in the top half on engagement within companies have 0.46 standard deviation units' higher composite performance compared with those in the bottom half on engagement.

Across companies, business units in the top half on engagement have 0.60 standard deviation units' higher composite performance compared with those in the bottom half on engagement.

After correcting for all available study artifacts (examining the true score relationship), business units in the top half on employee engagement have 0.73 standard deviation units' higher composite performance compared with those in the bottom half on engagement. This is the true score effect expected over time, across all business units.

As alluded to, some outcomes are the direct consequence of employee engagement (employee turnover, customer loyalty, safety, absenteeism, shrinkage and quality), and other outcomes are more of a downstream result of intermediary outcomes (sales and profit). For this reason, we have also calculated the composite correlation to short-term outcomes. Table 5 again indicates a substantial relationship between engagement and composite performance. Observed correlations and d-values are of approximately the same magnitude as those reported in Table 4 but slightly lower (most likely because the direct outcomes do not occupy all of the performance criterion space).

## Table 4: Correlation of Employee Engagement to Composite Business Unit Performance — All Outcomes

| Analysis | Correlation of Engagement to Performance |
|---|---|
| Observed r | 0.27 |
| d | 0.44 |
| r corrected for dependent-variable measurement error | 0.28 |
| d | 0.46 |
| r corrected for dependent-variable measurement error and range restriction across companies | 0.36 |
| d | 0.60 |
| ρ corrected for dependent-variable measurement error, range restriction and independent-variable measurement error | 0.43 |
| δ | 0.73 |

r = Correlation
d = Difference in standard deviation units
ρ = True score correlation
δ = True score difference in standard deviation units

Business units in the top half on engagement within companies have 0.44 standard deviation units' higher performance on direct outcomes compared with those in the bottom half. Across companies, the difference is 0.57 standard deviation units. After correcting for all available artifacts, the difference is 0.69 standard deviation units.

## Table 5: Correlation of Employee Engagement to Composite Business/ Work Unit Performance — Direct Outcomes (Customer Loyalty, Turnover, Safety, Absenteeism, Shrinkage, Quality)

| Analysis | Correlation of Engagement to Performance |
|---|---|
| Observed r | 0.25 |
| d | 0.41 |
| r corrected for dependent-variable measurement error | 0.27 |
| d | 0.44 |
| r corrected for dependent-variable measurement error and range restriction across companies | 0.34 |
| d | 0.57 |
| ρ corrected for dependent-variable measurement error, range restriction and independent-variable measurement error | 0.41 |
| δ | 0.69 |

r = Correlation
d = Difference in standard deviation units
ρ = True score correlation
δ = True score difference in standard deviation units

# UTILITY ANALYSIS: PRACTICALITY OF THE EFFECTS

## UTILITY ANALYSIS

In the past, studies of job satisfaction's relationship to performance have had limited analysis of the utility of the reported relationships. Correlations have often been discounted as trivial without an effort to understand the potential utility, in practice, of the relationships. The $Q^{12}$ includes items that Gallup researchers have found to be changeable by the local manager and others within the business/work unit. As such, understanding the practical utility of potential changes is crucial.

The research literature includes a great deal of evidence that numerically small or moderate effects often translate into large practical effects (Abelson, 1985; Carver, 1975; Lipsey, 1990; Rosenthal & Rubin, 1982; Sechrest & Yeaton, 1982). As shown in Table 6, this is, in fact, the case here. Effect sizes referenced in this study are consistent with or above other practical effect sizes referenced in other reviews (Lipsey & Wilson, 1993).

A more intuitive method of displaying the practical value of an effect is that of binomial effect size displays, or BESDs (Rosenthal & Rubin, 1982; Grissom, 1994). BESDs typically depict the success rate of a treatment versus a control group as a percentage above the median on the outcome variable of interest.

BESDs can be applied to the results of this study. Table 6 shows the percentage of business units above the median on composite performance for high- and low-scoring business/work units on the employee engagement ($Q^{12}$) composite measure. True validity estimates (correcting for measurement error only in the dependent variable) were used for analysis of business/work units both within and across organizations.

One can see from Table 6 that there are meaningful differences between the top and bottom halves. The top half is defined as the average of business/work units scoring in the highest 50% on the $Q^{12}$, and business/work units scoring in the lowest 50% constitute the bottom half. It is clear from Table 6 that management would learn a great deal more about success if it studied what was going on in top-half business units rather than bottom-half units.

With regard to composite business/work unit performance, business/work units in the top half on employee engagement have a 78% higher success rate in their own organization and a 113% higher success rate across business units in all companies studied. In other words, business/work units with high employee engagement nearly double their odds of above-average composite performance in their own organizations and increase their odds for above-average success across business/work units in all organizations by 2.1 times.

## Table 6: BESDs for Employee Engagement and Outcomes

| Employee Engagement | Business Units Within Company | Business Units Across Companies |
|---|---|---|
| | % Above Median Composite Performance (Total) | % Above Median Composite Performance (Total) |
| Top Half | 64 | 68 |
| Bottom Half | 36 | 32 |
| | % Above Median Composite Performance (Direct Outcomes) | % Above Median Composite Performance (Direct Outcomes) |
| Top Half | 63 | 67 |
| Bottom Half | 37 | 33 |

To illustrate this further, Table 7 shows the probability of above-average performance for various levels of employee engagement. Business units at the highest level of employee engagement across all business units in Gallup's database have an 80% chance of having high (above average) composite performance. This compares with a 20% chance for those with the lowest level of employee engagement. So it is possible to achieve high performance without high employee engagement, but the odds are substantially lower (in fact, four times as low).

## Table 7: Percentage of Business Units Above the Company Median on Composite Performance (Customer Loyalty, Profitability, Productivity, Turnover, Safety, Absenteeism, Shrinkage, Quality) for Different Employee Engagement Percentiles

| Employee Engagement Percentile | Percentage Above Company Median |
|---|---|
| Above 99th | 80% |
| 95th | 72% |
| 90th | 68% |
| 80th | 62% |
| 70th | 58% |
| 60th | 54% |
| 50th | 50% |
| 40th | 46% |
| 30th | 42% |
| 20th | 38% |
| 10th | 32% |
| 5th | 28% |
| Below 1st | 20% |

Other forms of expressing the practical meaning behind the effects from this study include utility analysis methods (Schmidt & Rauschenberger, 1986). Formulas have been derived for estimating the dollar-value increases in output as a result of improved employee selection. These formulas take into account the size of the effect (correlation), the variability in the outcome being studied and the difference in the independent variable (engagement in this case) and can be used in estimating the difference in performance outcomes at different levels in the distribution of $Q^{12}$ scores. Previous studies (Harter et al., 2002; Harter & Schmidt, 2000) provided utility analysis examples, comparing differences in outcomes between the top and bottom quartiles on the Q[12]. For companies included in this meta-analysis, it is typical to see differences between top and bottom engagement quartiles of two to four points on customer loyalty, one to four points on profitability, hundreds of thousands of dollars on productivity figures per month, and four to 10 points in turnover for low-turnover companies and 15 to 50 points for high-turnover companies.

Gallup researchers recently conducted utility analysis across multiple organizations with similar outcome metric types (an update of analyses presented in Harter et al., 2002, p. 275, Table 6). Comparing top-quartile with bottom-quartile engagement business units resulted in median percentage differences of:

- 10% in customer loyalty/engagement
- 21% in profitability
- 20% in productivity — sales
- 17% in productivity — production records and evaluations
- 24% in turnover for high-turnover companies (those with more than 40% annualized turnover)
- 59% in turnover for low-turnover companies (those with 40% or lower annualized turnover)
- 70% in safety incidents
- 28% in shrinkage
- 41% in absenteeism
- 58% in patient safety incidents
- 40% in quality (defects)

The above differences and their utility in dollar terms should be calculated for each organization, given the organization's unique metrics, situation and distribution of outcomes across business units. The median estimates represent the midpoint in the distribution of utility analyses conducted across many studies (83 for productivity, 92 for turnover, 48 for safety, 57 for customer, 48 for profitability, 29 for absenteeism, 14 for quality, 11 for shrinkage and 10 for patient safety), depending on the outcome and availability of organizational data with similar outcome types.

One can see that the above relationships are nontrivial if the business has many business/work units. The point of the utility analysis, consistent with the literature that has taken a serious look at utility, is that the relationship between employee engagement and organizational outcomes, even conservatively expressed, is meaningful from a practical perspective.

# DISCUSSION

Findings reported in this updated meta-analysis continue to provide large-scale cross-validation to prior meta-analyses conducted on the Q[12] instrument. The present study expands the size of the meta-analytic database by 32,320 business/work units (an increase of 65%), as well as the number of countries and work unit types studied. The relationship between engagement and performance at the business unit level continues to be substantial and highly generalizable across companies. Differences in correlations across companies can be attributed mostly to study artifacts. For outcomes with sample sizes of 10,000 or more business units in 2013 (customer, profitability, productivity and turnover), the results of this updated meta-analysis are almost completely replicated. For these outcomes, differences in effect sizes from 2013 to 2015 ranged from 0.01-0.02, and evidence of generalizability remained substantial. The size of this database gives us confidence in the direction of the true relationship between employee engagement and business outcomes but also confidence in the size of the relationship, which can be helpful in calculating potential return on investment from performance management initiatives. The consistent findings across many iterations of meta-analysis also speak to the importance and relevance of workplace perceptions for businesses across different economic times and even amid massive changes in technology since 1997 when this study series began.

These findings are important because they mean generalizable tools can be developed and used across different organizations with a high level of confidence that they elicit important performance-related information. The data from the present study provide further substantiation to the theory that doing what is best for employees does not have to contradict what is best for the business or organization.

It is also worth noting that, as Gallup consultants have educated managers and partnered with companies on change initiatives, organizations have experienced (between the first and second year), on average, one-half standard deviation growth on employee engagement and often a full standard deviation growth and more after three or more years. An important element in the utility of any applied instrument and improvement process is the extent to which the variable under study can be changed. Our current evidence is that employee engagement is changeable and varies widely by business unit or workgroup.

As we demonstrated in the utility analyses presented here and in other iterations of this analysis, the size of the effects observed has important practical implications, particularly given that engagement, as measured here, is quite changeable.

Current and future Gallup research is focusing on expanding the base of outcomes to include health and wellbeing variables. For instance, one study found substantial linkages between employee engagement in 2008 and sick days in 2009, after controlling for demographics and prior health conditions, including body mass index. In worldwide samples, we have found consistent associations between engagement at work and life satisfaction, daily experiences and health (Gallup, 2010). Another longitudinal study found that changes in engagement predicted changes in cholesterol and triglycerides (via blood samples) after controlling for demographics, health history and medication use (Harter, Canedy, & Stone, 2008). And even more recently, we have observed differences in momentary affect and cortisol when comparing engaged and disengaged employees (Harter & Stone, 2011). Yet another study found engagement at work predicts likelihood of involvement in organization-sponsored health programs (Agrawal & Harter, 2009). Others have found engagement to be integral to perceptions of inclusiveness across diverse groups (Jones & Harter, 2004; Badal & Harter, 2014). All together, these studies suggest that the boundaries for the effect of an engaging workplace are quite wide.

# REFERENCES

Abelson, R. P. (1985). A variance explanation paradox: When a little is a lot. *Psychological Bulletin, 97*(1), 129-133.

Agrawal, S., & Harter, J. K. (2009, October). *Employee engagement influences involvement in wellness programs.* Omaha, NE: Gallup.

Badal, S., & Harter, J. K. (2014). Gender diversity, business-unit engagement, & performance. *Journal of Leadership & Organizational Studies, 2(*4), 354-365.

Bangert-Drowns, R. L. (1986). Review of developments in meta-analytic method. *Psychological Bulletin, 99*(3), 388-399.

Batt, R. (2002). Managing customer services: Human resource practices, quit rates, and sales growth. *Academy of Management Journal, 45*(3), 587-597.

Carver, R. P. (1975). The Coleman Report: Using inappropriately designed achievement tests. *American Educational Research Journal, 12*(1), 77-86.

Denison, D. R. (1990). *Corporate culture and organizational effectiveness.* New York: John Wiley.

Edmans, A. (2012, November 1). The link between job satisfaction and firm value, with implications for corporate social responsibility. *Academy of Management Perspectives, 26*(4), 1-19.

Fleming, J. H., Coffman, C., & Harter, J. K. (2005, July-August). Manage your Human Sigma. *Harvard Business Review, 83*(7), 106-114.

Gallup (2010). *The state of the global workplace: A worldwide study of employee engagement and wellbeing.* Omaha, NE: Gallup.

Gallup, G. H. (1976, Winter). Human needs and satisfactions: A global survey. *Public Opinion Quarterly, 40*(4), 459-467.

Gallup, G. H., & Hill, E. (1959). *The secrets of long life.* New York: Bernard Geis.

The Gallup Organization (1992-1999). *Gallup Workplace Audit* (Copyright Registration Certificate TX-5 080 066). Washington, D.C.: U.S. Copyright Office.

Grissom, R. J. (1994). Probability of the superior outcome of one treatment over another. *Journal of Applied Psychology, 79*(2), 314-316.

Harter, J. K., & Agrawal, S. (2011). *Cross-cultural analysis of Gallup's $Q^{12}$ employee engagement instrument.* Omaha, NE: Gallup.

Harter, J. K., Asplund, J. W., & Fleming, J. H. (2004, August). *HumanSigma: A meta-analysis of the relationship between employee engagement, customer engagement and financial performance.* Omaha, NE: The Gallup Organization.

Harter, J. K., Canedy, J., & Stone, A. (2008). A longitudinal study of engagement at work and physiologic indicators of health. Presented at Work, Stress, & Health Conference. Washington, D.C.

Harter, J. K., & Creglow, A. (1997). *A meta-analysis and utility analysis of the relationship between core GWA employee perceptions and business outcomes.* Lincoln, NE: The Gallup Organization.

Harter, J. K., & Creglow, A. (1998, July). *A meta-analysis and utility analysis of the relationship between core GWA employee perceptions and business outcomes.* Lincoln, NE: The Gallup Organization.

Harter, J. K., Hayes, T. L., & Schmidt, F. L. (2004, January). *Meta-analytic predictive validity of Gallup Selection Research Instruments (SRI).* Omaha, NE: The Gallup Organization.

Harter, J. K., & Schmidt, F. L. (2000, March). *Validation of a performance-related and actionable management tool: A meta-analysis and utility analysis.* Princeton, NJ: The Gallup Organization.

Harter, J. K., & Schmidt, F. L. (2002, March). *Employee engagement, satisfaction, and business-unit-level outcomes: A meta-analysis.* Lincoln, NE: The Gallup Organization.

Harter, J. K., & Schmidt, F. L. (2006). Connecting employee satisfaction to business unit performance. In A. I. Kraut (Ed.), *Getting action from organizational surveys: New concepts, technologies, and applications* (pp. 33-52). San Francisco: Jossey-Bass.

Harter, J. K., & Schmidt, F. L. (2008). Conceptual versus empirical distinctions among constructs: Implications for discriminant validity. *Industrial and Organizational Psychology, 1*, 37-40.

Harter, J. K., Schmidt, F. L., Agrawal, S., & Plowman, S. K. (2013, February). *The relationship between engagement at work and organizational outcomes: 2012 $Q^{12}$ meta-analysis.* Omaha, NE: Gallup.

Harter, J. K., Schmidt, F. L., Asplund, J. W., Killham, E. A., & Agrawal, S. (2010). Causal impact of employee work perceptions on the bottom line of organizations. *Perspectives on Psychological Science, 5*(4), 378-389.

Harter, J. K., Schmidt, F. L., & Hayes, T. L. (2002). Business-unit-level relationship between employee satisfaction, employee engagement, and business outcomes: A meta-analysis. *Journal of Applied Psychology, 87*(2), 268-279.

Harter, J. K., Schmidt, F. L., & Killham, E. A. (2003, July). *Employee engagement, satisfaction, and business-unit-level outcomes: A meta-analysis.* Omaha, NE: The Gallup Organization.

Harter, J. K., Schmidt, F. L., Killham, E. A., & Agrawal, S. (2009). *$Q^{12}$ meta-analysis.* Gallup. Omaha, NE.

Harter, J. K., Schmidt, F. L., Killham, E. A., & Asplund, J. W. (2006). *$Q^{12}$ meta-analysis.* Gallup. Omaha, NE.

Harter, J. K., & Stone, A. A. (2011). Engaging and disengaging work conditions, momentary experiences, and cortisol response. *Motivation and Emotion, 36*(2), 104-113.

Hunter, J. E., & Schmidt, F. L. (1983). Quantifying the effects of psychological interventions on employee job performance and work-force productivity. *American Psychologist, 38*(4), 473-478.

Hunter, J. E., & Schmidt, F. L. (1990). *Methods of meta-analysis: Correcting error and bias in research findings.* Newbury Park, CA: Sage.

Hunter, J. E., & Schmidt, F. L. (2004). *Methods of meta-analysis: Correcting error and bias in research findings* (2nd ed.). Newbury Park, CA: Sage.

Hunter, J. E., Schmidt, F. L., & Le, H. A. (2006). Implications of direct and indirect range restriction for meta-analysis methods and findings. *Journal of Applied Psychology, 91*, 594-612.

Huselid, M. A. (1995). The impact of human resource management practices on turnover, productivity, and corporate financial performance. *Academy of Management Journal, 38*(3), 635-672.

Iaffaldano, M. T., & Muchinsky, P. M. (1985). Job satisfaction and job performance: A meta-analysis. *Psychological Bulletin, 97*(2), 251-273.

Johnson, J. W. (1996). Linking employee perceptions of service climate to customer satisfaction. *Personnel Psychology, 49*, 831-851.

Jones, J. R., & Harter, J. K. (2004). Race effects on the employee engagement-turnover intention relationship. *Journal of Leadership & Organizational Studies, 11*(2), 78-87.

Judge, T. A., Thoresen, C. J., Bono, J. E., & Patton, G. K. (2001). The job satisfaction-job performance relationship: A qualitative and quantitative review. *Psychological Bulletin, 127*(3), 376-407.

Lipsey, M. W. (1990). *Design sensitivity: Statistical power for experimental research.* Newbury Park, CA: Sage.

Lipsey, M. W., & Wilson, D. B. (1993). The efficacy of psychological, educational, and behavioral treatment: Confirmation from meta-analysis. *American Psychologist, 48*(12), 1181-1209.

Mosier, C. I. (1943). On the reliability of a weighted composite. *Psychometrika, 8*, 161-168.

National Technical Information Services. (1987). *Standard Industrial Classification manual.* Washington, D.C.: Executive Office of the President, Office of Management and Budget.

Ostroff, C. (1992). The relationship between satisfaction, attitudes, and performance: An organizational level analysis. *Journal of Applied Psychology, 77*(6), 963-974.

Reynierse, J. H., & Harker, J. B. (1992). Employee and customer perceptions of service in banks: Teller and customer service representative ratings. *Human Resource Planning, 15*(4), 31-46.

Rosenthal, R., & Rubin, D. B. (1982). A simple, general purpose display of magnitude of experimental effect. *Journal of Educational Psychology, 74*, 166-169.

Schmidt, F. L. (1992). What do data really mean? Research findings, meta-analysis, and cumulative knowledge in psychology. *American Psychologist, 47*(10), 1173-1181.

Schmidt, F. L., & Hunter, J. E. (1977). Development of a general solution to the problem of validity generalization. *Journal of Applied Psychology, 62*, 529-540.

Schmidt, F. L., & Hunter, J. E. (1996). Measurement error in psychological research: Lessons from 26 research scenarios. *Psychological Methods, 1*(2), 199-223.

Schmidt, F. L., & Hunter, J. E. (2015). *Methods of meta-analysis: Correcting error and bias in research findings.* (3rd ed.). Thousand Oaks, CA: Sage.

Schmidt, F. L., Hunter, J. E., McKenzie, R. C., & Muldrow, T. W. (1979). Impact of valid selection procedures on work-force productivity. *Journal of Applied Psychology, 64*(6), 609-626.

Schmidt, F. L., Hunter, J. E., Pearlman, K., & Rothstein-Hirsh, H. (1985). Forty questions about validity generalization and meta-analysis. *Personnel Psychology, 38*, 697-798.

Schmidt, F. L., & Le, H. A. (2004). Software for the Hunter-Schmidt meta-analysis methods. Iowa City, IA: Tippie College of Business, University of Iowa.

Schmidt, F. L., & Rader, M. (1999). Exploring the boundary conditions for interview validity: Meta-analytic validity findings for a new interview type. *Personnel Psychology, 52*, 445-464.

Schmidt, F. L., & Rauschenberger, J. (1986, April). *Utility analysis for practitioners.* Paper presented at the First Annual Conference of The Society for Industrial and Organizational Psychology, Chicago, IL.

Schmit, M. J., & Allscheid, S. P. (1995). Employee attitudes and customer satisfaction: Making theoretical and empirical connections. *Personnel Psychology, 48*, 521-536.

Schneider, B. (1991). Service quality and profits: Can you have your cake and eat it too? *Human Resource Planning, 14*(2), 151-157.

Schneider, B., Ashworth, S. D., Higgs, A. C., & Carr, L. (1996). Design, validity, and use of strategically focused employee attitude surveys. *Personnel Psychology, 49*(3), 695-705.

Schneider, B., & Bowen, D. E. (1993). The service organization: Human resources management is crucial. *Organizational Dynamics, 21*, 39-52.

Schneider, B., Parkington, J. J., & Buxton, V. M. (1980). Employee and customer perceptions of service in banks. *Administrative Science Quarterly, 25*, 252-267.

Sechrest, L., & Yeaton, W. H. (1982). Magnitudes of experimental effects in social science research. *Evaluation Review, 6*(5), 579-600.

Ulrich, D., Halbrook, R., Meder, D., Stuchlik, M., & Thorpe, S. (1991). Employee and customer attachment: Synergies for competitive advantage. *Human Resource Planning, 14*(2), 89-103.

Wagner, R., & Harter, J. K. (2006). *12: The elements of great managing.* New York: Gallup Press.

Whitman, D. S., Van Rooy, D. L., & Viswesvaran, C. (2010). Satisfaction, citizenship behaviors, and performance in work units: A meta-analysis of collective construct relations. *Personnel Psychology, 63*(1), 41-81.

Wiley, J. W. (1991). Customer satisfaction: A supportive work environment and its financial cost. *Human Resource Planning, 14*(2), 117-127.

Zohar, D. (1980). Safety climate in industrial organizations: Theoretical and applied implications. *Journal of Applied Psychology, 65*(1), 96-102.

Zohar, D. (2000). A group-level model of safety climate: Testing the effect of group climate on microaccidents in manufacturing jobs. *Journal of Applied Psychology, 85*(4), 587-596.

# APPENDIX 4

## The Relationship Between Strengths-Based Employee Development and Organizational Outcomes

### Strengths Meta-Analysis

Jim Asplund, M.A., Gallup
James K. Harter, Ph.D., Gallup
Sangeeta Agrawal, M.S., Gallup
Stephanie K. Plowman, M.A., Gallup

# EXECUTIVE SUMMARY

## OBJECTIVES

To date, the evidence from numerous organizational studies suggests that strengths-based employee development leads to more engaging and productive workplaces. The purpose of this study was to apply meta-analysis to a collection of research studies on strengths-based development and examine evidence of generalizability.

Specifically, this study will examine the:

1. true relationship between strengths-based employee development and performance in 22 organizations
2. consistency or generalizability of the relationship between strengths-based employee development and performance across organizations
3. practical meaning of the findings for executives and managers

# META-ANALYSIS, HYPOTHESIS, METHODS AND RESULTS

## META-ANALYSIS

Meta-analyses can be conducted on cumulative studies of the relationships between two or more variables of interest or the impact of two-group experimental interventions. The former are meta-analyses of r values whereas the latter are meta-analyses of d values (the difference between treatment and control groups divided by the pooled standard deviation). Meta-analytic mathematics, which uses advanced statistical methods such as reliability and range restriction distributions, are much more amenable to use of r values than d values. Since d values can be directly transformed into point-biserial r values, and vice versa, it is easiest to convert d values into r values, conduct the meta-analysis and then convert the true score r values back into d values for interpretative purposes. That process was used for this study.

For this meta-analysis, we corrected for artifactual sources of variation such as sampling error, measurement error and range restriction, where possible. Measurement error was corrected in most dependent variables based on artifact distributions obtained for previous Gallup meta-analyses. Test-retest reliability estimates were used based on Scenario 23 in Schmidt and Hunter (1996). Scenario 23 takes into account that some change in dependent variables (stability) is a function of real change.

## STRENGTHS-BASED INTERVENTIONS

The most general definition of a Gallup strengths-based intervention is one where a respondent completes the CliftonStrengths assessment and is made aware of their top natural talents. In practice, strengths-based interventions vary in the objective, type and magnitude. In some cases, respondents are given more advanced coaching and training, and in other cases, they are given more basic information such as a book or website description and tutorial. In some organizations, the interventions were designed for managers of teams, while in other organizations, individual contributors were given interventions.

Gallup researchers accumulated research studies comparing the intensity of strengths-based development interventions by business/work unit. In some studies, business units that had been given a strengths-based intervention were compared to those that had not. In other studies, business units with a low (but non-zero) percentage of employees receiving a strengths intervention were compared to business units where a higher percentage of employees learned to develop their strengths. These studies included randomized experimental designs, but the large majority were quasi-experimental, utilizing wait list control groups rather than randomized treatment and control groups. Where possible, variables that were hypothesized to explain possible differences between non-randomized treatment and control groups were utilized as statistical controls in analyses (e.g., baseline engagement, geography, business/work unit age, trade area market statistics, product type).

## STRENGTHS-BASED INTERVENTION TYPES

Researchers categorized the strengths-based interventions into four general types.

1. Business/work units included at least one person who completed the CliftonStrengths assessment. Dependent variables were compared to business/work units where no one completed the assessment.
2. The percentage of individuals who completed the CliftonStrengths assessment within a business/work unit was recorded. In this case, the treatment group independent variable could range from 1% to 100%.
3. An individual manager completed the CliftonStrengths assessment along with a manager developmental course. Business/work unit dependent variables were compared to those of managers who had not completed the course.

4. An individual manager completed the CliftonStrengths assessment. Business/work unit dependent variables were compared to those of managers who did not complete the assessment.

## DEPENDENT VARIABLES

Six general dependent variables were identified across studies: sales, profit, customer engagement, turnover, employee engagement and safety (accidents). The following is a description of each of the six dependent variable outcomes included in the studies.

- Sales: Sales, close rates, units per transaction, revenue growth, revenue per labor hours, sales in comparison to budget or goal, comparable sales growth, and productive utilization
- Profit: Overall percentage profit of revenue, profit increase, gross profit growth, margin erosion (reverse scored), margin versus target or goal, profit of existing customers, earnings before interest and taxes (EBIT)
- Employee engagement: Business-unit-level average scores on engagement surveys
- Customer engagement: Customer perceptions of quality
- Turnover: Annualized business/work unit turnover rate, first 90-day turnover rate
- Safety: Workers' compensation costs, workers' compensation incidents, patient falls, accident frequency, accident severity

Across studies, there was substantial variation in the proportion of the overall sample in organizations that were administered a strengths intervention. These values ranged from less than 1% to 99% (proportions of less than 0.01 to 0.99). With any proportion, the variance is maximized at 0.50. As such, departure from 0.50 reduces the possible effect size. Range restriction corrections were made based on an artifact distribution of independent variable estimates of U (sd/SD) across studies. Different artifact distributions were created for outcome-intervention combinations. In this case, correction for range restriction makes the size of true effect estimates more similar in magnitude to what one would expect in equally sized treatment and control group designs.

In an exhaustive review of Gallup's inferential databases, organizations with both CliftonStrengths assessment data and performance data were accumulated. Researchers limited their scrutiny to organizations with a minimum of 30 complete CliftonStrengths assessment responses, and a few studies had to be removed due to lack of identifiable contrast groups. In the end, a total of 43 studies were conducted in 22 organizations and included 1.2 million individuals.

Study organizations came from a wide range of industries, including heavy equipment and vehicle manufacturing, retail and commercial banking, mass and specialty retail, electric utilities, finance and insurance, healthcare, aerospace, food and other agriculture products, building materials, investment services, education, and pharmaceuticals.

The total study population was geographically diverse as well, with business/work units from 45 countries. The number of countries per study ranged from one to 36.

The following steps were followed in conducting this meta-analysis:

1. Studies were categorized by type of outcome, type of strengths intervention, and whether the study utilized control variables or not.
2. d values from experimental and quasi-experimental studies were converted to r's or pointbiserial r's, depending on the nature of the treatment effect variable (in one intervention type, the treatment variable was continuous — percentage of people within a business/work unit who were administered the CliftonStrengths assessment).
3. Meta-analyses using artifact distributions were conducted, reporting observed and true score effect sizes, standard deviations and generalizability statistics.
4. r values were converted back to d value effect sizes.
5. Utility analysis was conducted to estimate the practical value of the effect size estimates of the various intervention-outcome combinations.

## RESULTS

This study focuses on the relationships between learning or developing strengths and measures of organizational performance. Meta-analytic and validity generalization statistics for these relationships are shown in Table 1.

### Table I: Meta-Analysis of Relationship Between Outcomes and CliftonStrengths Assessment Intervention

| | Business Unit Level | | | | | |
|---|---|---|---|---|---|---|
| | Customer | Profit | Safety | Sales | Engagement | Turnover |
| Number of Business Units | 1,345 | 7,188 | 423 | 9,438 | 29,620 | 1,581 |
| Number of r's | 3 | 9 | 3 | 10 | 15 | 3 |
| | | | | | | |
| Mean Observed r | 0.053 | 0.129 | -0.119 | 0.082 | 0.086 | -0.214 |
| Observed SDr | 0.013 | 0.063 | 0.101 | 0.052 | 0.063 | 0.030 |
| Mean Observed d | 0.110 | 0.260 | -0.240 | 0.170 | 0.170 | -0.450 |
| | | | | | | |
| True Validity r[1] | 0.107 | 0.251 | -0.209 | 0.150 | 0.215 | -0.478 |
| True Validity SD[1] | 0.000 | 0.078 | 0.060 | 0.054 | 0.095 | 0.000 |
| True Validity d[1] | 0.220 | 0.540 | -0.440 | 0.310 | 0.450 | -1.240 |
| | | | | | | |
| % Variance Accounted for — Sampling Error | 1311.2 | 30.5 | 68.6 | 37.9 | 12.7 | 194.3 |
| % Variance Accounted for[1] | 1566.2 | 55.7 | 87.9 | 66.7 | 60.0 | 541.6 |
| | | | | | | |
| 90% CVr | 0.107 | 0.151 | -0.286 | 0.081 | 0.093 | -0.478 |
| 90% CVd | 0.220 | 0.310 | -0.620 | 0.160 | 0.190 | -1.240 |

SD = Standard Deviation
[1] Includes correction for direct range variation within organizations and dependent-variable measurement error

Mean observed correlations and standard deviations are shown, followed by estimated true validities, after correcting for dependent variable measurement error and within-organization range restriction. This range-restriction correction places all organizations on the same basis regarding variability in the independent variable. These results can be viewed as estimating the relationships across business/work units within the average organization.

The findings show generalizability across organizations, as indicated by the 90% credibility values, all of which match the direction of the hypothesized relationships (Schmidt & Hunter, 1977). That is, CliftonStrengths assessment completion effectively predicts these outcomes in the expected direction across organizations, including those in different industries and different countries.

For some of the measures, study artifacts explain most of the variance in correlations. For safety and sales, at least two-thirds of the variance in correlations is attributable to sampling error, range variation or measurement error. The results for profit measures were similar, but to a lesser degree; over half of the variability in these correlations is attributable to measurement artifacts.

In the case of customer and turnover measures, the sample of studies has much less variance between the effect sizes than would be expected by sampling error. This often happens with small numbers of studies per table entry, as was the case here. As a consequence, the estimated variance attributable to artifacts exceeded the total observed variability.

## CONTROL VARIABLES

As noted earlier, variables that were hypothesized to explain possible differences between nonrandomized treatment and control groups were utilized as statistical controls in analyses. As with the dependent variables themselves, the availability and quality of these control variables differed markedly both within and across organizations.

- Safety: All studies included control variables, including employee engagement, geographic identifiers, and employee and market demographic variables.
- Customer: Two of the three studies included control variables, including employee engagement, job and product types, and other employee demographic variables.
- Turnover: All three studies employed control variables, including employee engagement, geographic identifiers, manager tenure, employee tenure, number and type of competitors, and employee and market demographic characteristics.
- Engagement: All studies were controlled for engagement survey administration cohort (baseline engagement before intervention).
- Profit: Six of the nine studies used control variables, including employee and customer engagement, geographic identifiers, employee tenure, product type, employee and market demographic characteristics, business/work unit characteristics, and number and type of competitors.
- Sales: Seven of the 10 studies used control variables, including employee and customer engagement, geographic identifiers, employee tenure, product type, employee and market demographic characteristics, business/work unit characteristics, and number and type of competitors.

In total, 85% of studies in this meta-analysis utilized control variables of some type.

## DESIGN EFFECTS

As noted earlier, the studies included in the meta-analysis used four different research designs. One limitation of the meta-analysis is that the number of studies per design was not large. Table 2 shows the range of different study designs used for the analyses.

## Table 2

| Business Unit Level Meta-Analysis | Dependent Variable | Study Type | Control Variables Included? | Number of Correlations | Estimated True Validity: Mean | Lower 10% | Upper 10% | Range |
|---|---|---|---|---|---|---|---|---|
| 1 | Customer | 1 | mixed | 3 | 0.11 | 0.11 | 0.11 | 0.00 |
| 2 | Profit | mixed | mixed | 9 | 0.25 | 0.15 | 0.35 | 0.20 |
| 3 | Profit | mixed | yes | 6 | 0.29 | 0.29 | 0.29 | 0.00 |
| 4 | Profit | mixed | no | 3 | 0.14 | 0.14 | 0.14 | 0.00 |
| 5 | Profit | 1, 3 | mixed | 6 | 0.25 | 0.14 | 0.37 | 0.22 |
| 6 | Profit | 1, 3 | yes | 5 | 0.29 | 0.25 | 0.32 | 0.07 |
| 7 | Profit | 2, 4 | mixed | 3 | 0.25 | 0.25 | 0.25 | 0.00 |
| 8 | Safety | 1 | yes | 3 | -0.21 | -0.29 | -0.13 | 0.15 |
| 9 | Sales | mixed | mixed | 10 | 0.15 | 0.08 | 0.22 | 0.14 |
| 10 | Sales | mixed | yes | 7 | 0.14 | 0.05 | 0.23 | 0.18 |
| 11 | Sales | mixed | no | 3 | 0.26 | 0.26 | 0.26 | 0.00 |
| 12 | Sales | 1, 3 | mixed | 7 | 0.14 | 0.06 | 0.23 | 0.18 |
| 13 | Sales | 1, 3 | yes | 6 | 0.14 | 0.04 | 0.24 | 0.20 |
| 14 | Sales | 2, 4 | mixed | 3 | 0.20 | 0.20 | 0.20 | 0.00 |
| 15 | Turnover | 1, 3 | yes | 3 | -0.48 | -0.48 | -0.48 | 0.00 |
| 16 | Employee Engagement | 1, 2 | yes | 15 | 0.22 | 0.09 | 0.34 | 0.25 |

For most outcome measures, there was significant heterogeneity in study design. Given the small number of studies per design type, it is difficult to draw many inferences regarding the influence of different types of strengths intervention, for example.

# UTILITY ANALYSIS: PRACTICALITY OF THE EFFECTS

## UTILITY ANALYSIS

Effect sizes of the magnitude reported here are often difficult to interpret. Conventions regarding "small" or "large" effect sizes (Cohen, 1988) may not be informative since the practical significance of those effect sizes depends on the costs of improvement on the independent variable and the benefits of changes in the dependent variable. Rosenthal, et al. (2000) provide a classic example of a numerically small effect with large practical benefits: A study reporting the use of a beta blocker to increase heart attack survival (p. 27). The effect size of this study was 0.04, but this represented a 4% decrease in future heart attacks — a gain of some practical significance. The research literature includes a great many other examples of large practical benefits shown in studies with numerically moderate effect sizes (Abelson, 1985; Carver, 1975; Lipsey, 1990; Sechrest & Yeaton, 1982).

One can express the practical implications of the effects from this study by employing utility analysis methods (Schmidt & Rauschenberger, 1986). Formulas have been derived for estimating the dollar value increases in output as a result of improved employee selection. These formulas use the size of the effect, the variability in the outcome being studied and the difference in the independent variable to estimate the differences in performance outcomes.

The utility estimates for all outcomes are included in Table 3 and represent differences with considerable practical significance. Given that effect sizes varied, depending somewhat on whether or not control variables were used, we were conservative in our estimations of practical utility. We produced a range of likely utility estimates based on the 10$^{th}$ percentile (90% credibility value) of true score effects and the mean observed effect size. Variability of outcomes was estimated based on both literature and Gallup database values.

## Table 3

| | Business Unit Level | | | | | | |
|---|---|---|---|---|---|---|---|
| | Customer | Profit | Safety | Sales | Engagement | Low-Turnover Orgs. | High-Turnover Orgs. |
| Range Based on 90% CV and Observed | 3.4%-6.9% | 14.4%-29.4% | 22.9%-59.0% | 10.3%-19.3% | 9%-15% engaged employees | 5.8-16.1 pts. | 26.0-71.8 pts. |

## DISCUSSION

The present study is the first meta-analysis of the practical benefits of learning one's strengths using the CliftonStrengths assessment. These findings are important because they imply that interventions can be developed and used across different organizations with a high level of confidence. The data from the present study provide evidence that investing in employee development can provide material and psychological benefits to the organization, its customers and its owners.

# REFERENCES


Abelson, R. P. (1985). A variance explanation paradox: When a little is a lot. *Psychological Bulletin, 97*(1), 129-133. doi: 10.1037/0033-2909.97.1.129

Carver, R. P. (1975). The Coleman report: Using inappropriately designed achievement tests. *American Educational Research Journal, 12*(1), 77-86.

Cohen, J. (1988). *Statistical power analysis for the behavioral sciences* (2nd ed.). Hillsdale, NJ: Lawrence Earlbaum Associates.

Lipsey, M. W. (1990). *Design sensitivity: Statistical power for experimental research.* Newbury Park, CA: SAGE Publications.

Rosenthal, R., Rosnow, R. L., Rubin, D. B. (2000). *Contrasts and effect sizes in behavioral research: A correlational approach.* Cambridge: Cambridge University Press.

Schmidt, F. L., & Hunter, J. E. (1977). Development of a general solution to the problem of validity generalization. *Journal of Applied Psychology, 62*(5), 529.

Schmidt, F. L., & Hunter, J. E. (1996). Measurement error in psychological research: Lessons from 26 research scenarios. *Psychological Methods, 1*(2), 199-223.

Schmidt, F. L., & Rauschenberger, J. (1986, April). *Utility analysis for practitioners.* Paper presented at the first annual conference of The Society for Industrial and Organizational Psychology, Chicago, IL.

Sechrest, L., & Yeaton, W. H. (1982). Magnitudes of experimental effects in social science research. *Evaluation Review*, 6(5), 579-600. doi: 10.1177/0193841X8200600501

# APPENDIX 5

## Gallup Meta-Analytic Study of Managerial Hiring and Development Profiles

Yongwei Yang, Ph.D.
Joseph H. Streur, Ph.D.
James K. Harter, Ph.D.
Sangeeta Agrawal, M.S.

Nearly six decades ago, Gallup began studying management roles — the patterns of excellence and the innate tendencies that predict exceptional workplace performance for leaders of teams and organizations. Gallup has accumulated qualitative and quantitative findings of managerial success and maintained a database of more than 300 instrument development and validation studies of manager success across changing business and economic times.

In every organization or enterprise, all employees must meet the responsibilities of their respective roles. Each role exists to meet the needs of the people an enterprise serves, whether they are customers, students or patients. When serving these needs aligns with the enterprise's purpose and aims, sustainable growth occurs. This rationale holds true for all roles in an organization, from front-line employees to managers to leaders.

Management roles typically exist between the higher position levels of enterprise leadership and the roles of individual contributors and their immediate supervisors. The specific job titles within the management roles vary widely and often reflect organization-specific job-labeling conventions or the structure of a specific organizational hierarchy.

To delineate the types of management roles, Gallup researchers reviewed past studies of more than 200 roles from organizations across numerous industries that included retail, hospitality, manufacturing, finance and chemical. This allowed researchers to theorize the talent themes that enable successful fulfillment of manager responsibilities. These themes formed the content basis to select items for managerial assessments. Gallup's item bank includes more than 300 instrument development studies for managerial assessment content. Data from these studies are continually updated and reviewed based on psychometric properties — validity; reliability; and fairness of individual items, themes and dimensions. Based on qualitative and quantitative review of manager success characteristics, the following generalizable dimensions have been found to predict future managerial success:

1. Motivation — Inspiring teams to get exceptional work done
2. Workstyle — Setting goals and arranging resources for the team to excel
3. Initiation — Influencing others to act; pushing through adversity and resistance
4. Collaboration — Building committed teams with deep bonds
5. Thought process — Taking an analytical approach to strategy and decision-making

Systematic measurement of these innate tendencies can then be used — in conjunction with a critical review of experience and performance — to create an objective and complete picture of a manager's or leader's potential.

Gallup has historically collected performance data associated with managerial selection instruments after these instruments were used in the field. These instruments have included various levels of management, ranging from front-line management to executive leadership positions. From these data, Gallup has conducted concurrent (cross-validation) and predictive validity studies, studying the relationship between scores on the instruments and performance outcomes, including performance ratings, employee engagement of those directly reporting to the manager, financial performance of the business unit being managed, productivity, customer ratings of service quality, employee turnover of those directly reporting to the managers, and composite measures of performance (combined financial and nonfinancial metrics). Researchers have conducted various studies over the past several decades, including those referenced in two prior meta-analyses of Gallup selection instruments (Schmidt & Rader, 1999; Harter et al., 2004). The purpose of this meta-analysis is to update the previous meta-analyses, specifically for managerial selection instruments involving managerial positions with job demands that include the management of people toward organizational outcomes. Because Gallup developed the manager selection assessment that is the focus of this report based on content acquired from the previous Gallup studies, the meta-analytic validity estimates from past studies provide a basis for understanding the likely validity of the present tool and its generalizability across different settings.

*Method.* This meta-analysis contains only cross-validation samples of instruments that Gallup has historically developed, including in-depth assessments (structured interviews) and web-based assessments. For each performance outcome variable, the samples are independent. Observed validities are typically downward biased because of measurement error in the performance measurement and, in the case of predictive validity studies, range restriction because of the explicit use of instrument scores to select managers. Researchers used artifact distributions to correct for these downward biases.

Gallup researchers obtained 136 studies with 14,597 managers. Of these studies, 81 were predictive validity and 55 were concurrent cross-validation studies; 87 studies were from in-depth (structured) interviews, and 49 were obtained from web assessments. These studies included seven general performance outcomes, with some studies containing correlations from multiple outcomes. The most frequent outcome variable was a supervisory performance rating, followed by employee engagement survey responses from those reporting directly to each manager; financial performance measures such as sales and profit figures from the business units the managers managed; and productivity measures such as performance awards, bonuses, total accounts (financial) and room nights (hotel). Seven studies contained composite measures of performance based on combined financial performance, customer engagement and employee engagement measures. Five studies contained customer ratings of the quality of service provided by the managers' business units, and three studies contained employee retention data (the annualized turnover of employees reporting to the manager, reverse scored).

This accumulation of studies included managers across various industries, including agriculture, consumer goods, construction, financial services, retail, manufacturing, petroleum, insurance, healthcare, schools, hotels, restaurants, other hospitality, military and high-tech. We also included international data, consisting of managers from Africa, Canada, India, Malaysia, Singapore and other parts of Asia in addition to the United Kingdom and the United States. For some outcomes within studies, multiple measures were provided (such as multiple financial measures). In these cases, Gallup researchers followed some basic decision rules. In some cases where indistinguishably important criterion measures were provided for the same outcome, we averaged the correlation across studies and used this one average estimate for the study sample. In other cases, a particular measure was determined to be the most construct-valid measure of the outcome.

Hunter & Schmidt (2004) methods of meta-analysis were used in this study. A meta-analysis is a statistical integration of data accumulated across many different studies. As such, it provides powerful information because it controls for measurement and sampling errors and other idiosyncrasies that distort the results of individual studies. A meta-analysis seeks to eliminate biases and provides an estimate of true validity or true relationship between two or more variables. Statistics typically calculated during meta-analysis also allow the researcher to explore the presence, or lack, of moderators of relationships. For this study, researchers used the interactive procedure (Hunter & Schmidt, 1990) with refinements that increase accuracy of artifact distribution-based meta-analysis (Hunter & Schmidt, 2004; Hunter & Schmidt, 1994; Law, Schmidt, & Hunter, 1994; Schmidt et al., 1993). Gallup researchers used artifact distribution meta-analysis methods because not all studies had the necessary range restriction and dependent variable reliability estimates. Direct range restriction corrections were applied only to predictive validity studies, where direct range restriction is common. For concurrent validity studies, we have applied the indirect range restriction correction procedure to this meta-analysis (Hunter, Schmidt, & Le, 2006). Indirect range restriction is likely among incumbents used in concurrent cross-validation studies, as incumbent employees are likely to have been selected using some method that improves performance beyond chance, and criterion reliability estimates are then likely attenuated. We corrected for measurement error in the performance variables for both concurrent and predictive study designs.

*Artifact Distributions — Predictor Reliability Distribution.* The predictor (independent variable) reliability artifact distribution (mean = 0.82; s = 0.04) was taken from reported test-retest reliabilities of Gallup assessments, including both in-depth and web (Harter, 2003). For this meta-analysis, no corrections for predictor reliability were made to the mean true validity. Rather, for generalizability analyses, we used the predictor reliability artifact distributions to correct the true validity standard deviation.

*Artifact Distributions — Performance Ratings.* Supervisory performance ratings included ratings used for administrative purposes and those used for research only. Rating forms varied widely, but the dependent variable used in each study was a composite "overall" rating of an average across items contained in the rating. Where both were provided, the latter was used to increase reliability and content coverage. The inter-rater reliability of supervisory performance ratings has been studied extensively by Rothstein (1990) and Viswesvaran et al. (1996) in forming the artifact distribution with a mean of 0.52 (s = 0.10).

*Artifact Distributions — Employee Engagement.* Employee engagement was measured using Gallup's $Q^{12}$ measure, which has been extensively studied and reported on (Harter, Schmidt, Agrawal, & Plowman, 2013). The GrandMean (average of the 12 employee engagement items) was used as the criterion variable, once aggregated across the responses of employees who report to each manager. The artifact distribution was created based on test-retest reliabilities at the business-unit level based on the formula provided in Hunter and Schmidt (1996), scenario 23 (p. 219). Test-retest reliabilities for financial performance, productivity, customer ratings and employee turnover were computed using the same formula, which corrects for real change that is likely to occur from one time period to the next on these variables. The mean artifact distribution reliability for employee engagement was 0.73 (s = 0.14).

*Artifact Distributions — Financial Performance.* Financial variables included business-unit-level dollar sales, revenue, profit, profit growth, revenue per available room (hotel), profit percentage to goal and percentage gross margin to goal. The definition of financial performance is slightly different from that of prior Gallup meta-analyses because, in the current meta-analysis, we excluded studies with variables that were not pure financial variables, such as number of new accounts, units sold or room nights, which were instead included in the productivity category. We also included composite measures that were purely financial composites. In the "composite performance" category, we included composites of financial *and* nonfinancial outcomes. Because the financial outcomes represented a blended set of revenue, sales and profit, we combined the artifact distributions from business-unit-level productivity (revenue or sales) and profit from the Harter et al. (2013) meta-analysis. This resulted in a mean of 0.87 (s = 0.18).

*Artifact Distributions — Productivity.* As indicated previously, productivity measures included performance awards, bonuses, total accounts (financial) and room nights (hotel). For production records, we used the artifact distribution compiled for performance statistics and production records in Harter et al. (2004), with a mean of 0.98 (s = 0.01).

*Artifact Distributions — Composite Performance.* For the six studies that included composite measures of managerial performance, all included a sum of financial, customer and employee engagement outcomes. We used the artifact distribution of composite measures used in Harter et al. (2004) with a mean of 0.75 (s = 0.04).

*Artifact Distributions — Customer Ratings.* Measures of the service provided to customers through survey responses of customers were aggregated at the business-unit level. We used the artifact distribution compiled in Harter et al. (2013) with a mean of 0.68 (s = 0.20).

*Artifact Distributions — Employee Retention.* The artifact distribution for business-unit-level employee turnover was also compiled in Harter et al. (2013). It has a mean of 0.50 (s = 0.26).

*Range Restriction.* As noted previously, the studies in this analysis include both concurrent and predictive validity studies. Explicit range restriction commonly occurs in predictive validity studies, where organizations select applicants with higher scores. This leads to attenuated predictive validity estimates. For this study, we used the artifact distribution compiled based on Gallup studies (Harter et al., 2004) with a mean U (SD of hired employees/SD of applicants) of 0.77 (s = 0.16).

*Results.* The table below presents the meta-analysis results by study design (concurrent or predictive) within performance criterion variable type. Prior meta-analyses (Schmidt & Rader, 1999; Harter et al., 2004) found Gallup instruments to be predictive of various performance outcomes, including studies collected on manager selection instruments. This is also the case in the data reported here, with some variables added, including numerous studies conducted on the relationship between managerial talent and employee engagement, and five studies reporting the relationship between managerial talent and customer ratings of service quality. Additionally, four studies reported the relationship between managerial talent and the turnover of employees in the managers' business units.

## Meta-Analysis of Relationship Between Manager Talent and Manager Performance

| Criterion Type | Sample Type | Number of Cases | Number of Correlations | Mean Observed Correlation | Observed SD of Correlation | True Validity | True Validity SD | 90% Credibility Value | 10% Credibility Value |
|---|---|---|---|---|---|---|---|---|---|
| Composite Performance | Predictive | 256 | 6 | 0.26 | 0.07 | 0.37 | 0.00 | 0.37 | 0.37 |
| Performance Ratings | Concurrent | 2,995 | 29 | 0.19 | 0.13 | 0.36 | 0.11 | 0.22 | 0.51 |
| | Predictive | 5,662 | 26 | 0.16 | 0.11 | 0.28 | 0.14 | 0.10 | 0.46 |
| Employee Engagement | Concurrent | 1,765 | 22 | 0.19 | 0.14 | 0.30 | 0.12 | 0.15 | 0.46 |
| | Predictive | 1,013 | 9 | 0.18 | 0.15 | 0.26 | 0.15 | 0.06 | 0.47 |
| Productivity | Predictive | 685 | 11 | 0.17 | 0.13 | 0.24 | 0.01 | 0.22 | 0.26 |
| Financial Performance | Predictive | 880 | 21 | 0.21 | 0.20 | 0.29 | 0.17 | 0.07 | 0.51 |
| Customer Ratings | Predictive | 492 | 6 | 0.10 | 0.11 | 0.15 | 0.00 | 0.15 | 0.15 |
| Employee Retention | Predictive | 411 | 3 | 0.05 | 0.02 | 0.11 | 0.00 | 0.11 | 0.11 |

Across outcomes, there remains substantial evidence of generalizability in the relationship between manager talent and the seven performance outcomes. The distribution of true validities across studies is clearly in the hypothesized direction. Among the seven outcomes studied, the predictive validity was highest for composite performance (0.37), the magnitude of which was consistent across the six studies after correcting for measurement error, range restriction and sampling error. This makes sense because managers manage toward multiple outcomes. The impact of talent on organizational performance should be expected to be best expressed and evaluated through the combining of multiple variables, including financial and nonfinancial factors. For four outcomes (performance ratings, employee engagement, productivity and financial performance), the predictive validities were of similar magnitude, ranging from 0.24 to 0.29. These true validities were also largely generalizable, with some variance in predictive validity across studies, but a distribution that is clearly positive. This means one can expect to find a positive correlation to these performance outcomes across many situations. The most variance in predictive validities occurred regarding financial outcomes and employee engagement, but the 10$^{th}$ and 90$^{th}$ percentiles of validities ranged from 0.07 and 0.06 to 0.51 and 0.47, respectively. This indicates a distribution of prediction of financial performance and employee engagement that is clearly in the positive direction, but with some possible moderating factors regarding the magnitude of the relationship. It is possible that the financial outcome effect size is moderated by the type of financial measures available and the degree of managerial influence on those variables. It is also possible that the relationship between managerial talent and employee engagement is somewhat dependent on the specific constructs included in the talent measure for different organizations over time. Nonetheless, the various talent assessments used in historical research consistently positively predict both financial performance and employee engagement. The magnitude of effect size is only one factor in determining the practical utility. That is, a smaller effect size can explain higher dollar value practical effect if there is wide variability in performance across business units. The next section discusses practical utility in detail. The remaining outcomes (customer ratings and employee turnover) included fewer studies, but they also revealed true validities in the hypothesized direction. Higher manager talent is associated with more positive customer perceptions (0.15) and higher employee retention (0.11).

## INTERPRETING CRITERION VALIDITY COEFFICIENTS

Criterion-related validity evidence is usually expressed as correlations. Naturally, one may ask the question: Are these correlations "large"? Such a question needs to be answered within the relevant context. The first context is the findings in the literature regarding the criterion-related validity of personnel selection methods. Published meta-analytical studies regarding the predictability of dispositional factors to leadership or management effectiveness are limited. Judge, Bono, Ilies, and Gerhardt (2002) reported true score correlations (after correcting for unreliability in both predictor and criterion as well as for range restrictions) between measures of Big Five personality traits and leadership effectiveness measures ranging from 0.16 (Conscientiousness) to 0.24 (Extraversion and Openness to Experience). Judge, Colbert, and Ilies (2004) reported such true score correlations between paper-and-pencil intelligence measures and leadership effectiveness measures ranging from 0.17 to 0.33, and the relationship may vary depending on type of effectiveness measures. The estimated criterion validity with the manager assessments appears to be comparable to, and in some cases higher than, those reported by Judge et al. (2002) and Judge et al. (2004).

In the past two decades, various meta-analytic studies have explored the validity of employment interviews and other selection approaches (McDaniel, Whetzel, Schmidt, & Maurer, 1994; Schmidt & Hunter, 1998). As shown by these studies, the source of variance among validity coefficients is not limited to the type of selection assessments, the constructs being measured and the type of jobs; such variance can also arise from the type of criterion measures. In Judge et al. (2002), leadership effectiveness measures were based predominantly on supervisor and subordinate ratings. In Judge et al. (2004), "objective" effectiveness measures — defined by the authors as "based on a quantifiable score (e.g., team performance on a survival simulation ...)" (p. 544) — were also included. However, neither study appears to have included organizational or business outcome measures. In contrast, the criterion measures used to estimate the criterion-related validity for the manager assessments used composite measures that took into account multiple aspects of job performance. The diversity in criterion measures used in these studies and the appreciable validity estimates provide strong support for using the Gallup manager assessments for organizational interventions.

Another context for understanding the magnitude of a validity coefficient is to consider its practical business impact or potential utility. There are established methods to estimate impact from implementing a selection approach. Theoretical expectancy models (Taylor & Russell, 1939) show that, holding validity constant, the practical gain from a selection procedure may increase as a result of decreasing selection ratio and may also be affected by the base rate of success on the job (i.e., the rate of success without using the selection tool). For example, assuming a 50% base rate of success among people in managerial positions and applying the 0.37 composite performance predictive validity obtained from the meta-analysis, selecting the top 10% of applicants would improve the rate of success to 76%, or an improvement of 52%. A 30% selection ratio would result in a 67% success rate among those hired, or an improvement of 34%. Considering a 20% base rate of success and a 10% selection ratio, those hired would have a 42% success rate, or more than double the base rate. For a 30% selection ratio, those hired would have a 33% success rate.

Regarding financial performance, assuming an average level of predictive validity and a coefficient of variation (ratio of standard deviation to the mean) of 63% for business-unit-level revenue or sales in Gallup's database, selecting the top 10% of manager applicants on the Gallup instrument would relate to 32% improvement in revenue or sales per manager. Selecting the top 30% would relate to 21% higher revenue or sales per manager. Given the wide variation in profit across business units within organizations Gallup has studied (mean coefficient of variation of 94%), selecting the top 10% of manager candidates can relate to a difference of 48% in profit per manager. Selecting the top 30% of manager candidates can relate to a difference of 32% in profit per manager. These types of utility estimates can be calculated for many of the outcomes managers are responsible for. In short, if the Gallup manager selection instrument is used systematically, these examples show that an organization can expect sizable practical differences in business-unit performance over time.

## REFERENCES

Harter, J. K. (2003). *Test-retest reliability of Gallup selection assessments.* Gallup Technical Report. Omaha, NE.

Harter, J. K., Hayes, T. L., & Schmidt, F. L. (2004). *Meta-analytic predictive validity of Gallup Selection Research Instruments (SRI).* Gallup Technical Report. Omaha, NE.

Harter, J. K., Schmidt, F. L., Agrawal, S. A., & Plowman, S. K. (2013). *The relationship between engagement at work and organizational outcomes: 2012 $Q^{12}$ meta-analysis.* Gallup Technical Report. Omaha, NE.

Hunter, J. E., & Schmidt, F. L. (1990). *Methods of meta-analysis: Correcting error and bias in research findings.* Newbury Park, CA: Sage.

Hunter, J. E., & Schmidt, F. L. (1994). Estimation of sampling error variance in the meta-analysis of correlations: Use of average correlation in the homogeneous case. *Journal of Applied Psychology, 79*, 171-177.

Hunter, J. E., & Schmidt, F. L. (1996). Measurement error in psychological research: Lessons from 26 research scenarios. *Psychological Methods, 1,* 199-223.

Hunter, J. E., & Schmidt, F. L. (2004). *Methods of meta-analysis: Correcting error and bias in research findings (2nd ed.).* Newbury Park, CA: Sage.

Hunter, J. E., Schmidt, F. L., & Le, H. A. (2006). Implications of direct and indirect range restriction for meta-analysis methods and findings. *Journal of Applied Psychology, 91*, 594-612.

Judge, T. A., Bono, J. E., Ilies, R., & Gerhardt, M. W. (2002). Personality and leadership: A qualitative and quantitative review. *Journal of Applied Psychology, 87*, 765-780.

Judge, T. A., Colbert, A. E., & Ilies, R. (2004). Intelligence and leadership: A quantitative review and test of theoretical propositions. *Journal of Applied Psychology, 89*, 542-552.

Law, K. S., Schmidt, F. L., & Hunter, J. E. (1994). Nonlinearity of range corrections in meta-analysis: Test of an improved procedure. *Journal of Applied Psychology, 79*, 425-438.

McDaniel, M. A., Whetzel, D. L., Schmidt, F. L., & Maurer, S. D. (1994). The validity of employment interviews: A comprehensive review and meta-analysis. *Journal of Applied Psychology, 79*, 599-616.

Rothstein, H. R. (1990). Interrater reliability of job performance ratings: Growth to asymptote level with increasing opportunity to observe. *Journal of Applied Psychology, 75*, 322-327.

Schmidt, F. L., & Hunter, J. E. (1998). The validity and utility of selection methods in personnel psychology: Practical and theoretical implications of 85 years of research findings. *Psychological Bulletin, 124(2),* 262.

Schmidt, F. L., Law, K., Hunter, J. E., Rothstein, H. R., Pearlman, K., & McDaniel, M. (1993). Refinements in validity generalization methods: Implications for the situational specificity hypothesis. *Journal of Applied Psychology, 78*, 3-12.

Schmidt, F. L., & Rader, M. (1999). Exploring the boundary conditions for interview validity: Meta-analytic validity findings for a new interview type. *Personnel Psychology, 52*, 445-464.

Taylor, H. C., & Russell, J. T. (1939). The relationship of validity coefficients to the practical effectiveness of tests in selection: discussion and tables. *Journal of Applied Psychology, 23(5)*, 565.

Viswesvaran, C., Ones, D. S., & Schmidt, F. L. (1996). Comparative analysis of the reliability of job performance ratings. *Journal of Applied Psychology, 81*, 557-574.

# References and Notes

This book covers a wide range of research. For more details about Gallup's research and other studies referenced in the book's text, please see this expanded reference section.

For some references, we have included additional commentary.

Please note that any statistics not cited stem from Gallup research and studies.

## INTRODUCTION: THE NEW WILL OF THE WORLD

Bureau of Labor Statistics. (2018, January 19). *Labor force statistics from the current population survey.* Retrieved November 19, 2018, from https://www.bls.gov/cps/cpsaat08.htm

Clifton, J. (2015, December 10). *Killing small business.* Retrieved November 19, 2018, from https://news.gallup.com/opinion/chairman/186638/killing-small-business.aspx

Clifton, J. (2015, December 17). *What the whole world wants.* Retrieved November 19, 2018, from https://news.gallup.com/opinion/chairman/187676/whole-world-wants.aspx?g_source=link_NEWSV9&g_medium=&g_campaign=item_&g_content=What%2520the%2520Whole%2520World%2520Wants

Clifton, J. (2016, August 3). *Corporate boards: Failing at growth.* Retrieved November 19, 2018, from https://news.gallup.com/opinion/chairman/194132/corporate-boards-failing-growth.aspx?g_source=link_NEWSV9&g_medium=TOPIC&g_campaign=item_&g_content=Corporate%2520Boards%3a%2520Failing%2520at%2520Growth

Clifton, J. (2017, June 13). *The world's broken workplace.* Retrieved November 19, 2018, from https://news.gallup.com/opinion/chairman/212045/world-broken-workplace.aspx?g_source=link_NEWSV9&g_medium=TOPIC&g_campaign=item_&g_content=The%2520World%27s%2520Broken%2520Workplace

DeSilver, D. (2017, January 4). *5 facts about the minimum wage.* Retrieved November 19, 2018, from http://www.pewresearch.org/fact-tank/2017/01/04/5-facts-about-the-minimum-wage/

Desjardins, J. (2016, September 8). *Visualizing the size of the U.S. national debt.* Retrieved November 19, 2018, from http://money.visualcapitalist.com/visualizing-size-u-s-national-debt/

Drucker, P. F. (1954). *The practice of management: A study of the most important function in American society.* New York: Harper & Brothers.

Gallup. (2017). *State of the global workplace.* New York: Gallup Press.

Kamp, K. (2013, September 20). *By the numbers: The incredibly shrinking American middle class.* Retrieved November 19, 2018, from https://billmoyers.com/2013/09/20/by-the-numbers-the-incredibly-shrinking-american-middle-class/

Keng, C. (2014, June 22). *Employees who stay in companies longer than two years get paid 50% less.* Retrieved November 19, 2018, from https://www.forbes.com/sites/cameronkeng/2014/06/22/employees-that-stay-in-companies-longer-than-2-years-get-paid-50-less/#1d727e4e07fa

Rothwell, J. (2016). *No recovery: An analysis of long-term U.S. productivity decline.* Washington, D.C.: Gallup and the U.S. Council on Competitiveness.

Statista. (2018). *Number of full-time employees in the United States from 1990 to 2017 (in millions).* Retrieved November 19, 2018, from https://www.statista.com/statistics/192356/number-of-full-time-employees-in-the-usa-since-1990/

Trading Economics. (2018 December). *United States GDP.* Retrieved November 19, 2018, from https://tradingeconomics.com/united-states/gdp

# STRATEGY

## CHAPTER 1. WHAT EXACTLY SHOULD CEOs AND CHROs CHANGE?

Gallup. (2016). *How millennials want to work and live.* Retrieved December 7, 2018, from https://www.gallup.com/workplace/238073/millennials-work-live.aspx

## CHAPTER 2. WHY ORGANIZATIONAL CHANGE IS SO HARD

In a 2018 Gallup study of 4,000 full-time and part-time employees in France, Germany, Spain and the U.K., less than one in four employees strongly agreed that the leadership of their company makes them enthusiastic about the future.

---

Agrawal, S., & Harter, J. K. (2010). *The cascade effect of employee engagement: A longitudinal study: Technical report.* Omaha, NE: Gallup.

Dunbar, R. I. M. (1992). Neocortex size as a constraint on group size in primates. *Journal of Human Evolution, 20,* 469-493.

Fowler, J. H., & Christakis, N. A. (2008). Dynamic spread of happiness in a large social network: Longitudinal analysis over 20 years in the Framingham heart study. *BMJ,* 337, a2338+.

Gallup. (2016). *First, break all the rules: What the world's greatest managers do differently.* New York: Gallup Press.

Hernando, A., Villuendas, D., Vesperinas, C., Abad, M., & Plastino, A. (2010). Unravelling the size distribution of social groups with information theory in complex networks. *The European Physical Journal B, 76*(1), 87-97.

Liberty, E., Woolfe, F., Martinsson, P., Rokhlin, V., & Tygert, M. (2007). Randomized algorithms for the low-rank approximation of matrices. *Proceedings of the National Academy of Sciences, 104*(51), 20167-20172.

## CHAPTER 3. TWO NON-NEGOTIABLE TRAITS FOR LEADERS

In a five-decade review of Gallup leadership research, we found a wide range of successful leadership traits: intensity, catalyst, accountability, flexibility, goal orientation, planning, individualized perception, strategic networking, talent appreciation, team leading, business orientation, concept, knowledge seeking, strategic thinking, competitiveness, courage, orchestration, structure, enthusiasm, investment, concept and vision.

---

Emond, L. (2018, July 16). *Microsoft CHRO: A conversation about succession management.* Retrieved December 6, 2018, from https://www.gallup.com/workplace/237113/microsoft-chro-conversation-succession-management.aspx

Newport, F., & Harter, J. (2017, September 26). *What Americans value in the president, workers value in their CEO.* Retrieved December 6, 2018, from https://news.gallup.com/opinion/polling-matters/219932/americans-value-president-workers-value-ceo.aspx

## CHAPTER 4. BRING MULTIPLE TEAMS TOGETHER

To lead effectively, Gallup has found that executives inspire others through their vision; maximize the organization's values by creating accountability and leading change; and mentor and build a constituency by developing people, building relationships and communicating effectively.

---

Agrawal, S., & Harter, J. K. (2010). *The cascade effect of employee engagement: A longitudinal study: Technical report.* Omaha, NE: Gallup.

Wigert, B., & Maese, E. (2018). *The manager experience study.* Gallup Working Paper. Omaha, NE.

## CHAPTER 5. MAKE GREAT DECISIONS

In a 2018 Gallup study of 4,000 full-time and part-time employees in Europe, 41% in France, 33% in the U.K., 26% in Germany and 27% in Spain strongly agreed that their company has the right mentality to respond quickly to business needs.

---

Book summary of *Thinking, Fast and Slow* by Daniel Kahneman. (2016, September 10). Retrieved December 7, 2018, from http://www.hughflint.com/book-reviews/book-summary-by-thinking-fast-and-slow-by-daniel-kahneman/

Garamone, J. (2013, May 5). *Improving the science of decision making.* Retrieved December 7, 2018, from http://science.dodlive.mil/2013/05/05/improving-the-science-of-decision-making/

Greathouse, J. (2013, April 30). *5 time-tested success tips from Amazon founder Jeff Bezos.* Retrieved December 7, 2018, from https://www.forbes.com/sites/johngreathouse/2013/04/30/5-time-tested-success-tips-from-amazon-founder-jeff-bezos/#33db5d59370c

Kahneman, D. (2015). *Thinking, fast and slow.* New York: Farrar, Straus and Giroux.

# CULTURE

## CHAPTER 6. WHAT IS AN ORGANIZATIONAL CULTURE?

In a 2018 Gallup study of 4,000 full-time and part-time employees in France, Germany, Spain and the U.K., about one in three employees in each country strongly agreed that they would recommend their company as a place to work.

---

Gallup. (2018). *Gallup's approach to culture: Building a culture that drives performance.* Retrieved December 7, 2018, from https://www.gallup.com/workplace/232682/culture-paper-2018.aspx?g_source=link_WWWV9&g_medium=related_insights_tile1&g_campaign=item_229832&g_content=Get%2520the%2520Most%2520Out%2520of%2520Your%2520Culture

## CHAPTER 7. WHY CULTURE MATTERS

Gallup. (2016). *The relationship between engagement at work and organizational outcomes: 2016 Q12® meta-analysis: Ninth edition.* Retrieved December 7, 2018, from https://news.gallup.com/reports/191489/q12-meta-analysis-report-2016.aspx

Gallup. (2017). *State of the global workplace.* New York: Gallup Press.

## CHAPTER 8. HOW TO CHANGE A CULTURE

Koi-Akrofi, G. Y. (2016). Mergers and acquisitions failure rates and perspectives on why they fail. *International Journal of Innovation and Applied Studies, 17*(1), 150-158.

Ratanjee, V. (2018, February 27). *Why HR leaders are vital for culture change.* Retrieved December 7, 2018, from https://www.gallup.com/workplace/234908/why-leaders-vital-culture-change.aspx

# EMPLOYMENT BRAND

## CHAPTER 9. ATTRACTING THE NEW WORKFORCE

Most employees, not just millennials, prefer online job searches. A basic requirement is to make online job opportunities easy to find, user-friendly and visually appealing. Websites should include compelling content that clearly describes what differentiates your organization from the competition — your purpose, brand intentions and culture. Considering that 85% of millennials access the internet from their smartphones, if you are aiming to attract millennials, make sure your website offers a seamless mobile experience.

Only about one in four job seekers, mostly Gen Xers and baby boomers, still use newspapers to find job openings.

---

Gallup. (2016). *Gallup's perspective on: Designing your organization's employee experience.* Retrieved December 7, 2018, from https://www.gallup.com/workplace/242240/employee-experience-perspective-paper.aspx?g_source=link_wwwv9&g_campaign=item_242276&g_medium=copy

Gallup. (2016). *How millennials want to work and live.* Retrieved December 7, 2018, from https://www.gallup.com/workplace/238073/millennials-work-live.aspx

## CHAPTER 10. HIRING STAR EMPLOYEES

Ambady, N., & Rosenthal, R. (1992). Thin slices of expressive behavior as predictors of interpersonal consequences: A meta-analysis. *Psychological Bulletin, 111*(2), 256-274.

Bias. (n.d.). *Psychology Today.* Retrieved December 7, 2018, from https://www.psychologytoday.com/us/basics/bias

Buchanan, R. D., & Finch, S. J. (2005). *History of psychometrics.* Retrieved December 7, 2018, from https://www.researchgate.net/publication/230267368_History_of_Psychometrics

Christensen-Szalanski, J. J., & Beach, L. R. (1982). Experience and the base-rate fallacy. *Organizational Behavior & Human Performance, 29*(2), 270-278.

Dronyk-Trosper, T., & Stitzel, B. (2015). Lock-in and team effects: Recruiting and success in college football athletics. *Journal of Sports Economics, 18*(4), 376-387.

Gladwell, M. (2005). *Blink: The power of thinking without thinking.* New York: Little, Brown.

Grinnell, R. (2016). Availability heuristic. *Psych Central.* Retrieved December 7, 2018, from https://psychcentral.com/encyclopedia/availability-heuristic/

Moore, D. A. (2018, January 22). *Overconfidence: The mother of all biases.* Retrieved December 7, 2018, from https://www.psychologytoday.com/us/blog/perfectly-confident/201801/overconfidence

Pennsylvania State University. (2015, April 17). *Similar-to-me effect in the workplace.* Retrieved December 7, 2018, from https://sites.psu.edu/aspsy/2015/04/17/similar-to-me-effect-in-the-workplace/

Shahani-Denning, C. (2003). *Physical attractiveness bias in hiring: What is beautiful is good.* Retrieved from http://www.hofstra.edu/pdf/orsp_shahani-denning_spring03.pdf

The University of Texas at El Paso. (n.d.). *Master list of logical fallacies.* Retrieved December 7, 2018, from http://utminers.utep.edu/omwilliamson/ENGL1311/fallacies.htm

## CHAPTER 11. HIRING ANALYTICS — THE SOLUTION

Combining four hiring criteria (prior experiences and achievements, innate tendencies, multiple interviews, and on-the-job observations) can boost the success rate of hires from 20% to 70%.

The Schmidt et al. (2016) 100-year study found that many methods of selection can improve prediction of performance, including general mental ability tests, employment interviews (structured and unstructured), integrity and personality tests, reference checks, biographical data, prior experience, work sample, and those used in assessment centers. Researchers can use many of these methods to measure the five innate traits or tendencies (motivation, workstyle, initiation, collaboration, thought process) and combine them to maximize prediction of performance. The study found that general mental ability was the single strongest predictor of performance and that many of the other methods were substantially additive in predicting performance. General mental ability can be approximated in a variety of ways, including direct tests of mental ability or thought process, prior experiences and achievements, situational judgement knowledge tests, and job tryouts.

---

Harter, J. K., Hayes, T. L., & Schmidt, F. L. (2004). *Meta-analytic predictive validity of Gallup selection research instruments (SRI).* Omaha, NE: Gallup.

Schmidt, F. L., & Rader, M. (1999). Exploring the boundary conditions for interview validity: Meta-analytic validity findings for a new interview type. *Personnel Psychology,* 52, 445-464.

Schmidt, F. L., & Zimmerman, R. D. (2004). A counterintuitive hypothesis about employment interview validity and some supporting evidence. *Journal of Applied Psychology,* 89(3), 553-561.

Schmidt, F. L., Oh, I. S., & Shaffer, J. A. (2016). *The validity and utility of selection methods in personnel psychology: Practical and theoretical implications of 100 years of research findings.* Retrieved December 7, 2018, from https://www.testingtalent.net/wp-content/uploads/2017/04/2016-100-Yrs-Working-Paper-on-Selection-Methods-Schmit-Mar-17.pdf

Yang, Y., Harter, J. K., Streur, J. H., Agrawal, S., Dvorak, N., & Walker, P. (2013). *The Gallup manager assessment: Technical report.* Omaha, NE: Gallup.

## CHAPTER 12. WHERE TO FIND "GAME FILM" ON FUTURE STARS

Gallup. (2014). *Great jobs, great lives. The 2014 Gallup-Purdue Index report.* Retrieved December 7, 2018, from https://news.gallup.com/reports/197141/gallup-purdue-index-report-2014.aspx

Gallup. (2015). *Great jobs, great lives. The relationship between student debt, experiences and perceptions of college worth: Gallup-Purdue Index 2015 report.* Retrieved December 7, 2018, from https://news.gallup.com/reports/197144/gallup-purdue-index-report-2015.aspx

Gallup. (2017). *2017 college student survey: A nationally representative survey of currently enrolled students.* Retrieved December 7, 2018, from https://news.gallup.com/reports/225161/2017-strada-gallup-college-student-survey.aspx

## CHAPTER 13. FIVE QUESTIONS FOR ONBOARDING

Adkins, A. (2015, April 2). *Only 35% of U.S. managers are engaged in their jobs.* Retrieved December 7, 2018, from https://www.gallup.com/workplace/236552/managers-engaged-jobs.aspx

Gallup. (2017). *State of the American workplace.* Retrieved December 7, 2018, from https://www.gallup.com/workplace/238085/state-american-workplace-report-2017.aspx

Gallup. (2017). *State of the global workplace.* New York: Gallup Press.

Gallup. (2018). *Gallup's perspective on aligning compensation with your talent management strategy.* Omaha, NE: Gallup.

## CHAPTER 14. SHORTCUT TO DEVELOPMENT — STRENGTHS-BASED CONVERSATIONS

Engaged employees spend less time working alone and more time communicating with their manager. Unfortunately for organizations, their least engaged employees are spending more time with their customers, possibly infecting them with their negativity.

Gallup meta-analyses of experimental and quasi-experimental studies of strengths-based interventions across 49,495 business units show substantial improvements in employee engagement, productivity, profit, retention, safety and customer perceptions. Additionally, in meta-analyses of the engagement of 23,640 individuals and sales performance of 10,592 teams across 21 studies, those receiving feedback on both strengths and non-strengths achieved incremental performance improvement that was higher than that of those who received feedback on strengths alone. The studies indicate that the best form of feedback involves a primary focus on developing strengths along with an awareness of and discussion about how to manage non-strengths so they don't become weaknesses.

In addition, Gallup data suggest that employees today expect their manager to coach them primarily based on their strengths.

---

Asplund, J. A., & Agrawal, S. (2018). *The effect of CliftonStrengths 34 feedback on employee engagement and sales: 2018 CliftonStrengths meta-analysis.* Retrieved December 10, 2018, from https://www.gallup.com/workplace/243827/cliftonstrengths-meta-analysis-2018-effects-of-cliftonstrengths-34-feedback.aspx

Asplund, J., Harter, J. K., Agrawal, S., & Plowman, S. K. (2015). *The relationship between strengths-based employee development and organizational outcomes 2015 strengths meta-analysis.* Retrieved December 10, 2018, from https://news.gallup.com/reports/193427/strengths-meta-analysis-2015.aspx

Harter, J. K., & Stone, A. A. (2012). Engaging and disengaging work conditions, momentary experiences and cortisol response. *Motivation and Emotion, 36*(2), 104-113.

Rigoni, B., & Asplund, J. (2016, July 7). *Strengths-based employee development: The business results.* Retrieved December 10, 2018, from https://www.gallup.com/workplace/236297/strengths-based-employee-development-business-results.aspx

## CHAPTER 15. CLIFTONSTRENGTHS 34: A TAXONOMY OF HUMAN POTENTIAL

Asplund, J., Agrawal, S., Hodges, T., Harter, J., & Lopez, S. J. (2014 March). *The Clifton StrengthsFinder 2.0 technical report: Development and validation.* Omaha, NE: Gallup.

Clifton, D. O., & Harter, J. K. (2003). Investing in strengths. In K. S. Cameron, J. E. Dutton, & R. E. Quinn (Eds.), *Positive organizational scholarship: Foundations of a new discipline* (pp. 111-121). San Francisco: Berrett-Koehler.

Hodges, T. D., & Clifton, D. O. (2004). Strengths-based development in practice. In P. A. Linley & S. Joseph (Eds.), *Positive psychology in practice.* Hoboken, NJ: John Wiley and Sons.

Nebraska Human Resources Institute. (n.d.). *History of NHRRF: The Nebraska Human Resources Research Foundation.* Retrieved December 10, 2018, from https://alec.unl.edu/nhri/history-nhrrf

Piersol, R. (2015, June 1). Gallup's Clifton dies at age 79. *Lincoln Journal Star.* Retrieved December 10, 2018, from https://journalstar.com/gallup-s-clifton-dies-at-age-this-story-ran-in/article_cb499250-04a5-5852-b48f-282c047ff505.html

## CHAPTER 16. FIVE STEPS TO BUILDING A STRENGTHS-BASED CULTURE

1. *Start with the CEO or it doesn't work.* While this is the ideal starting point, most organizations Gallup has worked with start their strengths-based approach in divisions or departments, creating a strengths-based subculture in the organization. In these cases, to get executive buy-in, they need to treat these subcultures as test cases to demonstrate the return on investment by studying — both quantitatively and qualitatively — how a strengths-based approach is linked to achieving organizational outcomes.

2. *Require every employee to discover their strengths.* In some organizations, strengths discovery happens organically as they add a strengths-based approach to various programs over time. Ideally, every employee will discover their strengths sooner rather than later.

3. *Build an internal network of strengths coaches.* While HR will be vital to implement and support a strengths-based culture, Gallup has found that the most seamless adoptions occur when people from the business and other functional areas become strengths coaches. Becoming a strengths coach does not have to be a full-time job. The more integrated strengths coaches are into the mainstream organization, the more effective they will be.

4. *Integrate strengths into performance management.* For managers to be most effective as coaches, they first need to know how to use their own strengths. And they need to be engaged — they need a great employee experience themselves. Start with your managers, and as they see the impact of a strengths-based approach on their own lives, they'll be more effective at coaching their teams.

5. *Transform your learning programs.* Most organizations will have some programs or training that lead with fixing weaknesses. In some cases, making people aware of blind spots through compliance and ethics training is essential.

---

Crabtree, S. (2018, February 13). *Strengths-based cultures are vital to the future of work.* Retrieved December 10, 2018, from https://www.gallup.com/workplace/236177/strengths-based-cultures-vital-future-work.aspx

Gallup. (n.d.). *Strengths-based workplaces: The replacement for annual reviews.* Retrieved December 10, 2018, from https://www.gallup.com/services/192827/organization-greatest-potential-unlocked.aspx

Rigoni, B., & Asplund, J. (2016, September 29). *Strengths-based development: Leadership's role.* Retrieved December 10, 2018, from https://www.gallup.com/workplace/236378/strengths-based-development-leadership-role.aspx

Rigoni, B., & Asplund, J. (2017, January 3). *Strengths-based cultures attract top talent.* Retrieved December 10, 2018, from https://www.gallup.com/workplace/236270/strengths-based-cultures-attract-top-talent.aspx

## CHAPTER 17. THE RIGHT EXPECTATIONS — COMPETENCIES 2.0

Streur, J., Wigert, B., & Harter, J. (2018). *Competencies 2.0: The 7 expectations for achieving excellence: Technical report.* Omaha, NE: Gallup.

## CHAPTER 18. GETTING SUCCESSION PLANNING RIGHT

Casad, B. J. (2016, August 1). Confirmation bias. In *Encyclopædia Britannica.* Retrieved December 10, 2018, from https://www.britannica.com/science/confirmation-bias

Green, B. S., & Zwiebel, J. (2013 November). *The hot hand fallacy: Cognitive mistakes or equilibrium adjustments? Evidence from baseball.* Retrieved December 10, 2018, from https://www.gsb.stanford.edu/faculty-research/working-papers/hot-hand-fallacy-cognitive-mistakes-or-equilibrium-adjustments

Khoury, G., & Green, A. (2017, November 9). *Don't leave succession planning to chance.* Retrieved December 10, 2018, from https://www.gallup.com/workplace/236258/don-leave-succession-planning-chance.aspx

Ratanjee, V., & Green, A. (2018, June 14). *How to reduce bias in your succession and promotion plans.* Retrieved December 10, 2018, from https://www.gallup.com/workplace/235970/reduce-bias-succession-promotion-plans.aspx

Recency bias. [Quick Reference]. (n.d.). *Oxford Reference.* Retrieved December 10, 2018, from http://www.oxfordreference.com/view/10.1093/oi/authority.20110803100407676

## CHAPTER 19. THE EXIT

In a 2018 Gallup study of 4,000 full-time and part-time employees in France, Germany, Spain and the U.K., we found substantial variance across countries in employees' reported intentions to stay with their current employer. For example, 65% of employees in Germany and 60% in Spain strongly agreed that they plan to be with their current company three years from now. Only 38% in the U.K. and 36% in France strongly agreed.

---

Gallup. (2017). *State of the American workplace.* Retrieved December 7, 2018, from https://www.gallup.com/workplace/238085/state-american-workplace-report-2017.aspx

Gallup. (2018). *Gallup's perspective on exit programs that retain stars and build brand ambassadors.* Omaha, NE.

# BOSS TO COACH

## CHAPTER 20. THREE REQUIREMENTS OF COACHING

In a 2018 Gallup study of 4,000 full-time and part-time employees in Europe, 34% of employees in the U.K. strongly agreed that their manager includes them in goal setting. The percentage is lower in Germany (29%), France (25%) and Spain (19%). Across all four countries, 30% of employees or less strongly agreed that their performance is managed in a way that motivates them to do outstanding work.

---

Gallup. (2017). *State of the American workplace.* Retrieved December 7, 2018, from https://www.gallup.com/workplace/238085/state-american-workplace-report-2017.aspx

Wigert, B., & Harter, J. (2017). *Re-engineering performance management.* Gallup Position Paper. Omaha, NE.

## CHAPTER 21. THE FIVE COACHING CONVERSATIONS

In a 2018 Gallup study of 4,000 full-time and part-time employees in Europe, 22% of employees in Germany, 24% in the U.K., 22% in France and 12% in Spain strongly agreed that they have received meaningful feedback in the past week.

Multiple large-scale academic studies find that continual coaching has an impact on performance:

Brown, T. C., & Latham, G. P. (2002). The effects of behavioural outcome goals, learning goals, and urging people to do their best on an individual's teamwork behaviour in a group problem-solving task. *Canadian Journal of Behavioural Science, 34*(4), 276-285.

Cawley, B. D., Keeping, L., & Levy, P. E. (1998). Participation in the performance appraisal process and employee reactions: A meta-analytic review of field investigations. *Journal of Applied Psychology, 83*(4), 615-633.

Chen, S., Zhang, G., Zhang, A., & Xu, J. (2016). Collectivism-oriented human resource management and innovation performance: An examination of team reflexivity and team psychological safety. *Journal of Management & Organization, 22*(4), 535-548.

Colquitt, J. A., Conlon, D. E., Wesson, M. J., Porter, C. O. L. H., & Ng, K. Y. (2001). Justice at the millennium: A meta-analytic review of 25 years of organizational justice research. *Journal of Applied Psychology, 86*(3), 425-445.

Courtright, S. H., Thurgood, G. R., Stewart, G. L., & Pierotti, A. J. (2015). Structural interdependence in teams: An integrative framework and meta-analysis. *Journal of Applied Psychology, 100*(6), 1825-1846.

Harkin, B., et al. (2016). Does monitoring goal progress promote goal attainment? A meta-analysis of the experimental evidence. *Psychological Bulletin, 142*(2), 198-229.

Jeffrey, S. A., Schulz, A., & Webb, A. (2012). The performance effects of an ability-based approach to goal assignment. *Journal of Organizational Behavior Management, 32*(3), 221-241.

Klein, H. J., Wesson, M. J., Hollenbeck, J. R., & Alge, B. J. (1999). Goal commitment and the goal-setting process: Conceptual clarification and empirical synthesis. *Journal of Applied Psychology, 84*(6), 885-896.

Kluger, A. N., & DeNisi, A. S. (1996). The effects of feedback interventions on performance: A historical review, a meta-analysis, and a preliminary feedback intervention theory. *Psychological Bulletin, 119*(2), 254-284.

Koestner, R., Lekes, N., Powers, T. A., & Chicoine, E. (2002). Attaining personal goals: Self-concordance plus implementation intentions equals success. *Journal of Personality and Social Psychology, 83*(1), 231-244.

Konradt, U., Otte, K. P., Schippers, M. C., & Steenfatt, C. (2016). Reflexivity in teams: A review and new perspectives. *The Journal of Psychology, 150*(2), 153-174.

Locke, E. A., & Latham, G. P. (2002). Building a practically useful theory of goal setting and task motivation: A 35-year odyssey. *American Psychologist, 57*(9), 705-717.

McEwan, D., et al. (2015). The effectiveness of multi-component goal setting interventions for changing physical activity behaviour: A systematic review and meta-analysis. *Health Psychology Review, 10*(1), 67-88.

Mone, M. A., & Shalley, C. E. (1995). Effects of task complexity and goal specificity on change in strategy and performance over time. *Human Performance, 8*(4), 243-262.

Pearsall, M. J., Christian, M. S., & Ellis, A. P. J. (2010). Motivating interdependent teams: Individual rewards, shared rewards, or something in between? *Journal of Applied Psychology, 95*(1), 183-191.

Pichler, S. (2012). The social context of performance appraisal and appraisal reactions: A meta-analysis. *Human Resource Management, 51*(5), 709-732.

Pulakos, E. (2015, April). *Embedding high-performance culture through new approaches to performance management and behavior change.* Presented at Society for Industrial-Organizational Psychology Annual Conference, Philadelphia, PA.

Rodgers, R., & Hunter, J. E. (1991). Impact of management by objectives on organizational productivity. *Journal of Applied Psychology, 76*(2), 322-336.

Schippers, M. C., West, M. A., & Dawson, J. F. (2015). Team reflexivity and innovation: The moderating role of team context. *Journal of Management, 41*(3), 769-788.

Seifert, C. F., Yukl, G., & McDonald, R. A. (2003). Effects of multisource feedback and a feedback facilitator on the influence behavior of managers toward subordinates. *Journal of Applied Psychology, 88*(3), 561-569.

Sheldon, K. M., & Elliot, A. J. (1998). Not all personal goals are personal: Comparing autonomous and controlled reasons for goals as predictors of effort and attainment. *Personality and Social Psychology Bulletin, 24*(5), 546-557.

Smither, J. W., London, M., & Reilly, R. R. (2005). Does performance improve following multisource feedback? A theoretical model, meta-analysis, and review of empirical findings. *Personnel Psychology, 58*, 33-66.

Winters, D., & Latham, G. P. (1996). The effect of learning versus outcome goals on a simple versus a complex task. *Group & Organization Management, 21*(2), 236-250.

---

Wigert, B., & Harter, J. (2017). *Re-engineering performance management.* Gallup Position Paper. Omaha, NE.

## CHAPTER 22. PAY AND PROMOTION

Brosnan, S. F., & De Waal, F. B. (2003). Monkeys reject unequal pay. *Nature, 425*(6955), 297-299.

Cable, D. M., & Judge, T. A. (1994). Pay preferences and job search decisions: A person-organization fit perspective. *Personnel Psychology, 47*(2), 317-348.

Cawley, B. D., Keeping, L., & Levy, P. E. (1998). Participation in the performance appraisal process and employee reactions: A meta-analytic review of field investigations. *Journal of Applied Psychology, 83*(4), 615-633.

Cerasoli, C. P., Nicklin, J. M., & Ford, M. T. (2014). Intrinsic motivation and extrinsic incentives jointly predict performance: A 40-year meta-analysis. *Psychological Bulletin, 140*(4), 980-1008.

Chapman, D. S., Uggerslev, K. L., Carroll, S. A., Piasentin, K. A., & Jones, D. A. (2005). Applicant attraction to organizations and job choice: A meta-analytic review of the correlates of recruiting outcomes. *Journal of Applied Psychology, 90*(5), 928-944.

Dal Bó, E., Finan, F., & Rossi, M. A. (2013). Strengthening state capabilities: The role of financial incentives in the call to public service. *The Quarterly Journal of Economics, 128*(3), 1169-1218.

Deci, E. L., Koestner, R., & Ryan, R. M. (1999). A meta-analytic review of experiments examining the effects of extrinsic rewards on intrinsic motivation. *Psychological Bulletin, 125*(6), 627-668.

Dulebohn, J. H., & Martocchio, J. J. (1998). Employee perceptions of the fairness of work group incentive pay plans. *Journal of Management, 24*(4), 469-488.

Dweck, C. S. (2006). *Mindset: The new psychology of success.* New York: Random House.

Fehr, E., & Gächter, S. (2000). Fairness and retaliation: The economics of reciprocity. *The Journal of Economic Perspectives, 14*(3), 159-181.

Fehr, E., & Gächter, S. (2001 February). *Do incentive contracts crowd-out voluntary cooperation?* IEER Working Paper No. 34; and USC CLEO Research Paper No. C01-3.

Gallup. (2018). *Gallup's perspective on exit programs that retain stars and build brand ambassadors.* Omaha, NE.

Griffeth, R. W., Hom, P. W., & Gaertner, S. (2000). A meta-analysis of antecedents and correlates of employee turnover: Update, moderator tests, and research implications for the next millennium. *Journal of Management, 26*(3), 463-488.

Jenkins, G. D., Jr., Mitra, A., Gupta, N., & Shaw, J. D. (1998). Are financial incentives related to performance? A meta-analytic review of empirical research. *Journal of Applied Psychology, 83*(5), 777-787.

Judge, T. A., Piccolo, R. F., Podsakoff, N. P., Shaw, J. C., & Rich, B. L. (2010). The relationship between pay and job satisfaction: A meta-analysis of the literature. *Journal of Vocational Behavior, 77*(2), 157-167.

Nyberg, A. J., Pieper, J. R., & Trevor, C. O. (2016). Pay-for-performance's effect on future employee performance: Integrating psychological and economic principles toward a contingency perspective. *Journal of Management, 42*(7), 1753-1783.

PayScale. (2018). *2018 compensation best practices report.* Retrieved December 10, 2018, from https://www.payscale.com/cbpr

Pfeffer, J. (1998). Six dangerous myths about pay. *Harvard Business Review.* Retrieved December 10, 2018, from https://hbr.org/1998/05/six-dangerous-myths-about-pay

Rath, T., & Harter, J. (2010). *Wellbeing: The five essential elements.* New York: Gallup Press.

Rynes, S. L. (1987). Compensation strategies for recruiting. *Topics in Total Compensation, 2*(2), 185.

Wiersma, U. J. (1992). The effects of extrinsic rewards in intrinsic motivation: A meta-analysis. *Journal of Occupational and Organizational Psychology, 65*(2), 101-114.

Williams, M. L., McDaniel, M. A., & Nguyen, N. T. (2006). A meta-analysis of the antecedents and consequences of pay level satisfaction. *Journal of Applied Psychology, 91*(2), 392-413.

## CHAPTER 23. PERFORMANCE RATINGS: THE BIAS

Balzer, W. K., & Sulsky, L. M. (1992). Halo and performance appraisal research: A critical examination. *Journal of Applied Psychology, 77*(6), 975-985.

Cascio, W. F. (1989). *Managing human resources: Productivity, quality of work life, profits.* New York: McGraw-Hill.

Hoffman, B., Lance, C. E., Bynum, B., & Gentry, W. A. (2010). Rater source effects are alive and well after all. *Personnel Psychology, 63*(1), 119-151.

Lunenburg, F. C. (2012). Performance appraisal: Methods and rating errors. *International Journal of Scholarly Academic Intellectual Diversity, 14*(1), 1-9.

Mount, M. K., Judge, T. A., Scullen, S. E., Sytsma, M. R., & Hezlett, S. A. (1998). Trait, rater and level effects in 360-degree performance ratings. *Personnel Psychology, 51*(3), 557-576.

Neves, P. (2012). Organizational cynicism: Spillover effects on supervisor-subordinate relationships and performance. *The Leadership Quarterly, 23*(5), 965-976.

Scullen, S. E., Mount, M. K., & Goff, M. (2000). Understanding the latent structure of job performance ratings. *Journal of Applied Psychology, 85*(6), 956.

Wigert, B., & Harter, J. (2017). *Re-engineering performance management.* Gallup Position Paper. Omaha, NE.

## CHAPTER 24. PERFORMANCE RATINGS: THE FIX

Wigert, B., & Harter, J. (2017). *Re-engineering performance management.* Gallup Position Paper. Omaha, NE.

## CHAPTER 25. MAKE "MY DEVELOPMENT" THE REASON EMPLOYEES STAY

In a 2018 Gallup study of 4,000 full-time and part-time employees in Europe, fewer than one in four employees in France (23%), Germany (23%), the U.K. (17%) and Spain (17%) strongly agreed that there are clear opportunities for career advancement at their current employer.

---

Benko, C., & Anderson, M. (2010). *The corporate lattice: Achieving high performance in the changing world of work.* Boston: Harvard Business Review Press.

Biron, M. M., & Eshed, R. (2017). Gaps between actual and preferred career paths among professional employees: Implications for performance and burnout. *Journal of Career Development, 44*(3), 224-238.

Crawshaw, J. R., van Dick, R., & Brodbeck, F. C. (2012). Opportunity, fair process and relationship value: Career development as a driver of proactive work behaviour. *Human Resource Management Journal, 22*(1), 4-20.

Gallup. (2016). *How millennials want to work and live.* Retrieved December 7, 2018, from https://www.gallup.com/workplace/238073/millennials-work-live.aspx

Gallup. (2017). *State of the American workplace.* Retrieved December 7, 2018, from https://www.gallup.com/workplace/238085/state-american-workplace-report-2017.aspx

## CHAPTER 26. MONEYBALL FOR WORKPLACES

Gallup. (2016). *The relationship between engagement at work and organizational outcomes: 2016 Q12® meta-analysis: ninth edition.* Retrieved December 7, 2018, from https://news.gallup.com/reports/191489/q12-meta-analysis-report-2016.aspx

Global Happiness Council. (2018). Work and well-being: A global perspective. *Global Happiness Policy Report 2018.* Retrieved December 10, 2018, from https://s3.amazonaws.com/ghc-2018/GlobalHappinessPolicyReport2018.pdf

Harter, J. K., Schmidt, F. L., Agrawal, S., Plowman, S., & Blue, A. T. (2018). *Increased business value for positive job attitudes during economic recessions: A meta-analysis and SEM analysis.* Gallup Working Paper. Omaha, NE.

Harter, J. K., Schmidt, F. L., Asplund, J. W., Killham, E. A., & Agrawal, S. (2010). Causal impact of employee work perceptions on the bottom line of organizations. *Perspectives on Psychological Science, 5*(4), 378-389.

Harter, J. K., Schmidt, F. L., & Hayes, T. L. (2002). Business-unit-level relationship between employee satisfaction, employee engagement, and business outcomes: A meta-analysis. *Journal of Applied Psychology, 87*(2), 268-279.

Kornhauser, J. (n.d.). *Chicago Cubs utilizing "Moneyball" approach for early success.* Retrieved December 10, 2018, from http://www.rantsports.com/mlb/2015/04/23/chicago-cubs-utilizing-moneyball-approach-for-early-success/

Lewis, M. (2004). *Moneyball: The art of winning an unfair game.* New York: Norton.

Reiter, B. (2014, June 30). Houston's grand experiment. *Sports Illustrated.* Retrieved December 10, 2018, from https://www.si.com/vault/2014/06/30/106479598/astromatic-baseball-houstons-grand-experiment

St. John, A. (2013, October 31). *Powered by Bill James and friends, the Red Sox win (another) Moneyball World Series.* Retrieved December 10, 2018, from https://www.forbes.com/sites/allenstjohn/2013/10/31/powered-by-bill-james-and-friends-the-red-sox-win-another-moneyball-world-series/#76c13a857c64

## CHAPTER 27. THE TEAM LEADER BREAKTHROUGH

**The 34 CliftonStrengths themes sorted into the four strengths domains**

| Executing | Influencing | Relationship Building | Strategic Thinking |
|---|---|---|---|
| Achiever | Activator | Adaptability | Analytical |
| Arranger | Command | Connectedness | Context |
| Belief | Communication | Developer | Futuristic |
| Consistency | Competition | Empathy | Ideation |
| Deliberative | Maximizer | Harmony | Input |
| Discipline | Self-Assurance | Includer | Intellection |
| Focus | Significance | Individualization | Learner |
| Responsibility | Woo | Positivity | Strategic |
| Restorative | | Relator | |

In one study of 159 customer service teams, researchers found that the teams with the highest customer engagement levels had at least one person on the team with high "centrality" to the rest of the organization. Those who have high centrality are connected to others in the organization who are highly influential. Social network analytics calculates each person's centrality to the overall social network by considering their first-, second- and third-degree connections.

In another study of 821 employees, researchers found that the most highly engaged individuals tended to have managers who had high social network centrality to the rest of the organization.

The term "collective intelligence" is part of broad research literature that includes "shared mental models" and "shared cognition." Teams generally perform better when team members are on the same page or when they think differently but complement one another.

---

DeChurch, L. A., & Mesmer-Magnus, J. R. (2010). The cognitive underpinnings of effective teamwork: A meta-analysis. *Journal of Applied Psychology, 95*(1), 32-53.

Gallup. (2014). *Estimating the influence of the local manager on team engagement: Technical report.* Omaha, NE.

Mann, A., & McCarville, B. (2015, November 13). *What job-hopping employees are looking for.* Retrieved December 10, 2018, from https://news.gallup.com/businessjournal/186602/job-hopping-employees-looking.aspx

Mathieu, J. E., Hollenbeck, J. R., van Knippenberg, D., & Ilgen, D. R. (2017). A century of work teams in the Journal of Applied Psychology. *Journal of Applied Psychology, 102*(3), 452-467.

Woolley, A. W., Aggarwal, I., & Malone, T. W. (2015). Collective intelligence and group performance. *Current Directions in Psychological Science, 24*(6), 420-424.

## CHAPTER 28. WHY EMPLOYEE ENGAGEMENT PROGRAMS HAVEN'T WORKED

Based on a Gallup study of business unit performance outcomes across 82,248 business units in 230 companies, combining %4s and %5s on a 5-point agreement scale produces a less effective metric than one that focuses on %5s (strong agreement). A 10-percentage-point improvement on a %5 (strongly agree) metric results in nearly double the improvement in business outcomes (profit, productivity, customer loyalty, turnover and safety) compared with a 10-percentage-point improvement in %4s (general agreement).

---

Emond, L. (2017, August 15). *2 reasons why employee engagement programs fall short.* Retrieved December 10, 2018, from https://www.gallup.com/workplace/236147/reasons-why-employee-engagement-programs-fall-short.aspx

Gallup. (2017). *State of the global workplace.* New York: Gallup Press.

Harter, J. (n.d.). *Dismal employee engagement is a sign of global mismanagement.* Retrieved December 10, 2018, from https://www.gallup.com/workplace/231668/dismal-employee-engagement-sign-global-mismanagement.aspx

Harter, J. (2018, August 26). *Employee engagement on the rise in the U.S.* Retrieved December 10, 2018, from https://news.gallup.com/poll/241649/employee-engagement-rise.aspx

Pendell, R. (2018, August 28). *10 ways to botch employee surveys.* Retrieved December 10, 2018, from https://www.gallup.com/workplace/241253/ways-botch-employee-surveys.aspx

## CHAPTER 29. CREATING A CULTURE OF HIGH DEVELOPMENT

Flade, P., Harter, J., & Asplund, J. (2014, April 15). *Seven things great employers do (that others don't): Unusual, innovative, and proven tactics to create productive and profitable working environments.* Retrieved December 10, 2018, from https://news.gallup.com/businessjournal/168407/seven-things-great-employers-others-don.aspx

Harter, J. (2015, November 4). *Who drives employee engagement — manager or CEO?* Retrieved December 10, 2018, from https://news.gallup.com/opinion/gallup/186503/drives-employees-engagement-manager-ceo.aspx

O'Boyle, E., & Harter, J. (2018, April 18). *39 organizations create exceptional workplaces.* Retrieved December 10, 2018, from https://www.gallup.com/workplace/236117/organizations-create-exceptional-workplaces.aspx

## CHAPTER 30. THE FIVE TRAITS OF GREAT MANAGERS

With hundreds of in-depth studies in Gallup's database that spans five decades, our research team examined changes in the profile of great managing over time. Each of the hundreds of studies provided insight into which traits predicted success for the particular time when the study was conducted. We defined "success" as high team productivity, engagement, retention rates, customer service ratings and profit.

We combined the studies by decade to understand what has and has not changed. We found substantial consistency in many basic traits that predicted successful team performance. Many of the same traits that predicted success in the 1970s and 1980s still predict success today: Successful managers *are driven toward achieving performance outcomes* and *build close individual relationships with their employees* to achieve those outcomes.

We found that the same overall dimensions listed in Chapter 30 (motivation, workstyle, initiation, collaboration and thought process) were present in successful managers across time. But we also found important differences in *how* great managers today *initiate* their team and in how they solve problems and make decisions through their thought process.

Here are the two important differences our team uncovered through this research:

1. Managers of the past could influence others by laying down the law and exerting *control* over employees. These managers needed to be the central figure and architect of how work should get done. Today, managers play the role of *facilitator* or *coach* for their employees. We can think of these managers as coordinators or orchestrators. They must speak with authority while still being open to employees' input. Today's managers need to set clear systems of accountability in a world where work time and space are flexible and where work and life are blended.
2. Managers of the past solved problems by trying to understand the context their teams were working in and being aware of the larger circumstances in which decisions are made. This gave managers an *informed perspective* when making decisions. Today, successful managers are more *analytical decision-makers*. They are decidedly more future-focused and systems-oriented, naturally intrigued by possibilities and new ideas, and more objective and empirically grounded problem solvers and consumers of data.

These two differences between managers of the past and managers of the present are a reflection of the changes in the modern workplace — increased worker independence and substantial advancements in access to information. New profiles for selecting managers who lead high-performing teams should take these changes into consideration. Gallup has calibrated our hiring analytics to reflect these changes.

---

Bouchard, T. J., Lykken, D. T., McGue, M., Segal, N. L., & Tellegen, A. (1990). Sources of human psychological differences: The Minnesota study of twins reared apart. *Science, 250*(4978), 223-228.

Harter, J. K. (2000). Managerial talent, employee engagement, and business-unit performance. *The Psychologist-Manager Journal, 4*(2), 215.

Jang, K. L., Livesley, W. J., & Vemon, P. A. (1996). Heritability of the big five personality dimensions and their facets: A twin study. *Journal of Personality, 64*(3), 577-592.

Plomin, R., DeFries, J. C., & McClearn, G. E. (2008). *Behavioral genetics.* Macmillan.

Segal, N. L. (2012). *Born together—reared apart: The landmark Minnesota twin study.* Harvard University Press.

Yang, Y., Harter, J. K., Streur, J. H., Agrawal, S., Dvorak, N., & Walker, P. (2013). *The Gallup manager assessment: Technical report.* Omaha, NE: Gallup.

## CHAPTER 31. HOW TO DEVELOP YOUR MANAGERS

Gallup researchers studied 581 organizations that had (n = 309) or had not (n = 272) invested in Gallup training between their first and second administrations of employee engagement measurement. This included data from 2.5 million individuals who participated in employee engagement measurement from 2000-2016. Training included strengths-based education, employee engagement education and manager education.

Companies that invested in strengths training had an average increase of 17% more engaged employees compared with an 8% increase for those that measured $Q^{12}$ only, without training. Organizations that used employee engagement training without strengths training achieved a 12-percentage-point improvement. For a large organization with 10,000 people, for example, strengths training related to $23.3 million in estimated per-employee-productivity gains in the first year from a baseline — or a net of $12.1 million more than companies that did not use training and a net of $8.6 million more than those that used engagement training without the strengths component.

---

Meinert, D. (2014, July 22). *Leadership development spending is up.* Retrieved December 10, 2018, from https://www.shrm.org/hr-today/news/hr-magazine/pages/0814-execbrief.aspx

Wigert, B., & Agrawal, S. (2018, July 16). *Employee burnout, part 2: What managers can do.* Retrieved December 10, 2018, from https://www.gallup.com/workplace/237119/employee-burnout-part-2-managers.aspx

Wigert, B., & Maese, E. (2018). *The manager experience study.* Gallup Working Paper. Omaha, NE.

# THE FUTURE OF WORK

## CHAPTER 32. A QUICK REVIEW OF WHAT HAS CHANGED IN THE WORKPLACE

Gallup. (2016). *How millennials want to work and live.* Retrieved December 7, 2018, from https://www.gallup.com/workplace/238073/millennials-work-live.aspx

Gallup. (2017). *State of the American workplace.* Retrieved December 7, 2018, from https://www.gallup.com/workplace/238085/state-american-workplace-report-2017.aspx

Harter, J. (2014, September 9). *Should employers ban email after work hours?* Retrieved December 10, 2018, from https://www.gallup.com/workplace/236519/employers-ban-email-work-hours.aspx

Newport, F. (2017, May 10). *Email outside of working hours not a burden to U.S. workers.* Retrieved December 10, 2018, from https://news.gallup.com/poll/210074/email-outside-working-hours-not-burden-workers.aspx

## CHAPTER 33. THREE REQUIREMENTS FOR DIVERSITY AND INCLUSION

Bezrukova, K., Spell, C. S., Perry, J. L., & Jehn, K. A. (2016). A meta-analytical integration of over 40 years of research on diversity training evaluation. *Psychological Bulletin, 142*(11), 1227-1274.

Brenan, M. (2017, November 16). *Americans no longer prefer male boss to female boss.* Retrieved December 10, 2018, from https://news.gallup.com/poll/222425/americans-no-longer-prefer-male-boss-female-boss.aspx

Downey, S. N., van der Werff, L., Thomas, K. M., & Plaut, V. C. (2014). The role of diversity practices and inclusion in promoting trust and employee engagement. *Journal of Applied Social Psychology, 45*(1), 35-44.

Gallup. (2016). *How millennials want to work and live.* Retrieved December 7, 2018, from https://www.gallup.com/workplace/238073/millennials-work-live.aspx

Gallup. (2018). *Three requirements of a diverse and inclusive culture — and why they matter for your organization.* Retrieved December 10, 2018, from https://www.gallup.com/workplace/242108/diversity-inclusion-perspective-paper.aspx

Jones, J. M. (2015, May 20). *Majority in U.S. now say gays and lesbians born, not made.* Retrieved December 10, 2018, from https://news.gallup.com/poll/183332/majority-say-gays-lesbians-born-not-made.aspx

Kalev, A., Dobbin, F., & Kelly, E. (2006). Best practices or best guesses? Assessing the efficacy of corporate affirmative action and diversity policies. *American Sociological Review, 71*(4), 589-617.

Saad, L. (2017, November 3). *Concerns about sexual harassment higher than in 1998.* Retrieved December 10, 2018, from https://news.gallup.com/poll/221216/concerns-sexual-harassment-higher-1998.aspx

Swift, A. (2017, March 15). *Americans' worries about race relations at record high.* Retrieved December 10, 2018, from https://news.gallup.com/poll/206057/americans-worry-race-relations-record-high.aspx

Washington, E., & Patrick, C. (2018, September 17). *3 requirements for a diverse and inclusive culture.* Retrieved December 10, 2018, from https://www.gallup.com/workplace/242138/requirements-diverse-inclusive-culture.aspx

## CHAPTER 34. DIVERSITY AND INCLUSION: "TREAT ME WITH RESPECT"

Among workers in the U.S., 9% disagreed or strongly disagreed that they are treated with respect at work. Of those 9%, 90% indicated that they had experienced at least one of 35 discrimination or harassment experiences at work.

In a 2018 Gallup study of 4,000 full-time and part-time employees in Europe, 3% of employees in the U.K. disagreed or strongly disagreed that they are always treated with respect at work; 4% in Germany, 10% in Spain and 12% in France said the same.

---

Gallup. (2018). *Three requirements of a diverse and inclusive culture — and why they matter for your organization.* Retrieved December 10, 2018, from https://www.gallup.com/workplace/242108/diversity-inclusion-perspective-paper.aspx

Jones, J. R., & Harter, J. K. (2005). Race effects on the employee engagement-turnover intention relationship. *Journal of Leadership & Organizational Studies, 11*(2), 78-88.

Porath, C. (2014, November 19). Half of employees don't feel respected by their bosses. *Harvard Business Review.* Retrieved December 10, 2018, from https://hbr.org/2014/11/half-of-employees-dont-feel-respected-by-their-bosses

## CHAPTER 35. DIVERSITY AND INCLUSION: "VALUE ME FOR MY STRENGTHS"

Polzer, J. T., Milton, L. P., & Swarm Jr., W. B. (2002). Capitalizing on diversity: Interpersonal congruence in small work groups. *Administrative Science Quarterly, 47*(2), 296-324.

Riffkin, R., & Harter, J. (2016, March 21). *Using employee engagement to build a diverse workforce.* Retrieved December 10, 2018, from https://news.gallup.com/opinion/gallup/190103/using-employee-engagement-build-diverse-workforce.aspx

Washington, E. (2018, October 3). *How to use CliftonStrengths to develop diversity and inclusion.* Retrieved December 10, 2018, from https://www.gallup.com/workplace/243251/cliftonstrengths-develop-diversity-inclusion.aspx

## CHAPTER 36. DIVERSITY AND INCLUSION: "LEADERS WILL DO WHAT IS RIGHT"

In a 2018 Gallup study of 4,000 full-time and part-time employees in Europe, 57% in the U.K. strongly agreed that their employer would do what is right if they raised a concern about ethics and integrity; 36% in France, 32% in Spain and 31% in Germany said the same.

---

DiSciullo, M., & Jones, D. D. (2017, June 12). *More than 150 CEOs make unprecedented commitment to advance diversity and inclusion in the workplace.* Retrieved December 10, 2018, from https://www.ceoaction.com/media/press-releases/2017/more-than-150-ceos-make-unprecedented-commitment-to-advance-diversity-and-inclusion-in-the-workplace/

Miller, J. (2017, October 19). *It's not you, it's me: Supporting workplace inclusion.* Retrieved December 10, 2018, from https://www.gallup.com/workplace/236264/not-supporting-workplace-inclusion.aspx

Pendell, R. (2018, September 10). *How to reduce bias and hire the best candidate.* Retrieved December 10, 2018, from https://www.gallup.com/workplace/241955/reduce-bias-hire-best-candidate.aspx

Washington, E. (n.d.). *Starbucks after anti-bias training: Will it last?* Retrieved December 10, 2018, from https://www.gallup.com/workplace/235139/starbucks-anti-bias-training-last.aspx

Washington, E., & Newport, F. (2017, April 25). *Diversity and inclusion in the workplace after Trump election.* Retrieved December 10, 2018, from https://www.gallup.com/workplace/236324/diversity-inclusion-workplace-trump-election.aspx

## CHAPTER 37. THE GENDER GAP

Badal, S., & Harter, J. K. (2014). Gender diversity, business-unit engagement, and performance. *Journal of Leadership & Organizational Studies, 21*(4), 354-365.

Brenan, M. (2017, November 16). *Americans no longer prefer male boss to female boss.* Retrieved December 10, 2018, from https://news.gallup.com/poll/222425/americans-no-longer-prefer-male-boss-female-boss.aspx

Gallup. (2016). *Women in America: Work and life well-lived.* Retrieved December 10, 2018, from https://www.gallup.com/workplace/238070/women-america-work-life-lived-insights-business-leaders.aspx

Gallup and the International Labour Organization. (n.d.). *Towards a better future for women and work: Voices of women and men.* Retrieved December 10, 2018, from https://news.gallup.com/reports/204785/ilo-gallup-report-towards-better-future-women-work-voices-women-men.aspx

Miller, J. (2017, January 17). *The dwindling female labor force in the U.S.* Retrieved December 10, 2018, from https://news.gallup.com/businessjournal/201719/dwindling-female-labor-force.aspx

Ray, J., & Esipova, N. (2017, March 8). *Millions of women worldwide would like to join the workforce.* Retrieved December 10, 2018, from https://news.gallup.com/poll/205439/millions-women-worldwide-join-workforce.aspx

## CHAPTER 38. WOMEN IN THE WORKPLACE: THE #METOO ERA

Gallup and the International Labour Organization. (n.d.). *Towards a better future for women and work: Voices of women and men.* Retrieved December 10, 2018, from https://news.gallup.com/reports/204785/ilo-gallup-report-towards-better-future-women-work-voices-women-men.aspx

Newport, F., & Saad, L. (2017, November 14). *How widespread is sexual harassment in the U.S.?* [Audio blog post]. Retrieved December 10, 2018, from https://news.gallup.com/podcast/222344/widespread-sexual-harassment.aspx

Saad, L. (2017, November 3). *Concerns about sexual harassment higher than in 1998.* Retrieved December 10, 2018, from https://news.gallup.com/poll/221216/concerns-sexual-harassment-higher-1998.aspx

## CHAPTER 39. WOMEN IN THE WORKPLACE: WHY THE PAY GAP?

Bertrand, M., Goldin, C., & Katz, L. F. (2010). Dynamics of the gender gap for young professionals in the financial and corporate sectors. *American Economic Journal: Applied Economics, 2*(3), 228-255.

Bureau of Labor Statistics. (2016, January 15). Women's earnings 83 percent of men's, but vary by occupation. *TED: The Economics Daily.* Retrieved December 10, 2018, from https://www.bls.gov/opub/ted/2016/womens-earnings-83-percent-of-mens-but-vary-by-occupation.htm

Cook, C., Diamond, R., Hall, J., List, J. A., & Oyer, P. (2018). *The gender earnings gap in the gig economy: Evidence from over a million rideshare drivers.* Retrieved December 10, 2018, from https://www.gsb.stanford.edu/faculty-research/working-papers/gender-earnings-gap-gig-economy-evidence-over-million-rideshare

Gallup and the International Labour Organization. (n.d.). *Towards a better future for women and work: Voices of women and men.* Retrieved December 10, 2018, from https://news.gallup.com/reports/204785/ilo-gallup-report-towards-better-future-women-work-voices-women-men.aspx

Goldin, C. (2014). A grand gender convergence: Its last chapter. *American Economic Review, 104*(4), 1091-1119.

Goldin, C. (2015, July 27). How to achieve gender equality in pay. *Milken Institute Review.* Retrieved December 10, 2018, from http://www.milkenreview.org/articles/how-to-achieve-gender-equality-in-pay

Goldin, C., & Devani, T. (2017, August 7). Narrowing the wage gap: An interview with Claudia Goldin. *Harvard International Review*. Retrieved December 10, 2018, from http://hir.harvard.edu/article/?a=14544

Plumb, E. (2016, November 15). *The gender pay gap: An interview with Harvard economist Claudia Goldin*. Retrieved December 10, 2018, from https://www.workflexibility.org/gender-pay-gap-interview-economist-claudia-goldin/

## CHAPTER 40. WOMEN IN THE WORKPLACE: WORK-LIFE FLEXIBILITY

Gallup. (2016). *Women in America: Work and life well-lived*. Retrieved December 10, 2018, from https://www.gallup.com/workplace/238070/women-america-work-life-lived-insights-business-leaders.aspx

Gallup and the International Labour Organization. (n.d.). *Towards a better future for women and work: Voices of women and men*. Retrieved December 10, 2018, from https://news.gallup.com/reports/204785/ilo gallup report towards better future women work-voices-women-men.aspx

## CHAPTER 41. ARE BOOMERS A BURDEN?

Arnold, J., & Clark, M. (2016). Running the penultimate lap of the race: A multimethod analysis of growth, generativity, career orientation, and personality amongst men in mid/late career. *Journal of Occupational and Organizational Psychology, 89*(2), 308-329.

Case, A., & Deaton, A. (2015). Rising morbidity and mortality in midlife among white non-Hispanic Americans in the 21st century. *Proceedings of the National Academy of Sciences, 112*(49), 15078-15083.

Gallup. (2019). *Gallup's perspective on transitioning baby boomer employees*. Gallup Working Paper. Omaha, NE.

Harter, J., & Agrawal, S. (2015, January 27). *Older baby boomers more engaged at work than younger boomers*. Retrieved December 10, 2018, from https://news.gallup.com/poll/181298/older-baby-boomers-engaged-work-younger-boomers.aspx

Newport, F. (2018, May 9). *Update: Americans' concerns about retirement persist.* Retrieved December 10, 2018, from https://news.gallup.com/poll/233861/update-americans-concerns-retirement-persist.aspx

Newport, F. (2018, May 10). *Snapshot: Average American predicts retirement age of 66.* Retrieved December 10, 2018, from https://news.gallup.com/poll/234302/snapshot-americans-project-average-retirement-age.aspx

Norman, J. (2016, May 3). *Economic turmoil stirs retirement plans of young, old.* Retrieved December 10, 2018, from https://news.gallup.com/poll/191297/economic-turmoil-stirred-retirement-plans-young-old.aspx

Saad, L. (2016, May 13). *Three in 10 U.S. workers foresee working past retirement age.* Retrieved December 10, 2018, from https://news.gallup.com/poll/191477/three-workers-foresee-working-past-retirement-age.aspx

Swift, A. (2017, May 8). *Most U.S. employed adults plan to work past retirement age.* Retrieved December 10, 2018, from https://news.gallup.com/poll/210044/employed-adults-plan-work-past-retirement-age.aspx

## CHAPTER 42. BENEFITS, PERKS AND FLEXTIME: WHAT DO EMPLOYEES REALLY CARE ABOUT?

Gallup. (2016). *How millennials want to work and live.* Retrieved December 7, 2018, from https://www.gallup.com/workplace/238073/millennials-work-live.aspx

Gallup. (2017). *State of the American workplace.* Retrieved December 7, 2018, from https://www.gallup.com/workplace/238085/state-american-workplace-report-2017.aspx

## CHAPTER 43. HOW FLEXTIME AND HIGH PERFORMANCE CAN GO HAND IN HAND

Dvorak, N. (2017, September 15). *The working vacation.* Retrieved December 10, 2018, from https://news.gallup.com/opinion/gallup/218015/working-vacation.aspx

Gallup. (2012). *Engagement at work: Working hours, flextime, vacation time, and well-being.* Retrieved December 10, 2018, from https://www.gallup.com/services/176339/engagement-work-working-hours-flextime-vacation-time-wellbeing.aspx

Mann, A., & Nelson, B. (2017, December 12). *Thinking flexibly about flexible work arrangements.* Retrieved December 10, 2018, from https://www.gallup.com/workplace/236183/thinking-flexibly-flexible-work-arrangements.aspx

## CHAPTER 44. THE NEW OFFICE

Dvorak, N., & Sasaki, J. (2017, March 30). *Employees at home: Less engaged.* Retrieved December 10, 2018, from https://news.gallup.com/businessjournal/207539/employees-home-less-engaged.aspx

Gallup. (2017). *State of the American workplace.* Retrieved December 7, 2018, from https://www.gallup.com/workplace/238085/state-american-workplace-report-2017.aspx

Hickman, A. (2018, March 29). *Why friendships among remote workers are crucial.* Retrieved December 10, 2018, from https://www.gallup.com/workplace/236072/why-friendships-among-remote-workers-crucial.aspx

Hickman, A., & Fredstrom, T. (2018, February 7). *How to build trust with remote employees.* Retrieved December 10, 2018, from https://www.gallup.com/workplace/236222/build-trust-remote-employees.aspx

Hickman, A., & Pendell, R. (2018, May 31). *The end of the traditional manager.* Retrieved December 10, 2018, from https://www.gallup.com/workplace/236108/end-traditional-manager.aspx

Hickman, A., & Sasaki, J. (2017, April 5). *Can you manage employees you rarely see?* Retrieved December 10, 2018, from https://www.gallup.com/workplace/236372/manage-employees-rarely.aspx

Krueger, J., & Killham, E. (2006, March 9). *Why Dilbert is right: Uncomfortable work environments make for disgruntled employees — just like the cartoon says.* Retrieved December 10, 2018, from https://news.gallup.com/businessjournal/21802/Why-Dilbert-Right.aspx

Mann, A. (2017, June 22). *How to make an open office floor plan work.* Retrieved December 10, 2018, from https://www.gallup.com/workplace/236219/open-office-floor-plan-work.aspx

Mann, A. (2017, August 1). *3 ways you are failing your remote workers.* Retrieved December 10, 2018, from https://www.gallup.com/workplace/236192/ways-failing-remote-workers.aspx

Mann, A., & Adkins, A. (2017, March 15). *America's coming workplace: Home alone.* Retrieved December 10, 2018, from https://news.gallup.com/businessjournal/206033/america-coming-workplace-home-alone.aspx

Mann, A., & Adkins, A. (2017, March 22). *How engaged is your remote workforce?* Retrieved December 10, 2018, from https://www.gallup.com/workplace/236375/engaged-remote-workforce.aspx

MikeBloomberg. (2018, February 28). I've always believed that open, collaborative workspaces make a difference — in businesses and city halls alike. Glad to see this idea spreading to @BloombergDotOrg #iteams around the world. [Tweet]. Retrieved December 10, 2018, from https://twitter.com/MikeBloomberg/status/968952708542730241

## CHAPTER 45. CORPORATE INNOVATION: HOW TO MANAGE — AND NURTURE — CREATIVITY

In a 2018 Gallup study of 4,000 full-time and part-time employees in Europe, 55% of employees in the U.K. said they are allotted time to think creatively or discuss new ideas at work at least a few times a week; 48% in France and 38% in both Spain and Germany said the same. In Germany, 41% of employees strongly agreed that they feel encouraged to come up with new and better ways to do things; 36% in the U.K., 30% in France and 20% in Spain said the same.

According to a study of 25,257 U.S. employees aged 18 and older, higher engagement leads to more ideas:

- "In the last 12 months, did you or your work team have an idea for improving your company or organization?"
  - 61% said yes
- "What is the current status of implementing your idea?"
  - 46% said they had an idea, and it was implemented
- "Has your idea led to cost savings, increased revenue, or increased efficiency for your team or your company/organization?"
  - 20% said they had an idea, it was implemented and it led to improvement
- Engaged employees are:
  - 20% more likely than the average employee — and 66% more likely than actively disengaged employees — to say they (or their team) had an idea
  - 2.4 times as likely as the average employee — and 7.8 times as likely as actively disengaged employees — to say they had an idea, it was implemented and it led to improvement

---

Gallup. (2014, January 30). *Innovation: The new frontier for quality: Companies should use the tools they once used to prevent defects to promote fast, transformational change.* Retrieved December 10, 2018, from https://news.gallup.com/businessjournal/166958/innovation-new-frontier-quality.aspx

Reiter-Palmon, R., Wigert, B., & de Vreede, T. (2011). Team creativity and innovation: The effect of team composition, social processes and cognition. In M. Mumford (Ed.), *Handbook of organizational creativity* (pp. 295-326). Cambridge, MA: Academic Press.

Wigert, B. (2018). Constructing an evidence-based model for managing creative performance. In R. Reiter-Palmon, V. L. Kennel, & J. C. Kaufman (Eds.), *Individual creativity in the workplace* (pp. 339-369), Cambridge, MA: Academic Press.

## CHAPTER 46. YOU CAN'T BE "AGILE" WITHOUT GREAT MANAGERS

In a 2018 Gallup study of 4,000 full-time and part-time employees in Europe, about one in four employees in the U.K., Germany, France and Spain strongly agreed that they have the right tools and processes to respond quickly to business needs. Roughly the same proportion strongly agreed that they are satisfied with the cooperation between their department and other departments.

---

Emond, L. (2018, October 1). *Agility is both structural and cultural at Roche.* Retrieved December 10, 2018, from https://www.gallup.com/workplace/243167/agility-structural-cultural-roche.aspx

Gallup. (2018, August 29). *What does agility mean for business leaders?* Retrieved December 10, 2018, from https://www.gallup.com/workplace/241250/agility-mean-business-leaders.aspx

Gallup. (2018, September 7). *3 steps on the path to agility.* Retrieved December 10, 2018, from https://www.gallup.com/workplace/241793/steps-path-agility.aspx

Gallup. (2018, September 25). *2 key strategies for managing agile teams.* Retrieved December 10, 2018, from https://www.gallup.com/workplace/242387/key-strategies-managing-agile-teams.aspx

Krieger, J. (2010, October 5). *Creating a culture of innovation.* Retrieved December 10, 2018, from https://news.gallup.com/businessjournal/143282/Creating-Culture-Innovation.aspx

Ratanjee, V., & Dvorak, N. (2018, September 18). *Mastering matrix management in the age of agility.* Retrieved December 10, 2018, from https://www.gallup.com/workplace/242192/mastering-matrix-management-age-agility.aspx

## CHAPTER 47. GIG WORK: THE NEW EMPLOYER-EMPLOYEE RELATIONSHIP

Gallup. (2018). *Gallup's perspective on the gig economy and alternative work arrangements.* Retrieved December 10, 2018, from https://www.gallup.com/workplace/240878/gig-economy-paper-2018.aspx

Katz, L. F., & Krueger, A. B. (2016). *The rise and nature of alternative work arrangements in the United States, 1995-2015* (No. w22667). National Bureau of Economic Research.

McFeely, S. (2017, June 5). *Is the growing Uber-economy a threat to small businesses?* Retrieved December 10, 2018, from https://news.gallup.com/opinion/gallup/211739/growing-uber-economy-threat-small-businesses.aspx

McFeely, S. (2018, August 30). *7 ways your organization can capitalize on the gig economy.* Retrieved December 10, 2018, from https://www.gallup.com/workplace/241769/ways-organization-capitalize-gig-economy.aspx

McFeely, S., & Pendell, R. (2018, August 16). *What workplace leaders can learn from the real gig economy.* Retrieved December 10, 2018, from https://www.gallup.com/workplace/240929/workplace-leaders-learn-real-gig-economy.aspx

Newport, F., & McFeely, S. (2018, September 19). *What is the future of the U.S. gig economy?* [Audio blog post]. Retrieved December 10, 2018, from https://news.gallup.com/podcast/242315/future-gig-economy.aspx

## CHAPTER 48. GIG WORKERS: DESPERATE OR SATISFIED?

Deutschkron, S., & Pearce, C. (2017, October 17). *Freelancers predicted to become the U.S. workforce majority within a decade, with nearly 50% of millennial workers already freelancing, annual "Freelancing in America" study finds.* Retrieved December 10, 2018, from https://www.upwork.com/press/2017/10/17/freelancing-in-america-2017/

Gallup. (2018). *Gallup's perspective on the gig economy and alternative work arrangements.* Retrieved December 10, 2018, from https://www.gallup.com/workplace/240878/gig-economy-paper-2018.aspx

Manyika, J., Lund, S., Bughin, J., Robinson, K., Mischke, J., & Mahajan, D. (2016 October). Independent work: Choice, necessity, and the gig economy. *McKinsey Global Institute.* Retrieved December 10, 2018, from https://www.mckinsey.com/~/media/McKinsey/Featured%20Insights/Employment%20and%20Growth/Independent%20work%20Choice%20necessity%20and%20the%20gig%20economy/Independent-Work-Choice-necessity-and-the-gig-economy-Full-report.ashx

McFeely, S., & Pendell, R. (2018, August 16). *What workplace leaders can learn from the real gig economy.* Retrieved December 10, 2018, from https://www.gallup.com/workplace/240929/workplace-leaders-learn-real-gig-economy.aspx

## CHAPTER 49. ARTIFICIAL INTELLIGENCE HAS ARRIVED. NOW WHAT?

In a 2018 Gallup study of 4,000 full-time and part-time employees in Europe, 37% of German workers strongly agreed that their company readily implements new technologies that help them be more productive; 26% in France, 21% in the U.K. and 18% in Spain said the same. As in the U.S., the majority of employees in these European countries do not believe their job will be eliminated within the next five years as a result of new technology.

---

Brynjolfsson, E., & McAfee, A. (2012). *Race against the machine: How the digital revolution is accelerating innovation, driving productivity, and irreversibly transforming employment and the economy.* Lexington, MA: Digital Frontier Press.

Chang, S. (2017, September 2). *This chart spells out in black and white just how many jobs will be lost to robots.* Retrieved December 10, 2018, from http://www.marketwatch.com/story/this-chart-spells-out-in-black-and-white-just-how-many-jobs-will-be-lost-to-robots-2017-05-31

Daugherty, P., & Wilson, H. J. (2018). *Process reimagined: Together, people and AI are reinventing business processes from the ground up.* Retrieved December 10, 2018, from https://www.accenture.com/t20180424T033337Z__w__/us-en/_acnmedia/PDF-76/Accenture-Process-Reimagined.pdf

Dugan, A., & Nelson, B. (2017, June 8). *3 trends that will disrupt your workplace forever.* Retrieved December 10, 2018, from https://www.gallup.com/workplace/235814/trends-disrupt-workplace-forever.aspx

Frey, C. B., & Osborne, M. A. (2017). The future of employment: How susceptible are jobs to computerisation? *Technological Forecasting & Social Change, 114*, 254-280.

Levin, S. (2017, December 5). Google to hire thousands of moderators after outcry over YouTube abuse videos. *The Guardian.* Retrieved December 10, 2018, from https://www.theguardian.com/technology/2017/dec/04/google-youtube-hire-moderators-child-abuse-videos

Newport, F. (2017, May 17). *One in four U.S. workers say technology will eliminate job.* Retrieved December 10, 2018, from http://www.gallup.com/poll/210728/one-four-workers-say-technology-eliminate-job.aspx

Northeastern University & Gallup (2018). *Optimism and anxiety: Views on the impact of artificial intelligence and higher education's response.* Retrieved December 10, 2018, from https://www.northeastern.edu/gallup/pdf/OptimismAnxietyNortheasternGallup.pdf

Perez, S. (2017). *YouTube promises to increase content moderation and other enforcement staff to 10k in 2018.* Retrieved December 10, 2018, from https://techcrunch.com/2017/12/05/youtube-promises-to-increase-content-moderation-staff-to-over-10k-in-2018/

Reinhart, R. (2018, January 31). *Americans upbeat on artificial intelligence, but still wary.* Retrieved December 10, 2018, from https://news.gallup.com/poll/226502/americans-upbeat-artificial-intelligence-wary.aspx

Reinhart, R. (2018, February 8). *Most U.S. workers unafraid of losing their jobs to robots.* Retrieved December 10, 2018, from https://news.gallup.com/poll/226841/workers-unafraid-losing-jobs-robots.aspx

Reinhart, R. (2018, February 26). *Public split on basic income for workers replaced by robots.* Retrieved December 10, 2018, from https://news.gallup.com/poll/228194/public-split-basic-income-workers-replaced-robots.aspx

Reinhart, R. (2018, March 6). *Most Americans already using artificial intelligence products.* Retrieved December 10, 2018, from https://news.gallup.com/poll/228497/americans-already-using-artificial-intelligence-products.aspx

Reinhart, R. (2018, March 9). *AI seen as greater job threat than immigration, offshoring.* Retrieved December 10, 2018, from https://news.gallup.com/poll/228923/seen-greater-job-threat-immigration-offshoring.aspx

Rugaber, C. S. (2017, October 30). *Robots and automation likely to create more jobs in e-commerce.* Retrieved December 10, 2018, from https://www.inc.com/associated-press/e-commerce-automation-robots-create-more-jobs-amazon-effect.html

## CHAPTER 50. ARTIFICIAL INTELLIGENCE: PREPARING YOUR WORKPLACE

Herway, J. (2018, September 19). *How to set your company apart in a tech-driven world.* Retrieved December 10, 2018, from https://www.gallup.com/workplace/242186/set-company-apart-tech-driven-world.aspx

Northeastern University & Gallup. (2018). *Optimism and anxiety: Views on the impact of artificial intelligence and higher education's response.* Retrieved December 10, 2018, from https://www.northeastern.edu/gallup/pdf/OptimismAnxietyNortheasternGallup.pdf

Reinhart, R. (2018, February 12). *U.S. workers unsure about securing training if AI takes jobs.* Retrieved December 10, 2018, from https://news.gallup.com/poll/226868/workers-unsure-securing-training-takes-jobs.aspx

Semykoz, M. (2018, July 26). *Is your culture ready for the AI era?* Retrieved December 10, 2018, from https://www.gallup.com/workplace/237923/culture-ready-era.aspx

Semykoz, M. (2018, August 3). *How to manage the AI disruption: A culture of purpose.* Retrieved December 10, 2018, from https://www.gallup.com/workplace/238106/manage-disruption-culture-purpose.aspx

Semykoz, M. (2018, August 6). *Are you asking the right questions in the new AI era?* Retrieved December 10, 2018, from https://www.gallup.com/workplace/238151/asking-right-questions-new-era.aspx

Semykoz, M. (2018, August 8). *How to build a culture of confidence in the new age of AI.* Retrieved December 10, 2018, from https://www.gallup.com/workplace/238154/build-culture-confidence-new-age.aspx

Semykoz, M. (2018, August 15). *How to make expert ethical decisions in the AI era.* Retrieved December 10, 2018, from https://www.gallup.com/workplace/238157/expert-ethical-decisions-era.aspx

Semykoz, M. (2018, September 3). *Learn how to cultivate a culture of trust in the AI era.* Retrieved December 10, 2018, from https://www.gallup.com/workplace/238160/learn-cultivate-culture-trust-era.aspx

Semykoz, M. (2018, September 5). *AI is not magic: How to create the right AI culture.* Retrieved December 10, 2018, from https://www.gallup.com/workplace/238163/not-magic-create-right-culture.aspx

## CHAPTER 51. CAUGHT UP IN TECHNOLOGY — HCM SYSTEMS AND OTHER SOLUTIONS

A 2018 Gallup study of 4,000 full-time and part-time employees in Europe revealed that 55% of employees in Germany, 51% in the U.K., and 35% in both Spain and France strongly agreed that it is easy to access data that is relevant to their work.

---

Applin, S. A., & Fischer, M. D. (2015). Cooperation between humans and robots: Applied agency in autonomous processes. In *10th ACM/IEEE International Conference on Human-Robot Interaction, Workshop on the Emerging Policy and Ethics of Human-Robot Interaction,* Portland, OR.

Baraka, K., & Veloso, M. (2015). Adaptive interaction of persistent robots to user temporal preferences. In A. Tapus, E. Andre, J. C. Martin, F. Ferland, M. Ammi (Eds.), *Social robotics* (pp. 61-71). Switzerland: Springer.

Carpenter, T. J., & Zachary, W. W. (2017). Using context and robot-human communication to resolve unexpected situational conflicts. In *2017 IEEE Conference on Cognitive and Computational Aspects of Situation Management (CogSIMA),* Savannah, GA.

Faber, M., Butzler, J., & Schlick, C. M. (2015). Human-robot cooperation in future production systems: Analysis of requirements for designing an ergonomic work system. *Procedia Manufacturing, 3*, 510-517.

Faggella, D. (2018, November 29). *Machine learning in human resources — applications and trends.* Retrieved December 10, 2018, from https://www.techemergence.com/machine-learning-in-human-resources/

Fairchild, M. (n.d.). *The top 5 HRIS mistakes and how to avoid them.* Retrieved December 10, 2018, from http://www.hrlab.com/hris-mistakes.php

Hayes, B., & Scassellati, B. (2014). Discovering task constraints through observation and active learning. In *2014 IEEE/RSJ International Conference on Intelligent Robots and Systems,* Chicago.

Jain, D., & Sharma, Y. (2017). Adoption of next generation robotics: A case study on Amazon. *Perspectiva: A Case Research Journal, 3*, 9-23.

Kahneman, D. (2015). *Thinking, fast and slow.* New York: Farrar, Straus and Giroux.

Leite, I., McCoy, M., Ullman, D., Salomons, N., & Scassellati, B. (2015). Comparing models of disengagement in individual and group interactions. In *10th ACM/IEEE International Conference on Human-Robot Interaction, Workshop on the Emerging Policy and Ethics of Human-Robot Interaction,* Portland, OR.

Leite, I., Pereira, A., Castellano, G., Mascarenhas, S., Martinho, C., & Paiva, A. (2012). Modelling empathy in social robotic companions. In L. Ardissono, & T. Kuflik (Eds.) *Advances in user modeling*. UMAP 2011. Lecture Notes in Computer Science, vol. 7138. (pp. 135-147). Berlin: Springer.

Leyzberg, D., Spaulding, S., & Scassellati, B. (2014). Personalizing robot tutors to individuals' learning differences. In *Proceedings of the 2014 ACM/IEEE International Conference on Human-Robot Interaction,* Bielefeld, Germany.

Leyzberg, D., Spaulding, S., Toneva, M., & Scassellati, B. (2012). *The physical presence of a robot tutor increases cognitive learning gains.* CogSci.

Michalos, G., Karagiannis, P., Makris, S., Tokcalar, O., & Chryssolouris, G. (2016). Augmented reality (AR) applications for supporting human-robot interactive cooperation. *Procedia CIRP, 41*, 370-375.

Saerbeck, M., Schut, T., Bartneck, C., & Janse, M. D. (2010). Expressive robots in education — Varying the degree of social supportive behavior of a robotic tutor. In *Proceedings of the 28th ACM Conference on Human Factors in Computing Systems*, Atlanta, pp. 1613-1622.

Sharp, B. (2018). Policy implications of people analytics and the automated workplace. In R. Kiggins (Ed.), *The political economy of robots: Prospects for prosperity and peace in the automated 21st century* (pp. 61-80). Basingstoke, U.K.: Palgrave Macmillan.

Stoll, B., Reig, S., He, L., Kaplan, I., Jung, M. F., & Fussel, S. R. (2018). Wait, can you move the robot?: Examining telepresence robot use in collaborative teams. In *Proceedings of the 2018 ACM/IEEE International Conference on Human-Robot Interaction*, Chicago.

Strohkorb, S., Huang, C., Ramachandran, A., & Scassellati, B. (2016). Establishing sustained, supportive human-robot relationships: Building blocks and open challenges. In *AAAI Spring Symposia*, Palo Alto, CA.

Thomaz, A. L., & Breazeal, C. (2008). Teachable robots: Understanding human teaching behavior to build more effective robot learners. *Artificial Intelligence, 172*(6-7), 716-737.

Tsarouchi, P., Michalos, G., Makris, S., Athanasatos, T., Dimoulas, K., & Chryssolouris, G. (2017). On a human-robot workplace design and task allocation system. *International Journal of Computer Integrated Manufacturing, 30*(12), 1272-1279.

Unhelkar, V. V., & Shah, J. A. (2016). ConTCT: Deciding to communicate during time-critical collaborative tasks in unknown, deterministic domains. In *Thirtieth AAAI Conference on Artificial Intelligence*, Phoenix, AZ.

Xu, A., & Dudek, G. (2015). OPTIMo: Online Probabilistic Trust Inference Model for asymmetric human-robot collaborations. In *10th ACM/IEEE International Conference on Human-Robot Interaction, Workshop on the Emerging Policy and Ethics of Human-Robot Interaction*, Portland, OR.

## CHAPTER 52. BETTER DECISION-MAKING WITH PREDICTIVE ANALYTICS: MONEYBALL FOR MANAGERS

In a 2018 Gallup study of 4,000 full-time and part-time employees in Europe, 36% of German employees strongly agreed that their company makes good use of data that is available to make good decisions; 32% in France, 31% in Spain and 29% in the U.K. said the same.

---

Goasduff, L. (2015, September 15). *Gartner says business intelligence and analytics leaders must focus on mindsets and culture to kick start advanced analytics.* Retrieved December 10, 2018, from https://www.gartner.com/newsroom/id/3130017?utm_source=link_newsv9&utm_campaign=item_193574&utm_medium=copy

Kruse, W. E., & Dvorak, N. (2016, March 16). *Managing employee risk demands data, not guesswork.* Retrieved December 10, 2018, from https://news.gallup.com/businessjournal/189878/managing-employee-risk-demands-data-not-guesswork.aspx

Leonard, D., & Nelson, B. (2018, July 14). *Successful predictive analytics demand a data-driven workplace.* Retrieved December 10, 2018, from https://news.gallup.com/businessjournal/193574/successful-predictive-analytics-demand-data-driven-culture.aspx

Petti, B. (2018, May 3). *4 keys to becoming a data-driven HR leader.* Retrieved December 10, 2018, from https://www.gallup.com/workplace/236084/keys-becoming-data-driven-leader.aspx

Petti, B., & Williams, S. (2015, March 11). *Use different analytics to solve different problems.* Retrieved December 10, 2018, from https://news.gallup.com/opinion/gallup/181943/different-analytics-solve-different-problems.aspx

Schmarzo, B. (2014, February 6). *KPMG survey: Firms struggle with big data.* Retrieved December 10, 2018, from https://infocus.dellemc.com/william_schmarzo/kpmg-survey-firms-struggle-with-big-data/?utm_source=link_newsv9&utm_campaign=item_193574&utm_medium=copy

# IN CLOSING: HUMAN NATURE'S ROLE IN BUSINESS OUTCOMES


Asplund, J., Harter, J. K., Agrawal, S., & Plowman, S. K. (2015). *The relationship between strengths-based employee development and organizational outcomes 2015 strengths meta-analysis.* Retrieved December 10, 2018, from https://news.gallup.com/reports/193427/strengths-meta-analysis-2015.aspx

Fleming, J. H., & Asplund, J. (2007). *Human sigma: Managing the employee-customer encounter.* New York: Gallup Press.

Fleming, J. H., Coffman, C., & Harter, J. (2005). Manage your human sigma. *Harvard Business Review, 83*(7), 106-14.

Harter, J. K. (2000). Managerial talent, employee engagement, and business-unit performance. *The Psychologist-Manager Journal, 4*(2), 215-224.

Harter, J. K., Hayes, T. L., & Schmidt, F. L. (2004). *Meta-analytic predictive validity of Gallup selection research instruments (SRI).* Omaha, NE: Gallup.

Schmidt, F. L., Oh, I. S., & Shaffer, J. A. (2016). *The validity and utility of selection methods in personnel psychology: Practical and theoretical implications of 100 years of research findings.* Retrieved December 7, 2018, from https://www.testingtalent.net/wp-content/uploads/2017/04/2016-100-Yrs-Working-Paper-on-Selection-Methods-Schmit-Mar-17.pdf

Schmidt, F. L., & Rader, M. (1999). Exploring the boundary conditions for interview validity: Meta-analytic validity findings for a new interview type. *Personnel Psychology, 52*(2), 443-464.

Yang, Y., Harter, J. K., Streur, J. H., Agrawal, S., Dvorak, N., & Walker, P. (2013). *The Gallup manager assessment: Technical report.* Omaha, NE: Gallup.

Yu, D., Harter, J. K., Fleming, J. (2014). *The relationship between customer engagement and organizational outcomes in the business-to-consumer context: 2014 B2C customer engagement meta-analysis.* Omaha, NE: Gallup.

# Acknowledgements

*It's the Manager* is the product of decades of work conducted by Gallup scientists, consultants, client organizations and leading scientists from the academic community — based on the opinions and behaviors of tens of millions of employees from workplaces throughout the world. While we extracted findings and condensed them into the 52 short chapters of this book, the following much larger team provided direction, critical thinking, research and editorial guidance, and we are very grateful for their tireless efforts.

**Editor:** Geoff Brewer

**Gallup Press Publisher:** Seth Schuchman

**Chief of Staff for Jim Clifton:** Christine Sheehan

**Copy editing:** Kelly Henry

**Fact checking:** Trista Kunce

**Design:** Samantha Allemang

**Writing and editing contributions:** Ryan Pendell

**Administrative support:** Carissa Christensen, Shawna Hubbard-Thomas, Deann Wootton

**Writing and editing for websites and marketing:** Rachael Breck, Jessica Schatz, Kelly Slater, Jane Smith

**Gallup Press coordinator:** Christy Trout

**Marketing and project management:** Jessica Kennedy

**Communications:** Ashley Anderson, Anand Madhavan, Bryant Ott, Shari Theer

**Technology:** Katie Barton, Ryan Kronschnabel, Morgan Lubeck, Emily Ternus

**Internal project management:** Chelsea Boryca, Tiffany Saulnier

**Science team:** Sangeeta Agrawal, Jim Asplund, Kristin Barry, Anthony Blue, Nate Dvorak, Cheryl Fernandez, Ellyn Maese, Shane McFeely, Marco Nink, Stephanie Plowman, Joe Streur, Ben Wigert, Dan Witters, Daniela Yu

**Peer review:** Jon Clifton, Larry Emond, Vipula Gandhi, Dean Jones, Emily Meyer, Jane Miller, Scott Miller, Melissa Moreno, Matt Mosser, Tom Nolan, Steve O'Brien, Ed O'Boyle, Phil Ruhlman, John Wood

**Special thanks to:** The girl at United Gate F4 and RaLinda

Finally, we thank our mentor Don Clifton (1924-2003), the father of strengths-based psychology and inventor of the CliftonStrengths assessment, who taught us all to study what is *right* with people.

# About Gallup

Gallup is a global analytics, advisory and learning firm that helps leaders solve their organizations' biggest problems.

Gallup knows more about the will of employees, customers, students and citizens than any other organization in the world. We offer solutions, transformations and services in many areas, including:

- Culture change
- Leadership development
- Manager development
- Strengths-based coaching and culture
- Strategies for organic growth
- "Boss-to-coach" software tools
- Attracting and recruiting star team members
- Succession planning
- Performance management system and ratings
- Refining performance metrics
- Reducing defects and safety risks
- Evaluating internal programs
- Employee engagement and experience
- Predictive hiring assessments
- Retention forecasting
- Creating agile teams
- Improving the customer experience (B2B)
- Diversity and inclusion
- Well-being initiatives

To learn more, please contact Gallup at https://www.gallup.com/contact.

# About the Authors

Jim Clifton is Chairman and CEO of Gallup and bestselling author of *Born to Build* and *The Coming Jobs War*. His most recent innovation, the Gallup World Poll, is designed to give the world's 7 billion citizens a voice in virtually all key global issues. Under Clifton's leadership, Gallup has expanded from a predominantly U.S.-based company to a worldwide organization with 40 offices in 30 countries and regions. Clifton is currently a Distinguished Visiting Professor and Senior Fellow of the Frank Hawkins Kenan Institute of Private Enterprise at the University of North Carolina.

Jim Harter, Ph.D., is Chief Scientist, Workplace for Gallup. He has led more than 1,000 studies of workplace effectiveness, including the largest ongoing meta-analysis of human potential and business unit performance. The bestselling author of *12: The Elements of Great Managing* and *Wellbeing: The Five Essential Elements*, Harter has also published articles in many prominent business and academic journals.

Gallup Press exists to educate and inform the people who govern, manage, teach and lead the world's 7 billion citizens. Each book meets Gallup's requirements of integrity, trust and independence and is based on Gallup-approved science and research.